INTERNATIONAL DEVELOPMENT IN FOCUS

Toward Safer and More Productive Migration for South Asia

S. AMER AHMED AND LAURENT BOSSAVIE, EDITORS

WORLD BANK GROUP

Contents

Boxes

Figures

Tables

Foreword

International migration for temporary employment, leading to both jobs and remittance flows, is key to South Asia's development path. Remittances equate to between 6 percent and 30 percent of GDP in the region, which is many times the value of foreign direct investment and official development assistance combined, even well into the global COVID-19 (coronavirus) pandemic. These flows boost household consumption and support macroeconomic stability in countries of origin, playing an important role by building human capital through greater spending, especially on health and education. Temporary labor migration also provides higher-paying job opportunities for workers. The region currently faces the challenge of having to create good-quality jobs to keep up with the millions of people projected to enter the workforce every year for another generation. Overseas markets are a critical source of jobs when absorbing all these workers domestically can be difficult, despite a rapidly growing private sector. Migrants typically experience wage gains of at least three times their earnings back home, can acquire new skills, and accumulate savings with which to start up entrepreneurial activities after returning home, all of which can then benefit home labor markets by increasing labor productivity and contributing to job creation.

This book reminds us of the numerous benefits of temporary economic migration, but more importantly, helps identify the numerous challenges that keep migration from achieving its full potential for development. Temporary migrants face a series of problems when migrating overseas. The monetary costs for migration paid by migrants from the region are the highest globally, and are very large relative to household income before departure (and indeed subsequently). This cost barrier prevents the poorest from migrating overseas, even as the poorest would benefit the most from migration. It also places migrants in a situation of considerable vulnerability, leading at times to crippling indebtedness. In addition, migrants face increased risks to personal safety and welfare, given that current policies are insufficient to prepare workers for their migration experience or to protect them while at destination. Migrants' vulnerabilities are exacerbated by dangerous gaps or inaccuracies in information made available to them about employment opportunities in the main destinations.

This book shows that vulnerability can be reduced and the benefits of migration maximized for workers from South Asia. Building on rigorous analytics, it highlights policy actions that can be taken at all stages of the migration life cycle, including after return, to minimize the risks and maximize the benefits of migrating for the migrants themselves, for their families, and for the home economy. The book provides policy options for addressing information gaps on employment opportunities overseas at the departure stage and for preparing migrants adequately for their experience overseas.

Almost two years into the COVID-19 pandemic, the global economy is on the verge of a recovery. International temporary economic labor migration will play a critical role in this recovery. Countries throughout South Asia have been patiently building and enhancing their systems to ensure safer and more productive migration as soon as borders fully reopen. This book is therefore offered as a comprehensive resource for governments, development partners, and other stakeholders throughout South Asia.

Michal Rutkowski
Global Director
Social Protection and Jobs Global Practice
The World Bank

Lynne Sherburne-Benz
Regional Director
Human Development, South Asia
The World Bank

Acknowledgments

This book was prepared by a team jointly led by S. Amer Ahmed (Senior Economist, Social Protection and Jobs Global Practice) and Laurent Bossavie (Economist, Social Protection and Jobs Global Practice), under the overall supervision of Stefano Paternostro (Practice Manager, Social Protection and Jobs Global Practice). Çağlar Özden (Lead Economist, Development Economics Research Group) provided invaluable inputs throughout the preparation of the book. Amer Ahmed and Laurent Bossavie were colead authors responsible for chapters 1 and 2, Amer Ahmed was lead author for chapter 3, and Laurent Bossavie was lead author for chapter 4. The team that contributed to chapters 1, 2, and 3 included Esther Bartl, Laura Caron, Upasana Khadka, Maryem Khan, Csilla Lakatos, Sundas Liaqat, Sadia Sarwar, and Soonhwa Yi. The team that contributed to chapter 4 included Sundas Liaqat and He Wang. Joseph-Simon Görlach (Assistant Professor, Bocconi University) offered vital contributions on temporary migration in Bangladesh, particularly in chapter 4. Rubaba Anwar, Jyoti Pandey, Ali Qureshi, Aneeka Rahman, and Jasmine Rajbhandary facilitated policy dialogue and coordinated stakeholder consultations with government counterparts in Bangladesh, Nepal, and Pakistan.

The team is grateful for helpful feedback from officials at Bangladesh's Ministry of Expatriates' Welfare and Overseas Employment; Nepal's Ministry of Labor, Employment, and Social Security; and Pakistan's Ministry of Overseas Pakistanis and Human Resource Development. The team received useful feedback from several colleagues at development partners, including the International Labour Organization—Nilim Baruah, Deepa Bharthi, Richard Howard, Rahnuma Khan, Michelle Leighton, Shabarinath Nair, and Laetitia Weibel Roberts; the International Organization for Migration—Sajjad Ahmed, Sharon Dimanche, and Ishita Shruti; and the Swiss Agency for Cooperation and Development—Nazia Haider.

The team benefited from helpful conversations with, and comments from, several World Bank colleagues, including Andras Bodor, Yoon Cho, Supriyo De, Anastasiya Denisova, Manjula Luthria, Cem Mete, Sonia Plaza, Aneeka Rahman, Fahmina Rahman, Dhushyanth Raju, Martin Rama, Michal Rutkowski, Rebekah Smith, Mauro Testaverde, and Hans Timmer. Erwin Tiongson (professor of the practice, Georgetown University) also provided extensive comments and feedback. The team also benefited from helpful feedback from participants at the December 2019 conference "Safer and More Productive Migration for South Asia: A Forum for Knowledge to Action," organized by the World Bank, and the "Demographic Change and Labor Mobility Workshop," organized by the World Bank, the Italian Ministry of Economy and Finance, the Italian Center for International Development, and the Center for Economic and International Studies at the University of Rome Tor Vergata.

This book was supported by the Rapid Social Response Trust Fund, which financed the Bangladesh Return Migrant Survey, documented in a background paper by S. Amer Ahmed, Faizuddin Ahmed, Laurent Bossavie, Çağlar Özden, and He Wang. That survey was used for a series of background papers on temporary migration in Bangladesh—prepared with support from the World Bank's Research Support Budget—by Laurent Bossavie, Joseph Simon Görlach, Çağlar Özden, and He Wang that were used as inputs throughout the book. The Korea–World Bank Partnership Facility financed analytical work and stakeholder consultations that informed the findings. The updates to the analysis to reflect the implications of the COVID-19 (coronavirus) pandemic were supported by the Australian government through the Department of Foreign Affairs and Trade. The views expressed in this publication, however, are the authors' alone and are not necessarily the views of the Australian government.

About the Editors

S. Amer Ahmed is a Senior Economist in the Social Protection and Jobs Global Practice of the World Bank. He holds a PhD in agricultural economics from Purdue University, where he specialized in international trade, and where his research focused on trade-in-services. Since 2017, Ahmed has been working on South Asian economies, leading research and operational activities related to jobs and migration. He has published peer-reviewed research in the areas of climate change, labor, international trade, growth, and demographics. Aside from journal publications, Ahmed has co-authored flagship products such as the World Bank's biannual *Global Economic Prospects* series, and the World Bank's final *Global Monitoring Report 2015/2016* on the MDGs and demographics.

Laurent Bossavie is an Economist in the Social Protection and Jobs Global Practice of the World Bank. His main research areas are applied microeconomics, labor economics, and the economics of migration. His work studies the effects of employment and migration policies on workers' outcomes in both high-income and developing countries. His research on these topics has been published in leading peer-reviewed journals in labor economics, such as the *Journal of Human Resources*, among others. He holds a PhD in economics from the European University Institute (EUI) in Florence, Italy.

Abbreviations

ADD	Abu Dhabi Dialogue
BLA	bilateral labor agreement
BRMS	World Bank Bangladesh Return Migrant Survey 2018/19
CP	Colombo Process
EPS	Employment Permit System (Republic of Korea)
FDI	foreign direct investment
G2G	government-to-government
GCC	Gulf Cooperation Council
GCM	Global Compact for Safe, Orderly, and Regular Migration
GFMD	Global Forum for Migration and Development
GSP	Global Skills Partnership
ILO	International Labour Organization
IOM	International Organization for Migration
KNOMAD	Global Knowledge Partnership on Migration and Development
LA	labor attaché
MoEWOE	Ministry of Expatriates' Welfare and Overseas Employment (Bangladesh)
MOU	memorandum of understanding
MRA	Mutual Recognition Arrangement
ODA	official development assistance
OEC	Overseas Employment Certificate
OECD	Organisation for Economic Co-operation and Development
OFW	Overseas Filipino Workers
POEA	Philippines Overseas Employment Agency
RCI	recruitment cost index
TESDA	Technical Education and Skills Development Authority

Executive Summary

INTERNATIONAL MIGRATION: A CRUCIAL PART OF SOUTH ASIA'S DEVELOPMENT

International migration for temporary employment is a critical component of South Asia's development path, providing both jobs and remittance flows.[1] South Asian economies are at a stage of demographic transition in which people of working age still account for increasing shares of populations, with millions of people set to enter the working-age cohort every year for another generation. Overseas markets thus play an important role as a source of labor demand, especially because the private sector in some of these South Asian economies is under pressure to create decent jobs at a sufficient pace. For example, 27 percent of Nepali households have at least one person working abroad, equivalent to more than 2.8 million working-age Nepalis, amounting to three-quarters of the country's 3.8 million wage employees (Ruppert Bulmer, Shrestha, and Marshalian 2020). The larger economies in the region have several million migrants overseas, and these stocks have grown over time (figure ES.1). Focusing solely on the flows of temporary economic migrants during the period 2012–17, Bangladesh, India, Nepal, and Pakistan have sent hundreds of thousands of workers overseas every year—on average, roughly 597,000, 678,000, 463,000, and 713,000, respectively.

This book focuses on Bangladesh, Nepal, and Pakistan—three migrant-sending countries sharing similar characteristics, opportunities, and challenges. All three are lower-middle-income countries where sizable shares of the working-age population migrate overseas. Most migrants from these three countries are low skilled. When these low-skilled workers move to destinations such as the Gulf Cooperation Council (GCC) countries, they generally do so on a temporary basis through contractual labor arrangements before returning home after a few years abroad. They face similar vulnerabilities overseas and are subject to a range of possible abuses and shocks. In all three countries, migration is also largely male; female migration represents less than 5 percent of total international migration outflows. In contrast, outmigration from other countries in the region is dissimilar. In Afghanistan, migration systems are less mature, partly

FIGURE ES.1

International migration from South Asia

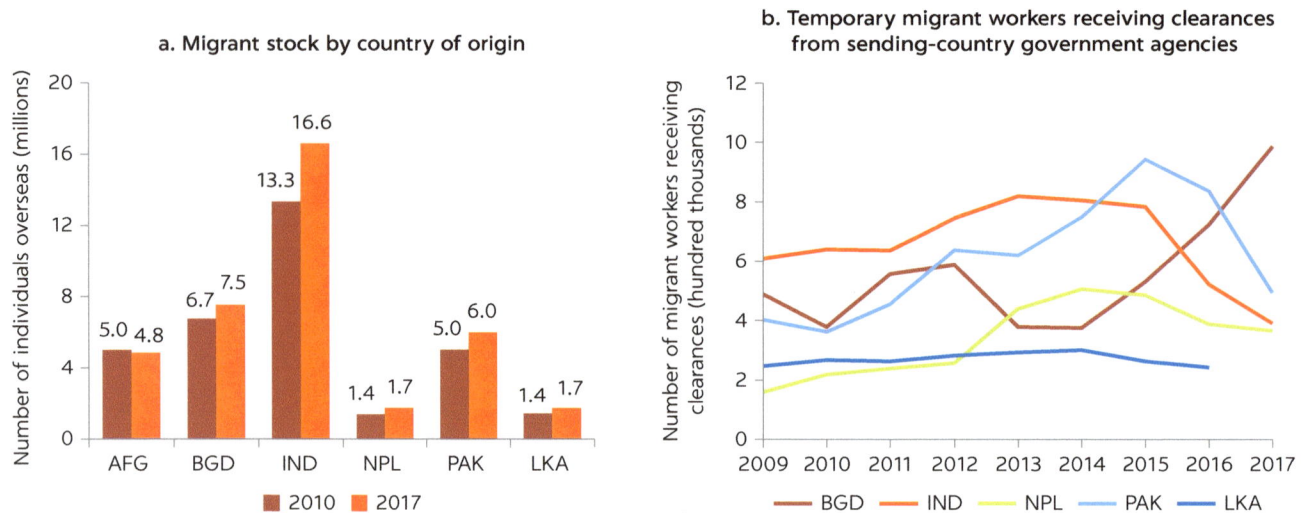

Sources: Panel a—UN DESA 2017; panel b—Bureau of Emigration and Overseas Employment (Pakistan); Bureau of Foreign Employment (Sri Lanka); Bureau of Manpower Employment and Training (Bangladesh); Department of Foreign Employment (Nepal); Ministry of External Affairs (India).

Note: Panel a illustrates migrant stock from a given country, regardless of reason for migration (for example, temporary economic migration, forced displacement, among others). Panel b includes data only for the five countries where governments maintain records of outbound temporary economic migrants. AFG = Afghanistan; BGD = Bangladesh; IND = India; LKA = Sri Lanka; NPL = Nepal; PAK = Pakistan.

because of the conflict and insecurity at origin, though it currently seeks to send more migrants overseas. In Sri Lanka, a lower-middle-income country, migration systems are considerably more advanced than in Bangladesh, Nepal, or Pakistan, and female migration represents a large share of outflows. In India, migrants tend to be increasingly higher skilled, and the implications for migration systems and policies are thus distinct.

Migration has large positive effects on South Asian economies overall, often marked by remittances that are high in relative and absolute terms. Remittances constitute an important fraction of the GDP of most South Asian economies (figure ES.2). In 2017, Nepal's remittances-to-GDP ratio of almost 28 percent was surpassed, worldwide, only by Tonga, the Kyrgyz Republic, Haiti, and Tajikistan (with ratios greater than 30 percent). The ratio is 11 percent in Bangladesh, 9 percent in Sri Lanka, and 7 percent in Pakistan. The ratios for Afghanistan, India, and Bhutan have always been less than 3 percent. Remittances are thus an important source of external financing for some countries (figure ES.3).

Migrating individuals benefit directly from international labor migration through higher wages abroad (figure ES.4). South Asian labor migrants earn a large wage premium compared with earnings at home because of the higher average wages and productivity in receiving countries. On average, monthly labor earnings of Bangladeshi migrants were, at 3,498 Bangladesh taka, almost four times higher in the receiving countries than in their home country (910 taka).[2] In 2016, labor migrants from India earned an average of US$362 in Saudi Arabia compared with US$112, on average, at home. Workers from Nepal earned almost five times more in Qatar than at home. Workers from Pakistan earned 3.6 times more in the United Arab Emirates, and 4.8 times more in

FIGURE ES.2

Remittances relative to the size of South Asian economies, 2018

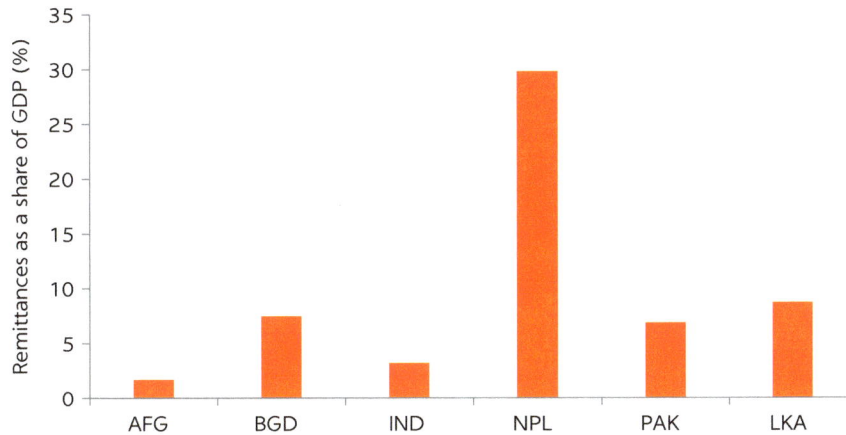

Sources: Data from World Development Indicators and KNOMAD Remittances Database.
Note: AFG = Afghanistan; BGD = Bangladesh; IND = India; LKA = Sri Lanka; NPL = Nepal;
PAK = Pakistan.

FIGURE ES.3

Remittance flows into major migrant-sending South Asian countries relative to FDI and ODA, 2019

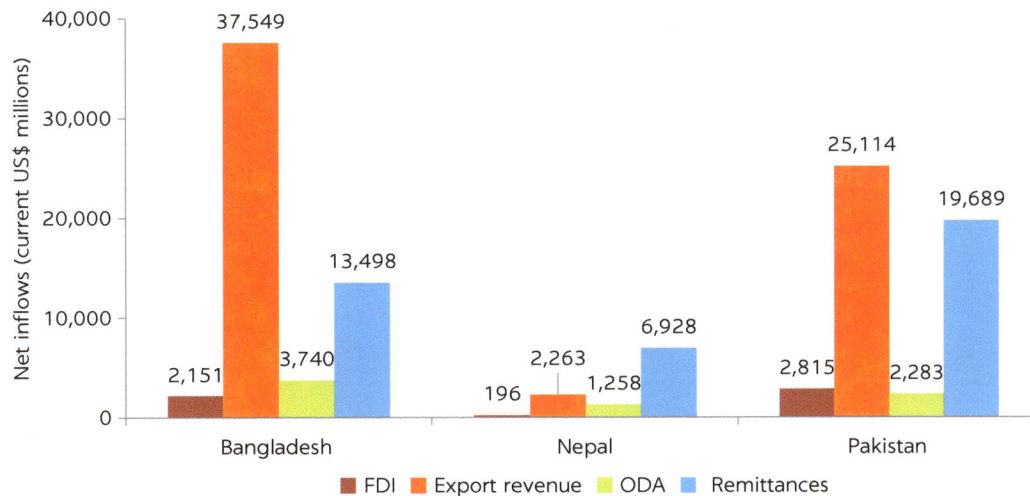

Sources: FDI, ODA, and export revenue data from World Development Indicators 2019; remittance inflow data from KNOMAD Remittances Database.
Note: FDI = foreign direct investment, net inflows (balance of payments, current US$); export revenue = exports of goods and services (current US$); ODA = net official development assistance (current US$); remittances = migrant remittance inflows (current US$).

Saudi Arabia. Higher wages abroad can help improve the welfare of households back home through remittances. In addition to these immediate static effects, this large positive income shock can increase savings and the ability to ensure against future negative shocks. It can also help increase lifetime earnings even after migrants have returned home, by allowing them to accumulate sufficient savings to start up entrepreneurial activities that could generate income for the remainder of their working lives (Bossavie et al. 2021).

FIGURE ES.4

Migrants' wage gains in destination countries

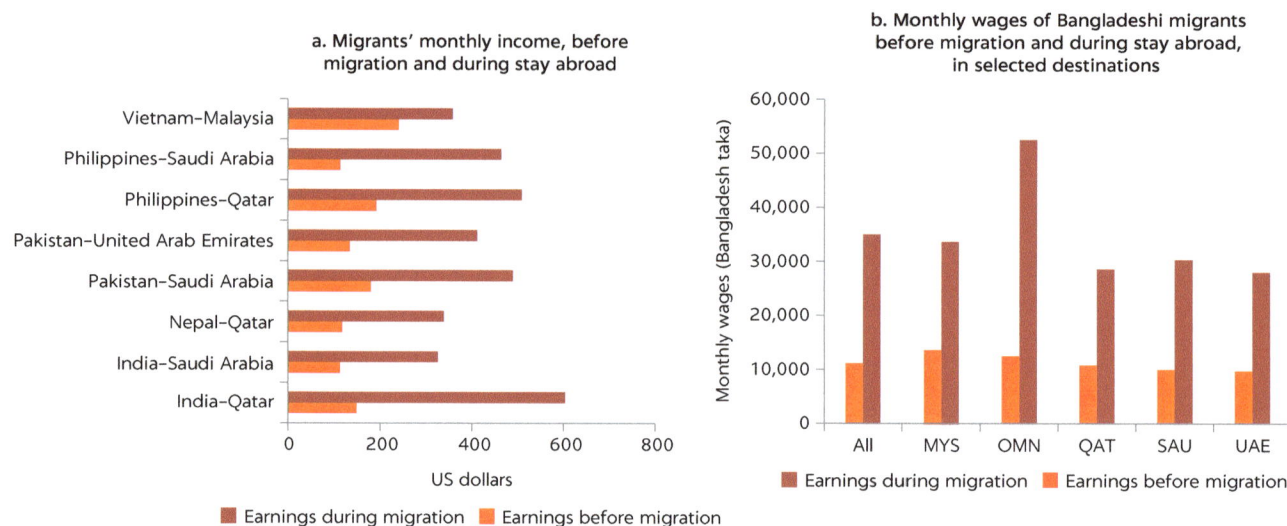

a. Migrants' monthly income, before migration and during stay abroad

b. Monthly wages of Bangladeshi migrants before migration and during stay abroad, in selected destinations

■ Earnings during migration ■ Earnings before migration

Sources: Data for panel a estimated from KNOMAD-ILO Migration Costs Surveys 2015 and 2016 for select corridors with South and East Asian origin countries. Data for panel b estimated from Bangladesh Return Migrant Survey 2018/19.
Note: All = all destinations; MYS = Malaysia; OMN = Oman; QAT = Qatar; SAU = Saudi Arabia; UAE = United Arab Emirates.

FACTORS PREVENTING MIGRATION FROM HAVING A HIGHER DEVELOPMENT IMPACT

Migrant workers from South Asia incur some of the highest migration costs in the world, and in some cases it takes them several months to recoup this outlay. Total migration costs vary substantially across migration corridors (figure ES.5). Pakistani migrants in Saudi Arabia incur the largest overall costs: almost US$5,000 on average. In comparison, migrants from Nepal spend less than US$1,000 to migrate to Malaysia, Qatar, or Saudi Arabia. When Filipinos migrate to Saudi Arabia, they pay only a very small fraction of the costs incurred by their Pakistani counterparts. Similarly, migrants from India pay in total less than a third of the expenditure incurred by Pakistani labor migrants when moving to the GCC countries. On average, Bangladeshi workers spent more than US$3,000 on migration costs.[3] For Bangladeshis, total migration costs are greatest for the Bangladesh-Qatar corridor, at almost US$4,000, and least for the Bangladesh-Malaysia corridor, at roughly US$2,900. Migration costs are invariably higher for workers from South Asia than for migrants from other countries of origin going to the same GCC countries, suggesting that features of the migrant recruitment market at home play an important systemic role in determining costs.

High migration costs present a substantial barrier to migrating for the poorest households. South Asia has the second-highest rate of extreme poverty in the world after Sub-Saharan Africa, but the poor are not generally the people who migrate. In Bangladesh, total migration costs equate to about two and a half years of the median household income in Bangladesh, and much more for the poorest households. As a result, only 2 percent of the households in the first and second consumption deciles have one or more migrating family members. The richer the household in Bangladesh and Nepal, the higher the likelihood that a family

Migration costs

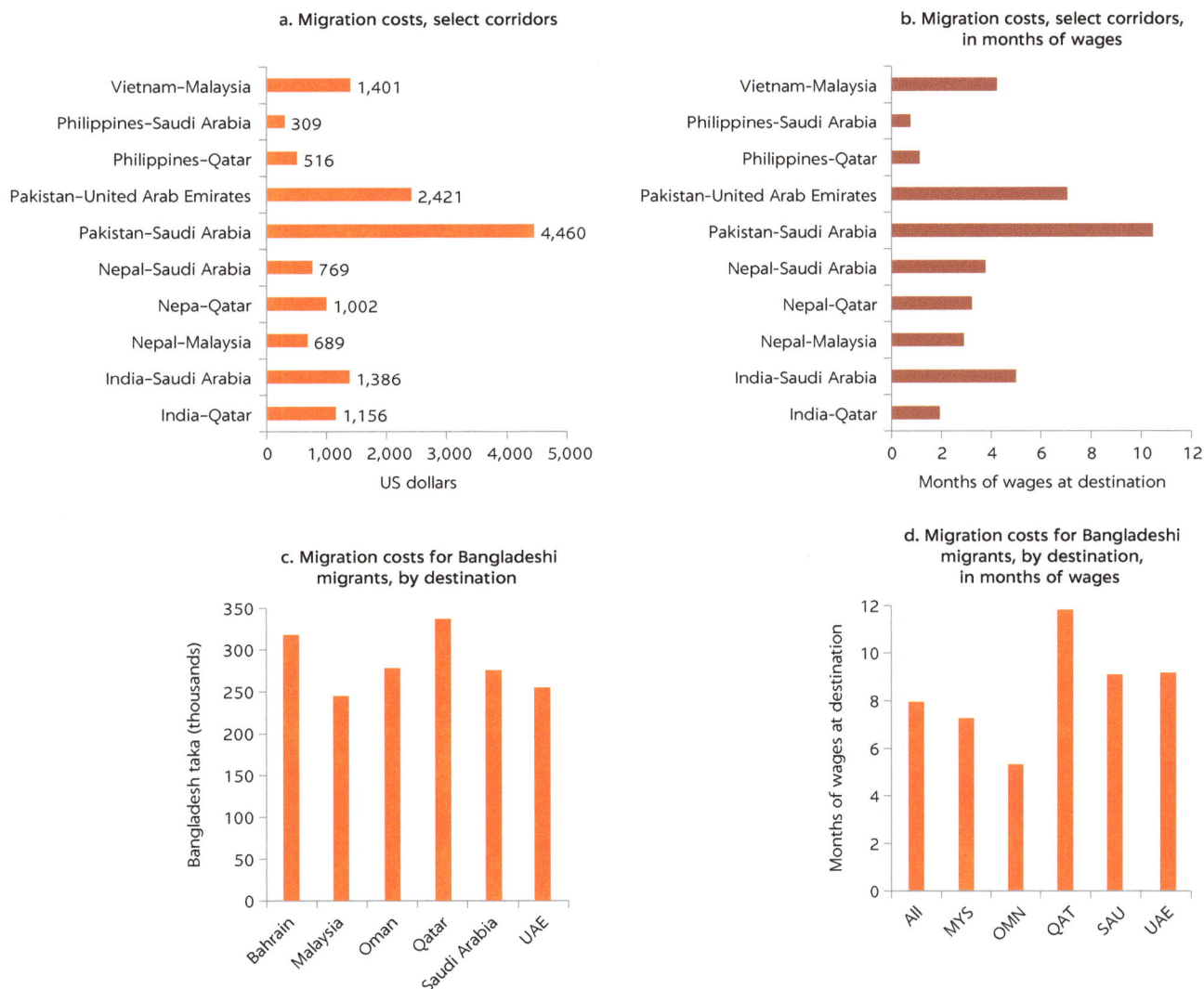

a. Migration costs, select corridors

Corridor	US dollars
Vietnam–Malaysia	1,401
Philippines–Saudi Arabia	309
Philippines–Qatar	516
Pakistan–United Arab Emirates	2,421
Pakistan–Saudi Arabia	4,460
Nepal–Saudi Arabia	769
Nepa–Qatar	1,002
Nepal–Malaysia	689
India–Saudi Arabia	1,386
India–Qatar	1,156

b. Migration costs, select corridors, in months of wages

c. Migration costs for Bangladeshi migrants, by destination

d. Migration costs for Bangladeshi migrants, by destination, in months of wages

Sources: For panels a and b, KNOMAD-ILO Migration Costs Surveys 2015 and 2016. For panels c and d, Bangladesh Return Migrant Survey 2018/19.
Note: For panels a and b, the migration cost indicator (MCI) is calculated as the average worker-incurred migration cost in 2016 US dollars divided by foreign monthly gross earnings in 2016 US dollars (KNOMAD-ILO Migration Costs Surveys 2015 and 2016). Migration costs include fees paid to recruitment agents, costs for documents (passport, visa, medical certificates, language test, security clearance), and transportation cost (KNOMAD-ILO Migration Costs Surveys 2015 and 2016). All = all destinations; MYS = Malaysia; OMN = Oman; QAT is Qatar; SAU = Saudi Arabia; UAE = United Arab Emirates.

member works as a migrant in another country (figure ES.6).[4] In addition, the income level of the migrating household also affects the incidence and amount of remittances.

High migration costs also reduce the propensity to remit and the amount of remittances sent. Migration costs significantly lower the disposable income of the migrant. Instead of transferring remittances to the household, the migrant uses earnings abroad to pay back migration-related expenses or loans taken from individuals outside the household. These effects are most pronounced in Pakistan, where migration costs are higher. For corridors originating in Pakistan, a 1 percent increase in migration costs is associated with a 0.11 percent to 0.16 percent decrease in remittances.[5] Other than reflecting differences in

FIGURE ES.6

International migrants in poorer and richer households in Bangladesh and Nepal

a. Share of Bangladeshi households with an international migrant (left axis) and remittances share of income in households with at least one migrant (right axis), by consumption decile

b. Share of Nepali households receiving remittances from an international migrant, by consumption quintile

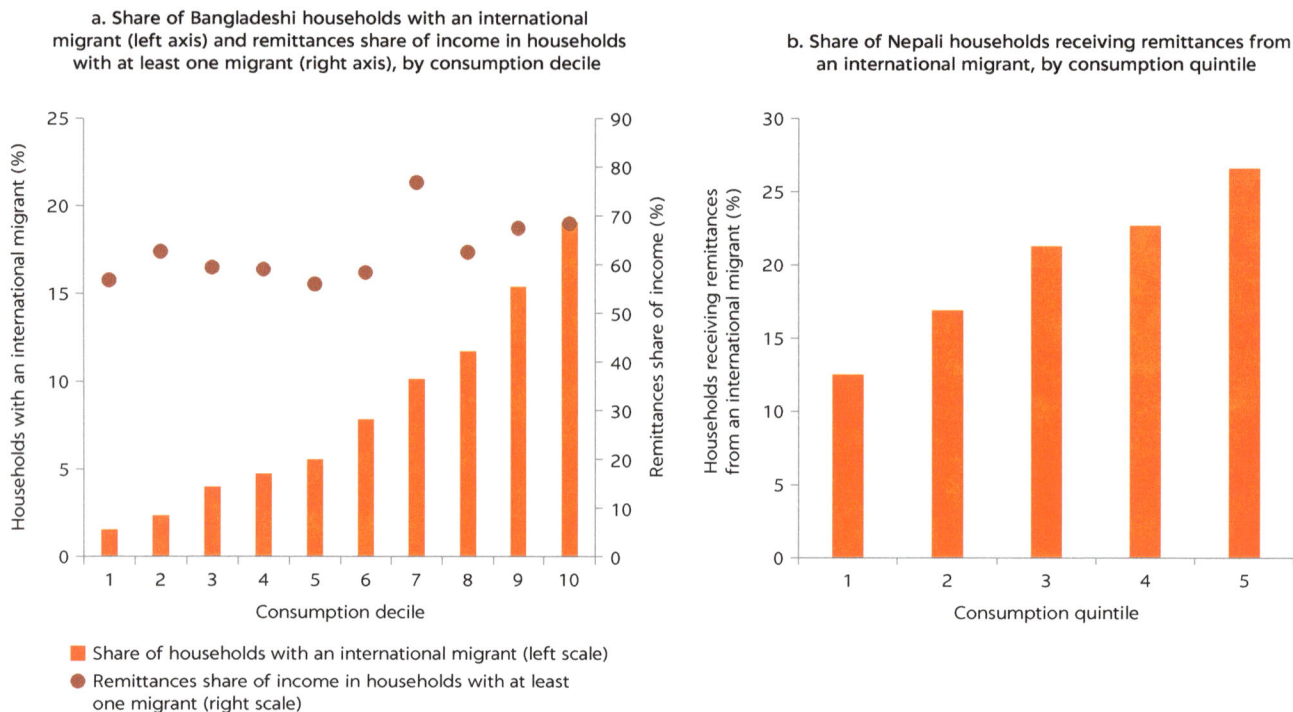

■ Share of households with an international migrant (left scale)
● Remittances share of income in households with at least one migrant (right scale)

Sources: Estimated from Household Income and Expenditure Survey Bangladesh 2016/17 and the Nepal Household Risk and Vulnerability Survey 2016. Higher consumption deciles and quintiles correspond to higher levels of household consumption.

statistical power, the fact that the negative effect of migration costs is larger in the Pakistani corridors may imply the existence of a threshold effect. That is, where migration costs are relatively lower (as in Nepal), they may be less important in determining remittance decisions, or their effect may be small relative to the total amount of remittances. It may be only at high levels that they have a detectable impact on total remittances.

High migration costs also have dynamic effects over the migrants' entire life cycle. Decisions about when and where to migrate, how long to stay at destination, and what to do after return are all interdependent and part of the same process of life-cycle optimization undertaken by migrants (Dustmann and Görlach 2016; Dustmann and Kirchkamp 2002). These decisions are affected both by the costs and by the benefits of temporary migration. Migration costs thus have an impact on when migrants leave—because they need to accumulate sufficient savings to finance upfront costs—on how long they need to stay at destination to generate sufficient net returns from the move, and on their economic activity after returning home. In particular, temporary migration can allow workers to accumulate savings relatively faster than they could at home, overcome credit constraints back home, and then start up entrepreneurial activities after return (Bossavie et al. 2021; Dustmann and Kirchkamp 2002; Wahba 2015). In this setting, higher migration costs increase the duration of the stay overseas required to achieve targeted savings, or, if migrants cannot stay longer at destination, total net savings are reduced. As a result, for lack of start-up capital, migrants may upon their return find themselves unable to begin self-employment or may have to postpone it and consequently experience lower lifetime earnings.

Intermediation costs account for large differences in total expenditures for South Asian labor migrants (figures ES.7 and ES.8). Pakistani migrants to Saudi Arabia and the United Arab Emirates spend more than 60 percent of their direct migration costs on visa fees. Without these high visa costs, the total expenditure would most likely be on par with the migration-related costs of their counterparts from other countries. Nepali migrants to Saudi Arabia and Malaysia spend about 60 percent and 40 percent, respectively, of their total migration expenditure on fees for brokers (agents). Agents' fees account for about 40 percent of the total expenditure of Nepali migrants in Qatar. Bangladeshi labor migrants spend on average more than 50 percent of the total migration cost on these intermediaries. On average, more than 20 percent of their total migration expenditure is used to obtain a passport and the visa of the relevant destination country.

Poor working conditions in receiving countries present nonpecuniary costs for South Asian labor migrants. Apart from financial costs, costs associated with deficiencies in the working conditions of migrants in host countries increase the overall costs of labor migration. These nonpecuniary costs, which are usually only revealed after arrival in the receiving country, need to be considered. They not only affect the overall well-being of migrants while at destination (Aleksynska, Aoul, and Petrencu 2017), but can also affect migrants' return decisions and thus the overall success (or failure) of the migration experience.

High migration costs contribute to high vulnerability in the host country. Given the very high total costs of migration, migrants from South Asia have to stay abroad about a year merely to break even on their initial investment.

FIGURE ES.7

Migration cost breakdown for select corridors

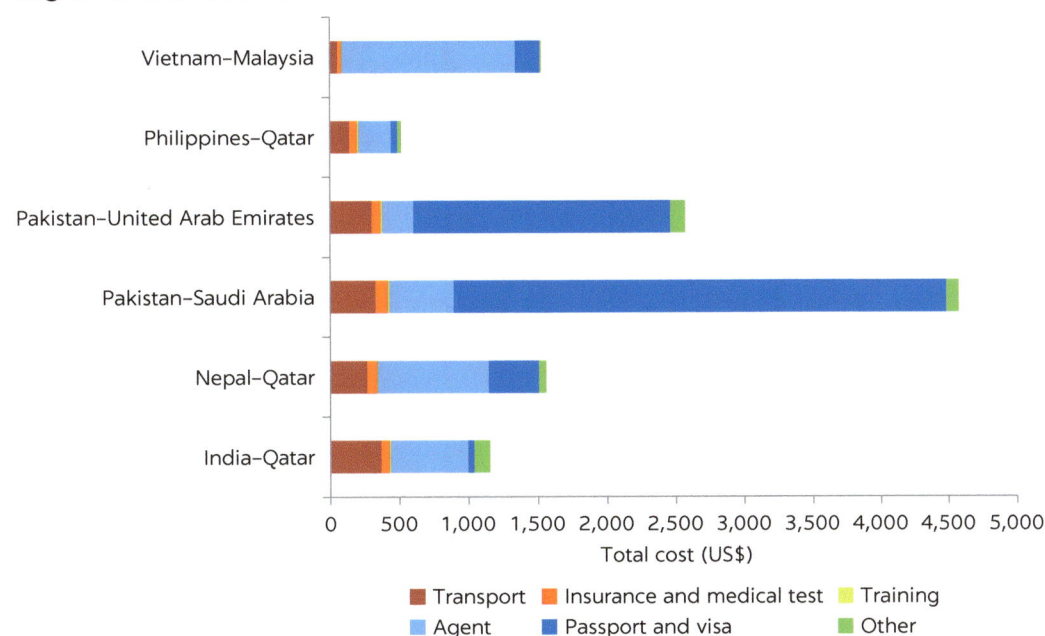

Source: KNOMAD-ILO Migration Costs Surveys 2015 and 2016.
Note: Costs that constitute less than 1 percent of total expenditures are dropped.
SAU = Saudi Arabia; UAE = United Arab Emirates.

FIGURE ES.8
Bangladesh, intermediation costs by component

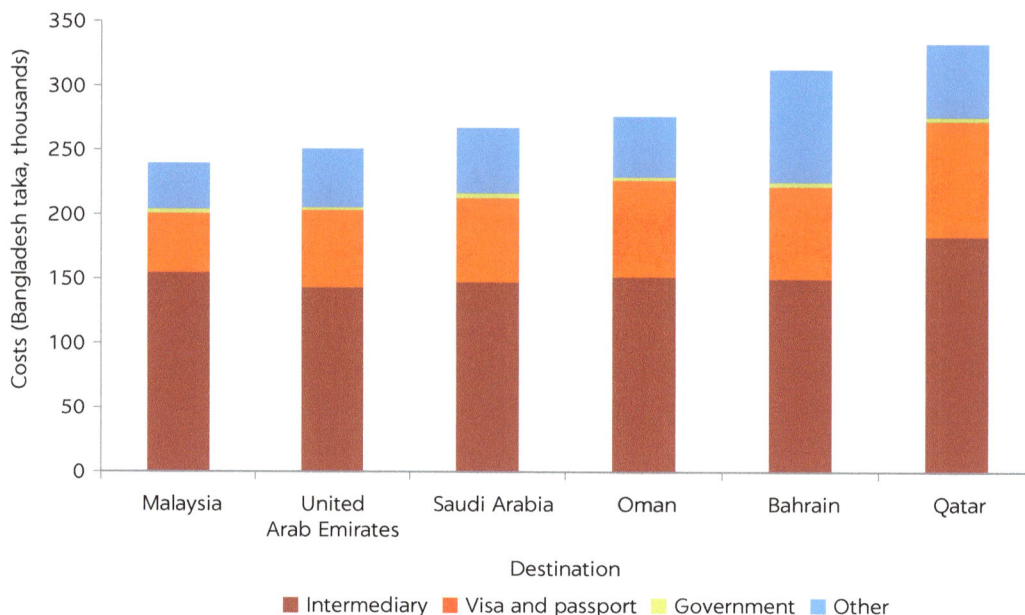

Source: Bangladesh Return Migrant Survey 2018/19.

Many migrants borrow to finance their migration, which further inflates costs and creates the additional pressure of loan repayment. Having repaid these very large fixed costs, migrants then need to stay long enough at destination to generate a return on their initial investment sufficient for them to accumulate savings and send remittances back home for consumption. These very large upfront costs greatly reduce the bargaining power of migrants, whose stay at destination is entirely tied to their sponsoring employer. In the absence of alternative options, migrants are obliged to stay with their employer, irrespective of their conditions of employment, leaving them exposed to abuse by the employer (Khan and Harroff-Tavel 2011). In addition, the high costs of migration can also serve as an incentive for migrants (who originally migrated legally) to overstay illegally if their employment contract and work permit are not renewed.[6]

EXPOSURE TO HIGH VOLATILITY AND FUTURE RISKS FROM HIGH CONCENTRATIONS IN FEW DESTINATIONS

Migrants from South Asia are concentrated in a few sectors and destinations. South Asian labor migration is regionally clustered in GCC countries and Malaysia (figure ES.9). A strong regional concentration of labor migration increases vulnerability to economic shocks in the migrants' home countries. In 2017, 2.7 million Bangladeshis worked as labor migrants abroad. Roughly 1 million of them worked in Saudi Arabia and another million in the United Arab Emirates. Among the 2.5 million Pakistani labor migrants abroad, 1.3 million worked in Saudi Arabia and roughly another million in the United Arab Emirates. Half of all Nepali temporary migrant workers are in Saudi Arabia. Labor migrants

FIGURE ES.9

Distribution of stock of migrants in major temporary economic migration destinations, 2017, and total migrants

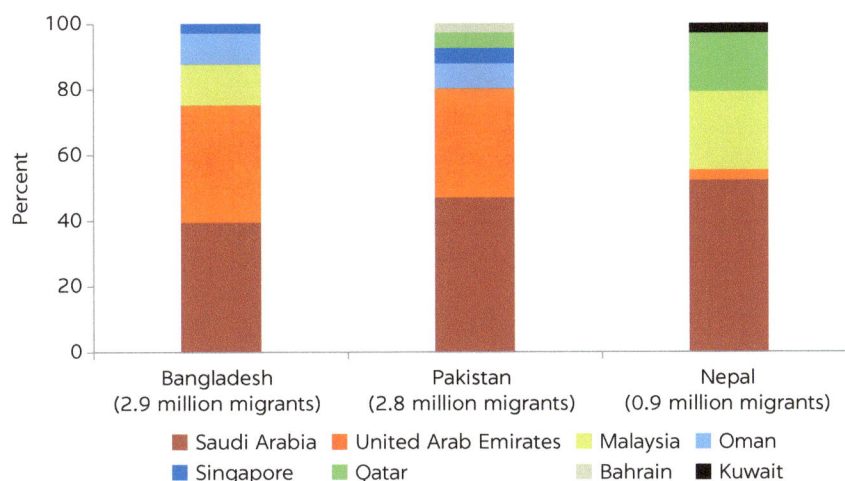

Source: UN DESA 2017.
Note: UN DESA figures include documented and undocumented migrants, and their families.

from South Asia are also concentrated in a few low-paying sectors of activity.[7] The majority of low-skilled male labor migrants from South Asia work in the construction sector in the receiving countries.

South Asia sends high volumes of temporary migrant workers to many economies, but the flows are highly volatile, and demand for low-skilled South Asian labor migrants in major destinations could continue to decline (figure ES.10). In the early and mid-2000s, volatile oil prices led to a reduction in government revenues and a decline in spending on new construction projects in the GCC region (Deloitte 2018). To sustain economic growth in the future, GCC countries will need to invest more heavily in new services and industries. These sectors usually require a more sophisticated skill set from workers than the construction sector (Callen et al. 2014). South Asian labor migrants, who are mostly low skilled and working in the construction sector, will be negatively affected by the economic changes under way in the GCC countries. Ultimately, because of changing economic structures in the GCC and associated uncertainties, South Asia's macroeconomic vulnerability will likely increase, at least in the short run.

The direct shocks to a corridor may have real or suspected externalities to other corridors, potentially leading to "races to the bottom." If South Asian economies send workers with similar skill profiles to the same destination, there is perceived competition for the positions available, and policy measures in some countries to increase the safety and protection of migrant workers may be thought to reduce the competitiveness of workers from that country. For example, India implemented its new e-Migrate system in 2015 to better manage its labor migrants and enhance their protection. Through the e-Migrate platform, the Indian Protector of Emigrants issues clearances for workers to leave the country after various conditions have been met, including the issuance of a contract that specifies that the worker will receive at least a minimum wage set by the Indian government. In the same year, Saudi Arabia signed memoranda of

FIGURE ES.10

Indicators of host country demand and sending country migration and remittances

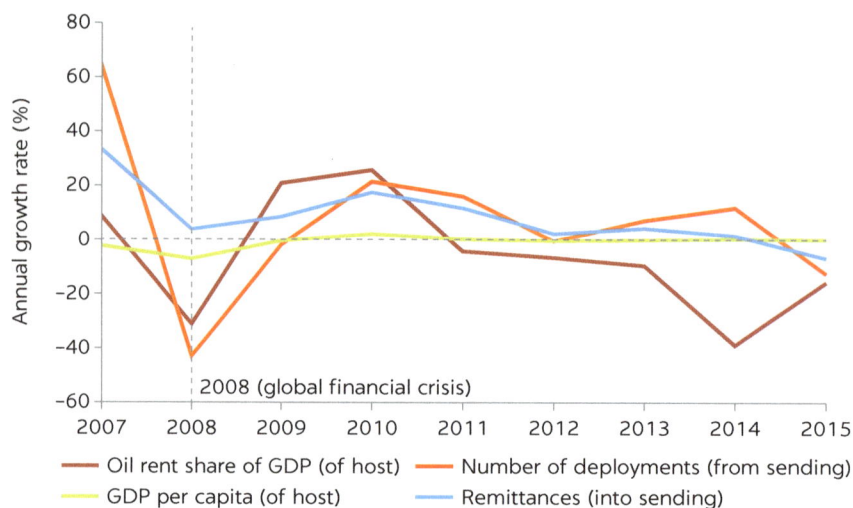

Sources: For data on oil rent share of GDP and GDP per capita, World Development Indicators; for data on remittances, KNOMAD Remittances Database; for deployments, Bangladeshi Bureau of Manpower Employment and Training; Sri Lankan Bureau of Foreign Employment; Pakistan Bureau of Emigration and Overseas Employment; Nepali Department of Foreign Employment; Indian Ministry of External Affairs.

Note: The figure shows growth rates during the period 2008–17. Number of deployments is calculated as average for Bangladeshi, Indian, Nepali, and Pakistani labor migrants in their respective top five destination countries. Data for Nepal's migration corridors are only available for the period 2009–17. Oil rent share of GDP is calculated as average for Bahrain, Kuwait, Malaysia, Oman, Qatar, Saudi Arabia, and the United Arab Emirates. Hong Kong SAR, China; and Singapore are excluded for lack of available data. GDP per capita is calculated as the average for the host countries with the largest shares of South Asian labor migrants (Bahrain, Kuwait, Malaysia, Oman, Qatar, Saudi Arabia, and the United Arab Emirates); remittances are defined as total amount of remittances that flow into Bangladesh, India, Nepal, and Pakistan.

understanding for workers from Bangladesh, including for female domestic workers. Subsequently, the flows of migrant workers from India to Saudi Arabia collapsed in that same year (2015), while flows from Bangladesh soared.

NEED FOR HOLISTIC POLICY ACTIONS TO MAKE MIGRATION SAFER AND MORE PRODUCTIVE

This book approaches migration not as a one-time event, but as part of the migrants' entire life cycle. The temporary nature of labor mobility is a prominent feature of migration from South Asia, which requires departing from the traditional migration framework that treats migration as a permanent, one-time episode. Instead, migration must be considered part of workers' entire life cycle, where all stages are interlinked and part of the same lifetime decisions (Bossavie et al. 2021; Dustmann and Görlach 2016). For example, premigration employment outcomes and age at departure are linked to duration of stay abroad. Duration of stay, in turn, is affected by migration costs and wages abroad, which also determine how long migrants need to stay overseas to achieve a given savings target. Closing the full cycle, the ability to finance a self-employment activity after return will be affected by the monetary costs of migration, wages abroad, and duration of stay at destination. Policy interventions that aim to influence any of these decisions or outcomes will thus, by the very nature of these links, also influence the others. It is thus critical for policy makers to consider these links when designing policies related to temporary migration.

Making migration for South Asia safer and more productive thus requires interventions across the migration life cycle (figure ES.11). The migration life cycle is generally described as having four stages (Cho and Majoka 2020). The first stage is predecision, when a worker decides to migrate based on an understanding of the costs and benefits of migrating. The second stage is predeparture, when, after the worker has decided to pursue an overseas job, he or she can take steps to improve employability, find and secure a job, and obtain the necessary legal documents to migrate (clearances from national authorities, visas, passports, and so forth), and complete the logistical preparations for migration (tickets, financing). The third stage is when the migrant is employed overseas, and the final stage is after return to the home country. The recruitment process and access to information are important factors that affect monetary and non-monetary migration costs specifically in the predecision and predeparture phases. However, migrant costs are also higher if the migrant travels to destinations with weaker labor laws and regulations, which is a significant issue during the third stage. At each stage of this process, migrants require information and support from the migration management system of both their country of origin and the destination country.

Reducing volatility and improving sustainability will ultimately require sending countries to diversify the destinations to which they send their workers. Despite the enormous economic capacity of countries in high-income Asia (mainly the Republic of Korea and Japan) and their sophisticated labor migration policies, these countries have received relatively few South Asian migrants in recent decades. However, because of changing demographics, high-income Asian countries might substantially increase the intake of labor migrants from South Asia in the future. Labor mobility through memoranda of understanding, such as for the Republic of Korea's Employment Permit System (EPS) program,

FIGURE ES.11

The four illustrative stages of the migration life cycle and common policy issues

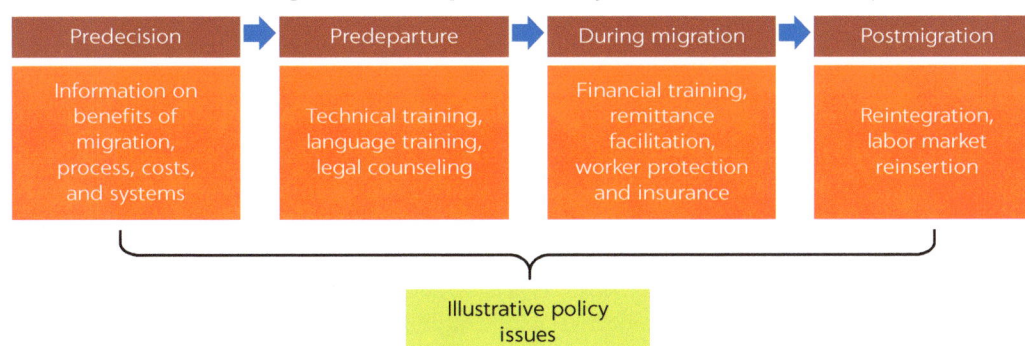

Predecision	Predeparture	During migration	Postmigration
Information on benefits of migration, process, costs, and systems	Technical training, language training, legal counseling	Financial training, remittance facilitation, worker protection and insurance	Reintegration, labor market reinsertion

Illustrative policy issues

Source: Adapted from Cho and Majoka (2020).

show that further diversification toward high-income Asia could be beneficial for South Asian migrants and their home countries because of much lower migration expenditures and a lower risk of human rights violations by employers than in the GCC countries.

Entering these newer markets will require changes in the profile of the migrants being sent. Currently, most migrants from South Asia are in lower-skilled occupations, reflecting the demands of current destinations (primarily GCC countries and Malaysia). Destinations that offer higher wages and better protections for workers—such as Korea—require additional skills, even for jobs in labor-intensive sectors such as agriculture. These skills include language knowledge in addition to noncognitive skills such as teamwork and collaboration. For other markets, such as Japan and Hong Kong SAR, China, where there is growing demand for caregivers (childcare and care of the elderly), the supply of such professionals will have to increase, as will the supply of skills development services to train aspiring migrants to become caregivers. Line agencies responsible for managed labor migration may also need to have the capacity to take proactive measures, such as identifying potential demand for different types of workers from new and existing markets. This information will be critical for reorienting the skills development architecture and gaining a detailed understanding of the scope for foreign labor offered by those markets.

Some institutional frameworks, such as high-quality bilateral labor agreements, can serve to reduce costs while also providing avenues into new markets, both new destinations and new types of professions. One is the Korean EPS, which is managed directly by Human Resource Development Korea and open to Bangladesh and Nepal. Migrating to Korea for temporary work through this program costs the Bangladeshi migrant approximately US$900. Migrants are paid Korean minimum wages, are able to change employers, have access to grievance redressal mechanisms, are covered by Korean labor laws against abuse and exploitation, and receive reintegration support (including a lump-sum payment) to Bangladesh upon completion of the contract period. The program is managed entirely by the Korean government, and it offers high-quality intermediation, whereby employers' needs for skills and workforce size are closely monitored to facilitate rigorous matching of migrant workers to employers.

Administrative capacity in the sending countries will need to increase if government-to-government programs such as the EPS or the Bangladesh-Malaysia government-to-government program are to be used further in the future. The improved migration outcomes and lower costs of intermediation are attributed to the public provision of services such as job matching and screening. However, this public provision requires substantial investments in government capacity for sustained service delivery. The Bangladesh-Malaysia government-to-government program experienced excess demand from aspiring migrants, with about 1.4 million eligible candidates applying for the 30,000 vacancies. The Ministry of Expatriates' Welfare and Overseas Employment's in-house recruitment agency, Bangladesh Overseas Employment and Services Limited, administers programs that are similar to, albeit smaller than, the Korean EPS. However, the EPS is a channel for relatively modest migrant labor demand from Korea (relative to labor demand from GCC countries, for example), with a total of roughly 30,000 workers needed from all sending countries combined.

WAYS TO HARNESS THE DEVELOPMENT POTENTIAL OF RETURN MIGRANTS MORE EFFECTIVELY

Given contractual labor arrangements in the main destinations, low-skilled migrants from South Asia must ultimately return home. The main host countries of labor migrants from South Asia—primarily in the GCC countries and Southeast Asia—only grant temporary residence rights to low-skilled labor migrants. Stay at destination is strictly conditional on holding a valid employment contract and work permit, and expiry of the employment contract without renewal, or a layoff by the employer at destination, automatically entails a return to the home country. In the GCC countries, the acquisition of citizenship is effectively prohibited, irrespective of duration of stay (Lucas 2008; Wahba 2015).[8] Low-skilled contractual migrants can have their labor contracts and work permits renewed at destination—if the employer still wants their services—but they cannot retire at destination.

Many temporary migrants return earlier than originally planned or specified by their contract term, indicating that shocks and imperfect information affect return decisions. The main reason for returning among migrants from South Asia is the end of their employment contract at destination. However, unanticipated returns—that is, migrants returning earlier than they had originally planned—are common among temporary migrants: 43 percent of return migrants in Bangladesh report that they returned earlier than originally planned or before the end of their employment contract term. The leading reasons for returning earlier are being expelled from the host country, low wages at destination, and being laid off by the employer. The fact that many migrants return earlier because of low wages suggests imperfect information on earnings overseas at the time of migration.

Temporary labor migrants overestimate earnings and savings at destination before departure, which affects migration and return decisions. More than three-quarters of return migrants in Bangladesh expected to earn higher wages at destination than they actually did. The gap between expected earnings at destination and actual wages is substantial (figure ES.12). Median actual labor earnings at destination are, on average, only two-thirds of what temporary migrants expected before departure. Similarly, the majority of return migrants report being able to save less at destination than they expected before departure. Additionally, despite the large differentials between wages at home and at destination, low earnings are often a reason for unanticipated returns. Former Bangladeshi migrants report this as one of the leading reasons for returning earlier than they planned. In Nepal and Pakistan, return migrants also report having been systematically promised a higher wage than they were actually paid, as evidenced by the KNOMAD-ILO Migration Costs Surveys 2015 and 2016.

Return migrants are less likely to be employed shortly after return than nonmigrants, but these lower employment rates are transitory. Immediately after return, employment rates of return migrants are lower than those of the nonmigrant population. However, within roughly two years the employment rates of return migrants in Nepal, Pakistan, and Bangladesh almost caught up with those of nonmigrants (figure ES.13). Evidence from Nepal and Bangladesh indicates that temporarily lower employment rates are driven by a lower

FIGURE ES.12

Wage levels expected before departure compared with wages actually earned overseas by temporary migrants from Bangladesh

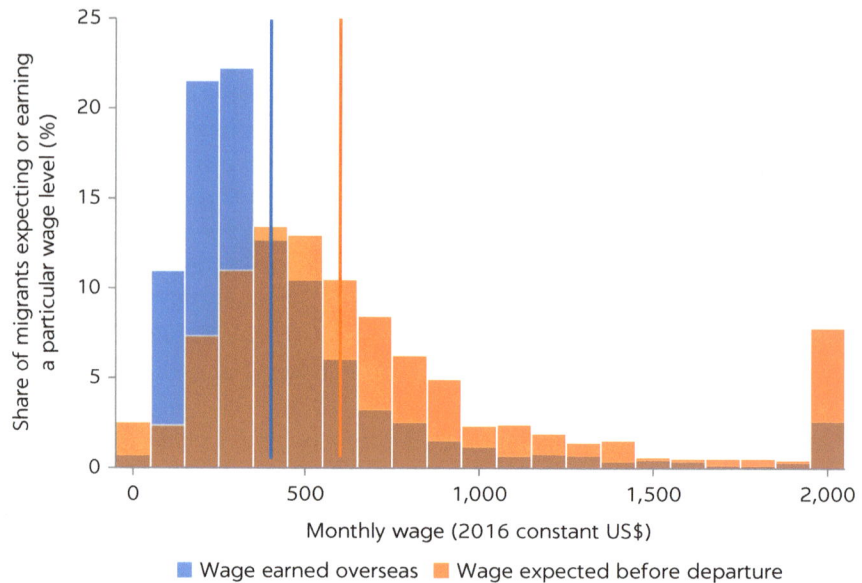

Sources: Bossavie et al. (2021) based on the Bangladesh Return Migrant Survey 2018/19.
Note: Statistics are for males ages 18–59. Orange and blue vertical lines represent median values for expected and actual wages overseas, respectively.

willingness to work immediately after return, as well as job search frictions. Job search frictions suggest that interventions targeted at temporary migrants in the months following return can support their transition back into home labor markets.

Many return migrants are able to start up in self-employment after return, thanks to savings accumulated abroad. Evidence from Bangladesh shows massive movements of workers—who were not in employment before migrating—into nonagricultural self-employment after return (figure ES.14). Similar transitions into nonagricultural self-employment after return have been documented in Pakistan (Ilahi 1999). The likelihood of becoming self-employed after return is positively associated with duration of stay overseas and wages abroad, and negatively associated with migration costs (Bossavie et al. 2021; Ilahi 1999). This finding is consistent with the idea that temporary migration helps alleviate credit constraints back home through the accumulation of savings coupled with entrepreneurial perspectives and abilities developed while abroad.

Policies targeted at return migrants must distinguish between planned and unplanned returns and, equally important, between forced and voluntary returns. The circumstances behind migrants' returns have very different implications for the type of policies needed to maximize the benefits of return migration for both the migrant and the home country. The interventions needed to support return temporary migrants who voluntarily returned after accumulating sufficient savings overseas are very different from those needed for migrants who were expelled from the host country, returned earlier than expected after

FIGURE ES.13

Labor market status of return migrants, by number of years since returning

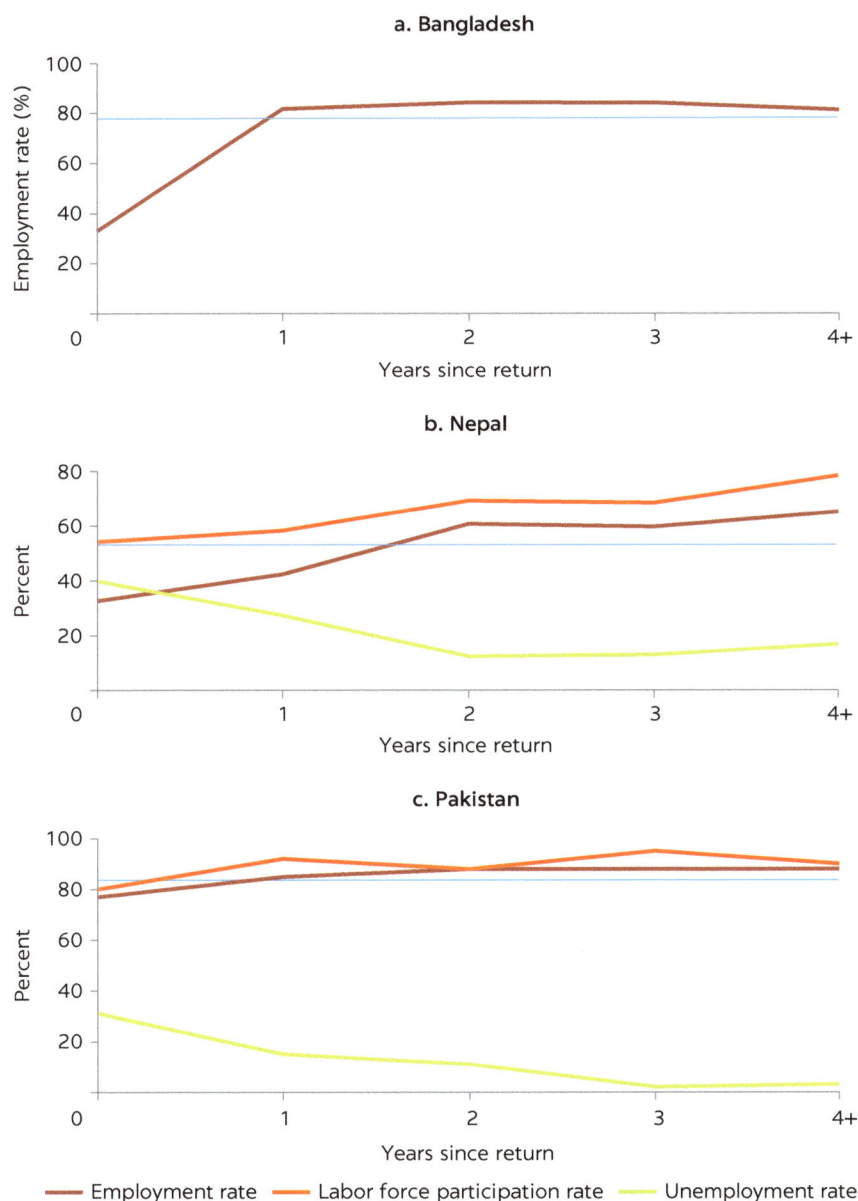

a. Bangladesh

b. Nepal

c. Pakistan

— Employment rate   — Labor force participation rate   — Unemployment rate

Source: World Bank calculations based on the World Bank Bangladesh Return Migrant Survey 2018/19, the Household Income and Expenditure Survey 2016/17 for Bangladesh, and the 2017/18 Labor Force Survey for Nepal and Pakistan.
Note: Statistics are for males ages 18–59 and account for sampling weights. Statistics for Bangladesh are restricted to rural and semi-urban areas. The horizontal straight blue line reports the employment rate of the nonmigrant population. The employment rate is calculated as the ratio of the number of individuals employed to the working-age population. The labor force participation rate is calculated as the ratio of number of individuals who are either employed or looking for a job to the working-age population. The unemployment rate is calculated as the ratio of the number of individuals who are looking for employment to the number of individuals who are economically active, that is, who are either employed or looking for employment.

FIGURE ES.14

Employment status of temporary migrants from Bangladesh before migration and after return (as a percentage of all return migrants surveyed)

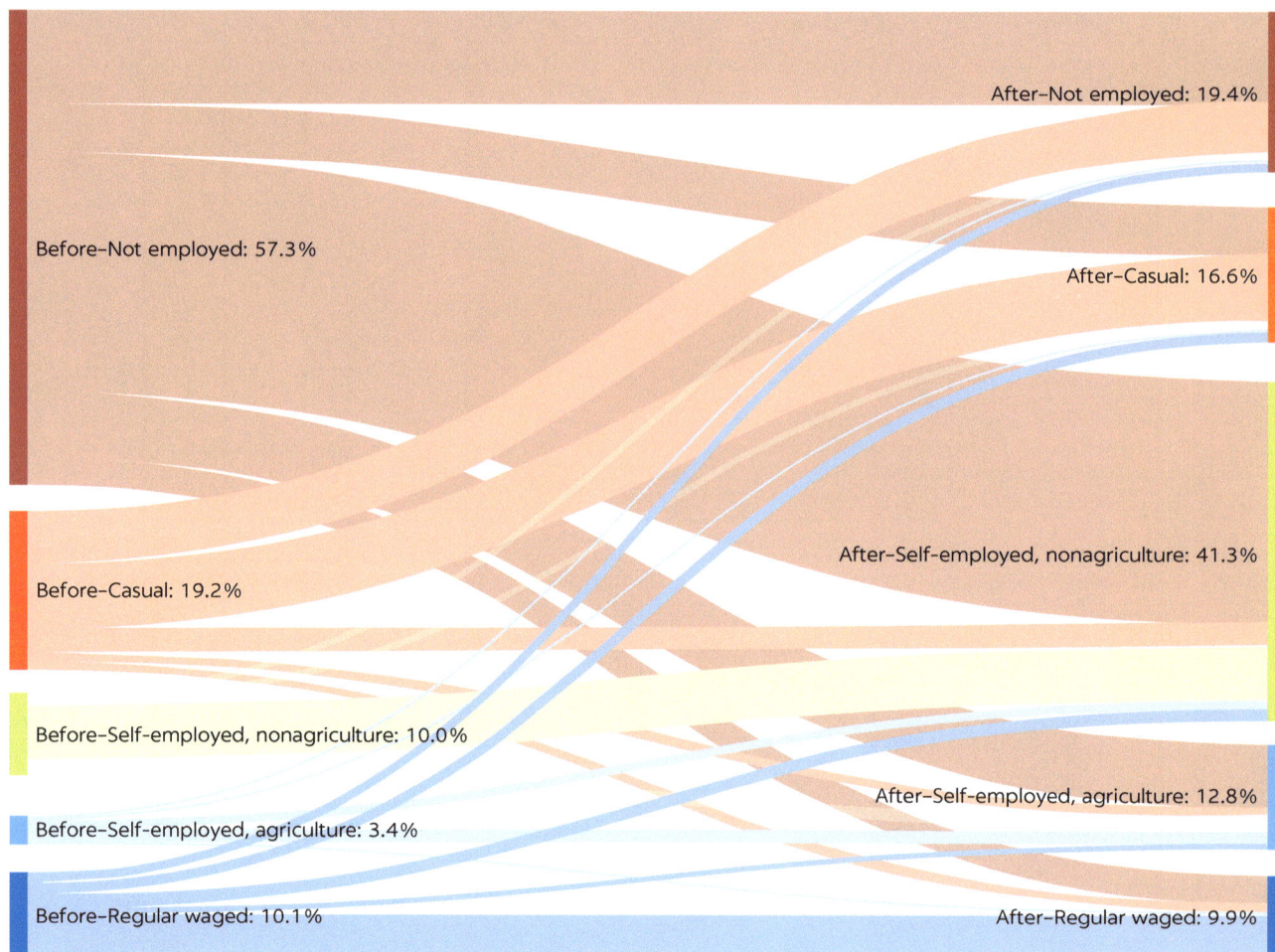

Before–Not employed: 57.3%
Before–Casual: 19.2%
Before–Self-employed, nonagriculture: 10.0%
Before–Self-employed, agriculture: 3.4%
Before–Regular waged: 10.1%

After–Not employed: 19.4%
After–Casual: 16.6%
After–Self-employed, nonagriculture: 41.3%
After–Self-employed, agriculture: 12.8%
After–Regular waged: 9.9%

Sources: Ahmed et al. (2021) based on data from the Bangladesh Return Migrant Survey 2018/19.
Note: Statistics are for males ages 18–59.

disenchantment, or were laid off by their employer at destination. Whereas voluntary returns can be accompanied by more standard labor interventions, such as labor intermediation or support for entrepreneurship, forced returns can require additional policy support. Such interventions include support for repatriation and cash grants to meet basic needs and commence the process of livelihood restoration. Interventions aimed at improving savings management and financial literacy throughout the migration life cycle, however, can serve to improve the welfare of migrants irrespective of the reason for their return (Doi, McKenzie, and Zia 2014).

Designing effective policies for temporary migrants requires systematic collection of data on their migration history and outcomes before, during, and after migration. Important knowledge gaps remain regarding temporary migrants in South Asia because the relevant data either do not exist or are unavailable in the form required. Administrative data sources in the region do not allow following the trajectories of migrants during migration and after return to the home country, given that basic background information on migrants is only recorded at the time of departure. In addition, the labor market outcomes of temporary migrants in destination countries are typically unknown because administrative data from host countries cannot be linked to home-country administrative data on migrants. As a result, administrative data are currently of very limited use in understanding temporary migration from South Asia and in designing adequate supporting policies. Some nationally representative surveys in origin countries have covered temporary migrants after their return, but sample sizes are typically small, and detailed information on labor market outcomes at destination is typically lacking (Ahmed et al. 2021; Bossavie and Özden 2022). National household surveys must therefore be expanded or modified so that detailed labor migration modules capture the necessary granularity of data on return migrants. In addition, surveys targeting return migrants, such as the World Bank Bangladesh Return Migrant Survey 2018/19, could be replicated and generalized to other migrant-sending countries. Those surveys allow the collection of in-depth information on the migration and employment histories of temporary migrants at a level of detail that cannot be achieved by standard national household surveys.

IMPLICATIONS OF THE COVID-19 PANDEMIC AND ITS AFTERMATH

The COVID-19 (coronavirus) pandemic generated new challenges for South Asian migrants, but mostly exacerbated and brought to light vulnerabilities and migration system insufficiencies that already existed prior to the pandemic. The lack of diversification of migrants' destinations and economic activities overseas greatly exposed them to the negative shocks associated with COVID-19. Indeed, South Asian migrants are concentrated in markets that have been severely hit by the COVID-19 (coronavirus) pandemic. The GCC countries, the main destination for South Asian migrant workers, have been affected by the pandemic as well as by the suppressed global demand for and price of oil (World Bank 2020). A reduction in labor as well as in materials, capital, and intermediate inputs due to disruptions in transport and business caused a powerful, immediate cascade of supply contractions (IMF 2020).[9] Those restrictions have been having a disproportionate impact on the construction sector (the main employment sector for low-skilled migrants from South Asia), which has been shown to expand the most during a boom and to contract the most during a recession (Dell'Ariccia et al. 2020). Many construction sites were closed because of potential infection and spread of the virus, and the risk of infection is high among migrants living in densely populated residential facilities. The hardest hit sectors include retail and wholesale trade, hospitality and leisure, manufacturing, and food service, where a large share of migrants from the region are also employed.

The sharp slowdown in economic activity and global mobility have affected temporary migrants from South Asia in numerous ways, enhancing the need for policies supporting safe and productive migration. First, in the short run, many migrant workers already in destination countries have been stranded, often with no jobs, access to health care, or ability to return (Guadagno 2020; Moroz, Shrestha, and Testaverde 2020; World Bank 2020). Second, aspiring migrants have been unable to depart because of travel restrictions imposed in a global effort to limit the spread of the pandemic, and limited demand for foreign labor in the main destinations—the number of new deployments from the region dropped sharply in 2020 as a result of the global pandemic. In Bangladesh, the number of departures for work overseas dropped from more than 700,000 in 2019 to only 217,000 in 2020. A similar drop in new deployments was observed in Pakistan, from 625,000 in 2019 to 224,705 in 2020. Initial figures for 2021 suggest that new deployments are recovering slightly, though they remain well below 2019 levels. Finally, the COVID-19 pandemic has also led to an unprecedented number of returns to the South Asia region, even though home economies' labor markets have been severely hit and thus have very limited capacity to absorb them. An estimated 250,000 Bangladeshis returned to the country between January and April of 2020, and estimates suggest that up to 2 million may have returned in the following months. Similarly, the government of Nepal has been preparing to repatriate 400,000 displaced workers (IOM 2020). By May of 2020, about 60,000 Pakistanis were registered to return from the United Arab Emirates alone (Al Jazeera 2020). Given the very high costs of migration from the region, migrants who had recently gone overseas and were forced to return prematurely find themselves indebted, at high rates of interest, at a time when labor market opportunities to restart economic activities at home are also quite limited. While the situation of forced returnees has been especially concerning in the context of COVID-19, the pandemic brought to light preexisting vulnerabilities among this population, which need to be addressed beyond the specific context of the pandemic.

Longer-run impacts will depend on the persistence of the pandemic and the pace of labor market recovery once the pandemic is contained. The numbers of COVID-19 cases in the GCC countries and Malaysia—the principal destinations for South Asian workers—have risen since the beginning of 2021. Implementation of vaccines is expected to bring case numbers down, though the shape of relevant epidemiological curves cannot be predicted with any accuracy. It is thus likely that the mobility restrictions will persist for some time. In any case, the global labor market is expected to recover only very gradually from the COVID-19 pandemic. Demand for services, and thereby for many types of migrant labor, will probably remain low in the short and medium terms. If and when demand for migrant labor rises again, sending countries will need support to restart managed migration systems, respond quickly, and ensure safe and productive migration amid the recovery from the pandemic.

Structural shifts in destination economies in response to the pandemic could also have longer-lasting impacts for South Asian migrant workers by shifting the type of migrant workers demanded and their volumes. Occupations deemed essential—such as frontline health care professionals—have been largely exempted from restrictions on current economic activity or new deployment. For example, health care workers from India (and the Philippines) were exempt from Saudi Arabia's recent widespread travel ban. More generally, there are public discussions under way in higher-income economies about the growing need for more foreign health care personnel. South Asian migrant-sending countries have already been investing in the skills of their migrant workers and have been trying to diversify into higher-wage markets such as care services in East Asian economies. More intensively focusing on health care workers as potential migrants may be an effective additional way for South Asian countries to diversify the opportunities available to prospective migrant workers.[10] In the future, there may also be lower aggregate migrant labor demand in host countries due to both technological change and policy shifts. For example, there may be a greater move toward automation of tasks that are routine and do not require cognitive thinking, or even labor market nationalization, such as the Saudization policy of Saudi Arabia.

NOTES

1. The World Bank (2019) provides a detailed description of the differences between the groups that are often collectively referred to as "migrants"—international migrants, refugees, irregular migrants, and temporary migrants. This book focuses almost exclusively on temporary, international, regular migrant workers. They are engaged in remunerated activity in a country of which they are not a national.
2. These data are from the Bangladesh Return Migrant Survey 2018/19 conducted for this book, described in Ahmed et al. (2021).
3. Current exchange rate was used for conversion.
4. These estimates are based on data from the Bangladesh Household Income and Expenditure Survey 2016/17 and the Nepal Household Risk and Vulnerability Survey 2016.
5. In the Nepal-Malaysia and Nepal–Saudi Arabia corridors, the results are not statistically significant, and the standard errors are large, possibly because of the small sample size.
6. About 12 percent of return migrants to Bangladesh report being expelled from the destination country because of visa or work permit issues as the main reason for returning (Bangladesh Return Migrant Survey 2018/19).
7. The sample from KNOMAD-ILO Migration Costs Surveys 2015 and 2016 might not be representative.
8. According to the sponsorship system that regulates migration to the GCC, labor migrants can only enter and stay in the country through a sponsor, a local employer who takes on both legal and economic responsibility for the migrant worker.
9. Annex A of IMF (2020) summarizes the current state of the outbreak in the major sending and receiving countries discussed. It also provides a list of mobility restrictions and other measures taken by GCC countries to address COVID-19 transmission.
10. Although there are valid misgivings about the possibility of resulting shortages of health care workers in sending countries ("brain drain"), recent papers in the "brain gain" literature suggest that workers invest in human capital in response to migration opportunities, including occupation-specific human capital, thus leading to a net domestic increase in skilled workers, despite labor outflow. See, for example, Khanna and Morales (2019) on the net increase in computer scientists in India, and Abarcar and Theoharides (2018) on the net increase in health care professionals in the Philippines.

REFERENCES

Abarcar, Paolo, and Caroline Theoharides. 2018. "The International Migration of Healthcare Professionals and the Supply of Educated Individuals Left Behind." Unpublished. https://economics.nd.edu/assets/289077/theoharides_amherst_intl_migration_of_healthcare_pros.pdf.

Al Jazeera. 2020. "Coronavirus Travel Bans Hit South Asia Migrant Workers." March 20. https://www.aljazeera.com/news/2020/03/coronavirus-travel-bans-hit-south-asia-migrant-workers-200320160840164.html.

Ahmed, S. Amer, Faiz Ahmed, Laurent Bossavie, Çağlar Özden, and He Wang. 2021. "Temporary Migration and Development: A New Dataset from Bangladesh." Background paper for *Toward Safer and More Productive Migration for South Asia*, World Bank, Washington, DC.

Aleksynska, Mariya, Samia Kazi Aoul, and Veronica Petrencu (Preotu). 2017. "Deficiencies in Conditions of Work as a Cost to Labor Migration: Concepts, Extent, and Implications." KNOMAD Working Paper 28, World Bank, Washington, DC.

Bossavie, Laurent, and Çağlar Özden. 2022. "Impacts of Temporary Migration on Development in Origin Countries." World Bank, Washington DC.

Bossavie, Laurent, Joseph-Simon Görlach, Çağlar Özden, and He Wang. 2021. "Temporary Migration for Long-Term Investment." Background paper for *Toward Safer and More Productive Migration for South Asia*, World Bank, Washington, DC.

Callen, Tim, Reda Cherif, Fuad Hasanov, Amgad Hegazy, and Padamja Khandelwal. 2014. "Economic Diversification in the GCC: Past, Present, and Future." Staff Discussion Note 14/12, International Monetary Fund, Washington, DC.

Cho, Yoonyoung, and Zaineb Majoka. 2020. *Pakistan Jobs Diagnostic: Promoting Access to Quality Jobs for All.* Jobs Series 20, World Bank, Washington, DC.

Dell'Ariccia, Giovanni, Ehsan Ebrahimy, Deniz O. Igan, and Damien Puy. 2020. "Discerning Good from Bad Credit Booms: The Role of Construction." Staff Discussion Note 20/02, International Monetary Fund, Washington, DC.

Deloitte. 2018. "Has the Industry Turned the Corner? Deloitte GCC Powers of Construction 2018." https://www2.deloitte.com/xe/en/pages/real-estate/articles/gcc-powers-construction-2018.html.

Doi, Yoko, David McKenzie, and Bilal Zia. 2014. "Who You Train Matters: Identifying Combined Effects of Financial Education on Migrant Households." *Journal of Development Economics* 109 (2): 33–55.

Dustmann, Christian, and Joseph-Simon Görlach. 2016. "The Economics of Temporary Migrations." *Journal of Economic Literature* 54 (1): 98–136.

Dustmann, Christian, and Oliver Kirchkamp. 2002. "Migration Duration and Activity Choice after Re-Migration." *Journal of Development Economics* 67 (2): 351–72.

Guadagno, Lorenzo. 2020. *Migrants and the COVID-19 Pandemic: An Initial Analysis.* Geneva: International Organization for Migration.

Ilahi, Nadeem. 1999. "Return Migration and Occupational Change." *Review of Development Economics* 3 (2): 170–86.

IMF (International Monetary Fund). 2020. *World Economic Outlook, April 2020: The Great Lockdown.* Washington, DC: IMF.

IOM (International Organization for Migration). 2020. "IOM Assists Vulnerable Returning Migrants Impacted by the COVID-19 Pandemic." Press Release, July 21.

Khan, Azfar, and Helene Harroff-Tavel. 2011. "Reforming the Kafala: Challenges and Opportunities in Moving Forward." *Asian and Pacific Migration Journal* 20 (3–4): 293–313.

Khanna, Gaurav, and Nicolas Morales. 2019. "The IT Boom and Other Unintended Consequences of Chasing the American Dream." Unpublished. https://ssrn.com/abstract=2968147 or http://dx.doi.org/10.2139/ssrn.2968147.

Lucas, Robert E. B. 2008. *International Migration and Economic Development: Lessons from Low Income Countries.* Cheltenham: Edward Elgar.

Moroz, Harry, Mahesh Shrestha, and Mauro Testaverde. 2020. "Potential Responses to the COVID-19 Outbreak in Support of Migrant Workers." World Bank, Washington, DC.

Ruppert Bulmer, Elizabet, Ami Shrestha, and Michelle Marshalian. 2020. "*Nepal Jobs Diagnostic*." Jobs Series 22, World Bank, Washington, DC.

UN DESA (United Nations Department of Economic and Social Affairs). 2017. *World Population Prospects: The 2017 Revision.* New York: UN DESA.

Wahba, Jackline. 2015. "Selection, Selection, Selection: The Impact of Return Migration." *Journal of Population Economics* 28 (3): 535–63.

World Bank. 2015, 2016, 2017. "KNOMAD-ILO Migration Costs Surveys." Global Knowledge Partnership on Migration and Development (KNOMAD), World Bank, Washington, DC.

World Bank. 2019. "World Development Indicators, 2019." World Bank, Washington, DC.

World Bank. 2020. "COVID-19 Crisis through a Migration Lens." Migration and Development Brief 32, World Bank, Washington, DC. http://hdl.handle.net/10986/33634.

1 Migration as an Engine of Development in South Asia

INTRODUCTION

South Asian economies have been struggling to create more and better jobs. Economies in the region are at a stage of demographic transition at which people of working age are generally still an increasing portion of the population. And millions of people will be entering the working-age cohort every year for another generation yet. This stage is an important window of opportunity to boost growth and development in South Asia. However, domestic job creation has been struggling to keep up with the massive influx of youth into the labor market. In particular, good-quality, formal, and higher-wage jobs have not been created rapidly enough to accommodate the numbers (Cho and Majoka 2020; Farole et al. 2017; Ruppert Bulmer, Shrestha, and Marshalian 2020). Labor earnings in South Asia remain quite low by international standards. These phenomena combine to provide important push factors toward employment opportunities in international labor markets.

In this context, international migration for temporary employment, for both jobs and remittance flows, is a critical component of South Asia's development path.[1] Overseas markets play an important role as a source of labor demand for South Asian workers. For example, 27 percent of Nepali households had at least one person working abroad, equivalent to more than 2.8 million working-age Nepalis (Ruppert Bulmer, Shrestha, and Marshalian 2020), equivalent to three-quarters of the country's 3.8 million wage employees. The larger economies in the region have several million migrants overseas, and these stocks have grown over time (figure 1.1). Migrants from South Asia account for 13 percent of all global migrants (not counting intraregional migrants), and two-thirds of migrants in major destinations such as the Gulf Cooperation Council (GCC) countries.[2] The 2012–17 period witnessed substantial flows of temporary economic migrants, with Bangladesh, India, Nepal, and Pakistan sending hundreds of thousands of workers overseas every year (approximately 597,000, 678,000, 463,000, and 713,000, on average, respectively).[3]

FIGURE 1.1

International migration from South Asia

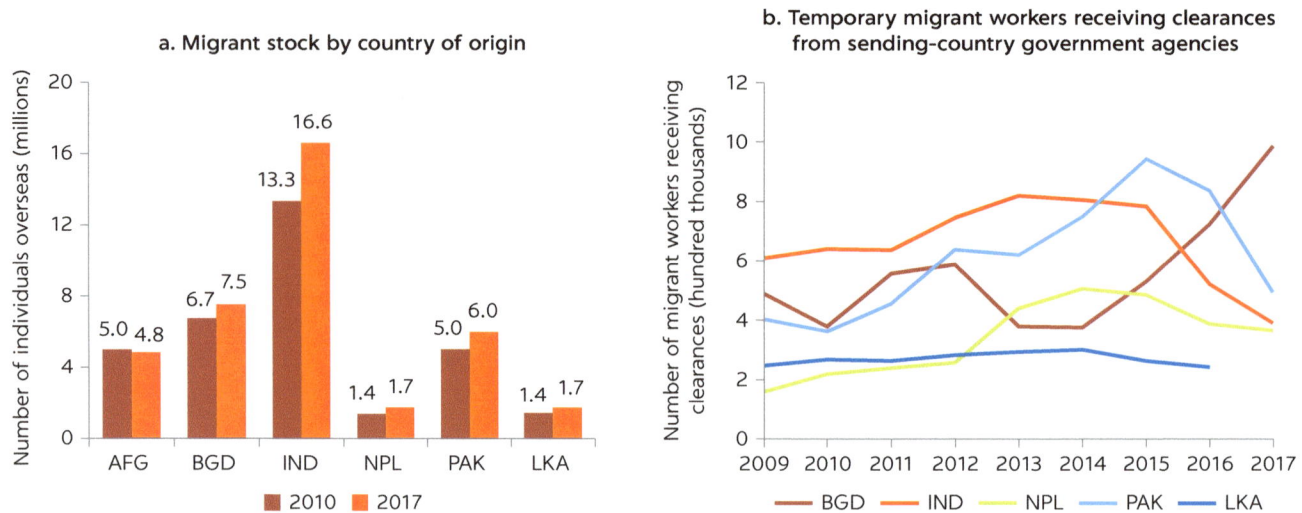

a. Migrant stock by country of origin

b. Temporary migrant workers receiving clearances from sending-country government agencies

Sources: Panel a: UN DESA 2017; panel b: Bangladeshi Bureau of Manpower Employment and Training; Sri Lankan Bureau of Foreign Employment; Pakistani Bureau of Emigration and Overseas Employment; Nepali Department of Foreign Employment; Indian Ministry of External Affairs.
Note: Panel a illustrates migrant stock from a given country, regardless of reason for migration (for example, temporary economic migration, forced displacement, among others). Panel b only includes data for the five countries where governments maintain records of outbound temporary economic migrants. AFG = Afghanistan; BGD = Bangladesh; IND = India; LKA = Sri Lanka; NPL = Nepal; PAK = Pakistan.

International migration and remittances have contributed to development by boosting consumption and reducing poverty at home and by increasing the incomes of the migrants themselves.[4] It is estimated that a 10 percent increase in the share of international migrants in a country's population leads to a 2.1 percent decline in the share of people living on less than US$1.00 per day (Adams and Page 2005).[5] A 10 percent increase per capita in international remittances based on official statistics was also estimated to lead to a 3.5 percent decline in the share of people living in poverty. The greater the share of low-skilled migrants in a country's migrant population, the greater the flow of remittances, with the greatest remittance flows coming from middle-income countries (Adams 2009). It thus follows that the poverty reduction impacts of migration can potentially be the greatest for South Asian economies, many of which are in the low- or middle-income brackets. For example, in Bangladesh, international remittances accounted for 11 percent of observed poverty reduction in 2000–10, and in Nepal, one-fifth of poverty reduction in 1995–2004 was estimated to be attributable to migration, primarily international (Lokshin, Bontch-Osmolovski, and Glinskaya 2011; World Bank 2013).

The inflow of South Asian labor migrants also has large positive effects on the economies of the receiving countries. Although opponents of migration in high-income countries have often argued that low-skilled migrants "crowd out" jobs for native workers, many studies have found that this is not the case. Ahmed, Go, and Willenbockel (2016) show that although migration can push down the wages of native workers in the short run, the effects on the incomes of native-born workers is positive in the long run. These short-term effects depend on the degree of substitutability of migrants' skills with those of natives. In the longer run, the wages of workers who were negatively affected not only recover but even exceed premigration wages. Overall, natives of high-income receiving countries gain the most because of larger increases in capital return and quicker capital formation (Ahmed, Go, and Willenbockel 2016). Although the wages of natives with skills similar to those of immigrants can decline in the short run, natives with complementary skills typically benefit from an inflow of migrants (World Bank 2018b).

In recent decades, the large inflows of lower-wage and low-skilled South Asian migrant workers have contributed significantly to the high growth rates seen by GCC and high-income Asian countries despite relatively small national labor forces. In Saudi Arabia, the wages of foreign labor migrants have been as modest as one-fifth that of citizens (Hertog 2012). The national labor forces of GCC countries are small, as many locals prefer not to work in low-skilled professions (and their economic circumstances typically permit them to act on that preference), and women usually do not participate in the labor force (Shediac, Haddad, and Klouche 2010). South Asian labor migration has also been beneficial for high-income Asian countries, such as the Republic of Korea, which have been facing declining labor forces because of aging and low fertility rates (Cho et al. 2018).

Labor migration from Bangladesh, Nepal, and Pakistan shares similar characteristics. All three countries are lower-middle-income economies where sizable shares of the working-age population migrate overseas. Most migrants from these three countries are low skilled. When they move to destinations such as the GCC countries, they do so on a temporary basis through contractual labor arrangements before returning home after a few years abroad. They face similar vulnerabilities overseas and are subject to a range of possible abuses and shocks. In all three countries, migration is also largely male; female migration accounts for less than 5 percent of total international migration outflows. In contrast, out-migration from other countries in the region is rather different. In Afghanistan, migration systems are less mature, partly because of the conflict and insecurity there, though it currently seeks to send more migrants overseas. In Sri Lanka, a lower-middle-income country, migration systems are considerably more advanced than the three countries that are the focus of this book and female migration accounts for a large share of outflows. In India, migrants are increasingly higher skilled, and the implications for migration systems and policies are thus distinct.

CHARACTERISTICS OF MIGRANT WORKERS: YOUNGER, LOW SKILLED, AND CONCENTRATED IN A SMALL NUMBER OF SECTORS AND DESTINATIONS

South Asian labor migration is regionally concentrated in the GCC countries and Malaysia (figure 1.2). There is strong demand for low- and semi-skilled labor in the nontraded services sector of high-income countries, particularly in the Middle East. The GCC countries, where national workers are mostly employed in the public sector, attract many foreign workers to fill labor shortages in occupations in the private sector that nationals are unwilling to take. After intraregional migration is excluded, the stock of migrants from South Asia is heavily concentrated in a handful of economies, particularly the GCC countries. Just five economies host 81.5 percent of Bangladesh's, 72.8 percent of Nepal's, and 66 percent of Pakistan's migrant stock. This high level of concentration increases the sending countries' exposure to the consequences of shocks experienced in the receiving country.[6] In 2017, 2.7 million Bangladeshis worked as labor migrants abroad. Roughly 1 million of them worked in Saudi Arabia and another million in the United Arab Emirates. Among the 2.5 million Pakistani labor migrants abroad, 1.3 million worked in Saudi Arabia and about another million in the United Arab Emirates. Half of all Nepali temporary migrant workers are in Saudi Arabia.

Migrant workers from South Asia are also concentrated in a few low-paying sectors.[7] The majority of low-skilled male labor migrants from South Asia work in the construction sector. More than 60 percent of Bangladeshi labor migrants work in the construction sector in the top six destination countries, followed by the "retail, hotel, restaurant" and "utility, transport" sectors, at roughly 10 percent each (figure 1.3). More than 50 percent of the Bangladeshi labor migrants who work in the construction sector in receiving countries had not worked in the sector before migrating (figure 1.4). Nepali labor migrants have a greater diversity of jobs than other South Asian migrants in receiving countries (figure 1.5). About 40 percent of Nepali labor migrants in Saudi Arabia work in the construction sector, followed by almost 40 percent in services (including domestic work). It is mostly Nepali women who are employed in domestic work in the destination countries. Most Nepali labor migrants in Malaysia work in low-skilled jobs, for instance, as factory workers, electricians, drivers, security guards, and so forth.

Given the regulation of low-skilled migration in the main destinations, migration from South Asia is temporary by design. Its temporary nature is largely dictated by regulations in the main host countries. Duration of stay of low-skilled migrants is strictly tied to temporary labor contracts, and for them there is no path to permanent legal residence in the main GCC and Southeast Asian destinations. Although migrants can extend their stay through labor contract extensions, they must ultimately return home.

FIGURE 1.2

Distribution of stock of migrants in major temporary economic migration destinations, 2017, and total migrants

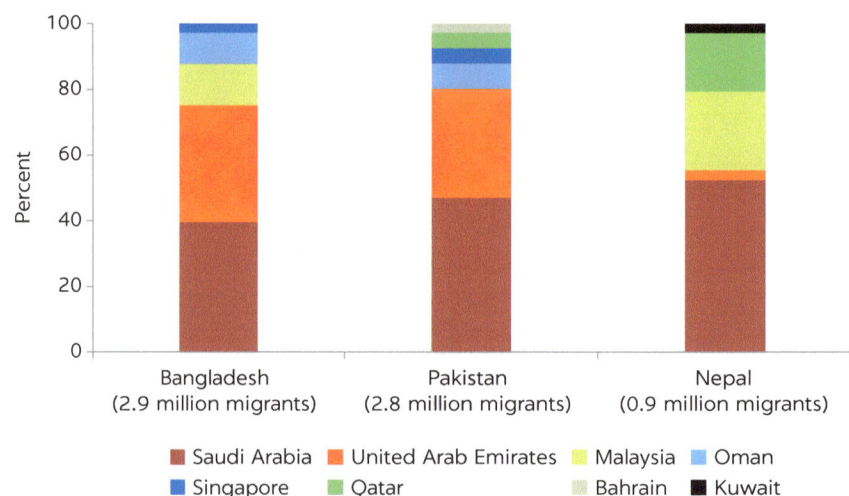

Source: UN DESA 2017.
Note: Distribution of migrants in major temporary economic migration destinations in 2017 (percentage share of total from each source country, respectively, as marked). UN DESA figures include documented and undocumented migrants, and their families.

FIGURE 1.3

Employment of Bangladeshi labor migrants by sector in top destination countries

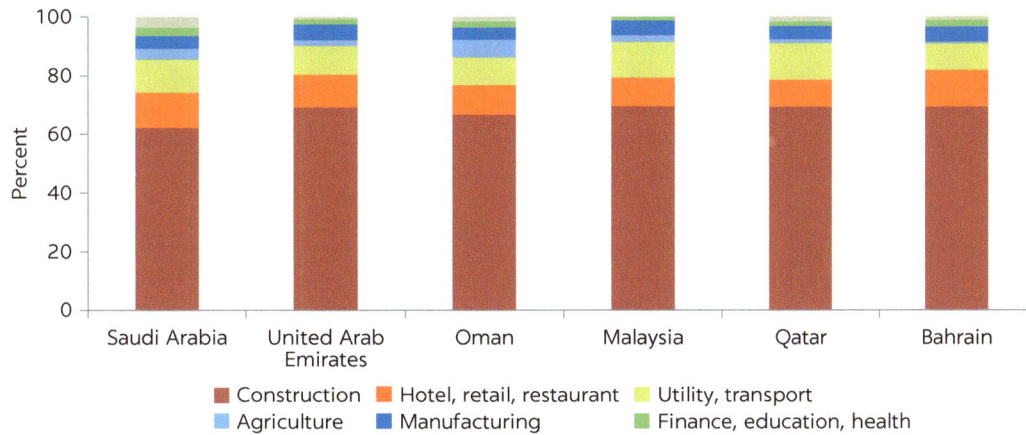

Source: Bangladesh Return Migrant Survey 2018/19.

FIGURE 1.4

Employment by sector, before migration and in destination country, of Bangladeshi migrants

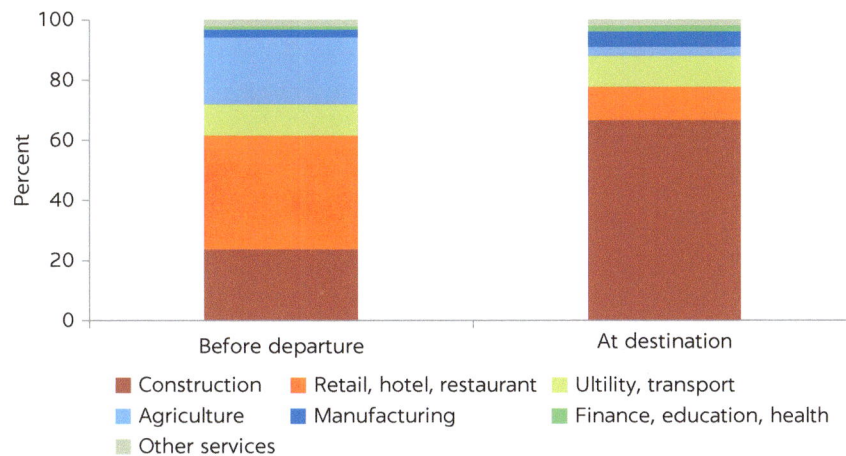

Source: Bangladesh Return Migrant Survey 2018/19.

Additionally, family migration is not permitted for low-skilled migrants, which increases incentives to return home. These features of low-skilled labor migration from South Asia have important implications for any policy intervention in the region.

Given the overall low levels of skills among the workforce in Bangladesh, Nepal, and Pakistan, temporary migration from South Asia is a low-skilled phenomenon by international standards. Whereas college-educated individuals are typically overrepresented among international migrants, the average migrant from Bangladesh, Nepal, or Pakistan has incomplete secondary education, and of these, significant numbers have completed primary education at most; for example, 40 percent of Pakistani labor migrants to the United Arab Emirates have low education, as do 70 percent of Nepali migrant workers to Qatar, and in Bangladesh, the share of international migrants who have at most completed primary

FIGURE 1.5

Employment of Nepali labor migrants by sector in host countries

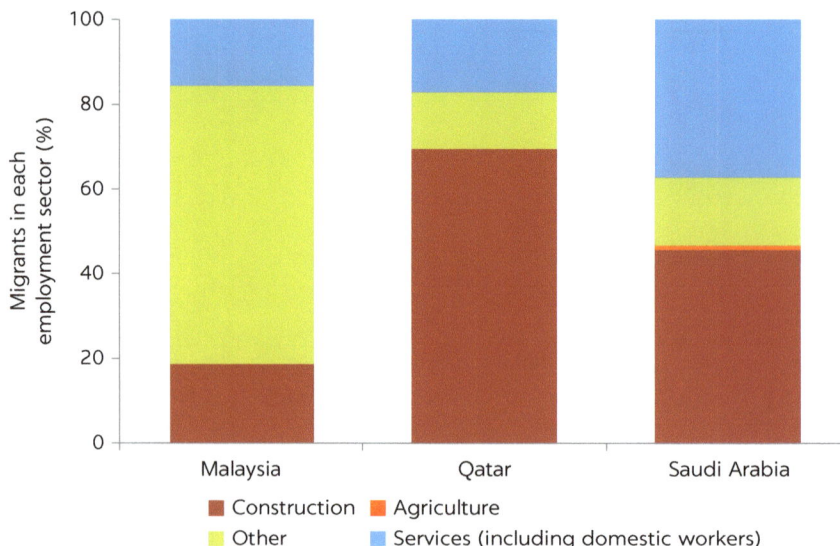

Source: KNOMAD-ILO Migration Costs Surveys 2015 and 2016.
Note: The category "Other" compromises low-skilled jobs such as factory workers, electricians, technicians, drivers, cleaning staff, painters, security guards, and so forth. (No data available for other migration corridors.)

education is 34 percent (Ahmed et al. 2021). In comparison, the share of low-skilled migrants from other sending countries is much lower. For example, low-skilled migrants represent only 6 percent and 5 percent of migrants from the Philippines in Qatar and Saudi Arabia, respectively (table 1.1).

However, workers from South Asia who migrate overseas are, on average, more skilled than workers who do not migrate. Although they are low skilled by international standards, they are "positively selected": they have attained, on average, higher levels of schooling than their counterparts who did not migrate (figure 1.6).[8] International migrants have, on average, completed two more years of schooling than nonmigrants in Bangladesh, and one and a half years more in Nepal. Those are substantial, statistically significant differences. These findings are consistent with global evidence showing that international migrants are positively selected with respect to the population of workers in the origin country (World Bank 2018b).

South Asian workers with intermediate levels of schooling are most likely to migrate. However, the relationship between years of schooling and the likelihood of migrating overseas is nonlinear (panels a and b of figure 1.7). The patterns for Nepal and Bangladesh, the two countries for which these types of data are available, are very similar. The likelihood of migrating abroad is lowest among workers who never attended school and those with only a few years of primary schooling. Although one would expect the returns (benefits) of migration to the GCC countries to be particularly tempting for low-skilled workers, these workers may also face strong liquidity and credit constraints that limit their ability to migrate in the face of strong competition and very high migration costs (Ratha and Seshan 2018). The likelihood of migrating overseas strongly increases for individuals who have completed primary school and have

FIGURE 1.6

Years of schooling completed by workers from Bangladesh and Nepal, by migration status

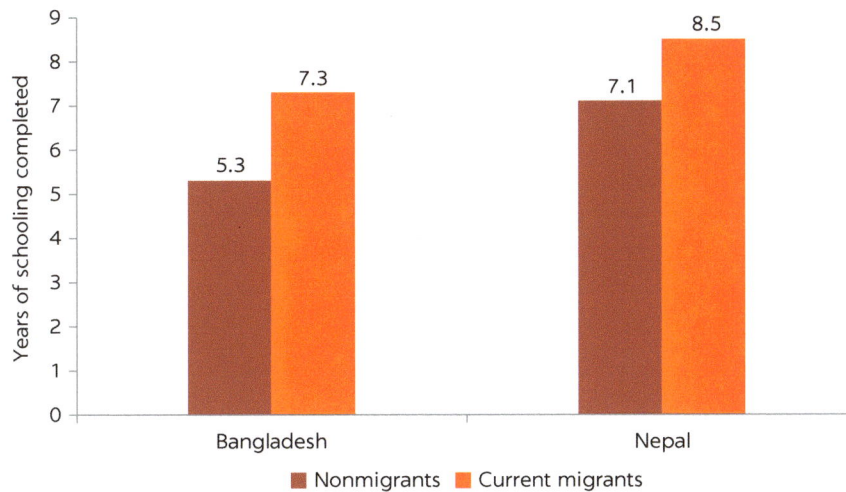

Sources: World Bank calculations based on the Household Income and Expenditure Survey 2016/17 for Bangladesh and on the Labor Force Survey 2017/18 for Nepal.
Note: Statistics are for males ages 15–64 and account for sampling weights. Current migrants are defined as household members who were absent from the household for work overseas at the time of the survey.

some secondary schooling. The incidence of migration is highest among this latter group in both Bangladesh and Nepal. Interestingly, however, the likelihood of migration declines for individuals who have completed secondary school and decreases sharply for those who have some tertiary education. This finding indicates that the benefits of migrating to the main destinations under consideration may be lower for workers with tertiary education, who have better access to higher-paying employment domestically, such as public sector jobs (Farole et al. 2017; Cho and Majoka 2020).

Educational attainment also influences wages at destination. Many of the Nepali and Pakistani labor migrants surveyed in the KNOMAD Migration Costs Surveys have only primary education (table 1.1). Among Pakistani labor migrants to the United Arab Emirates, 40 percent have low education, as do 70 percent of Nepali migrant workers to Qatar. Estimates derived by pooling data from multiple corridors reveal a strong association between wages and completion of primary education (table 1A.1 in annex 1A). More experienced workers—using age as a proxy—earn more, but the boost to their wages tends to decline as they grow older. This age-related decline also reflects the type of low-skill and labor-intensive work in which many migrants are engaged, where physical fitness and youth are important.

Temporary migrants from South Asia are young compared with the average working-age population in the country of origin (figure 1.8). Globally, migrants tend to be younger than the working-age population at origin (World Bank 2018b). The same pattern is observed in South Asia, where international migrants are disproportionally in the 20–35 age group compared with the overall working-age population at origin. Meanwhile, very young individuals, under age 20, are underrepresented among migrants, as are workers over age 40.

FIGURE 1.7

Share of the working-age male population that ever migrated abroad, by level of educational attainment

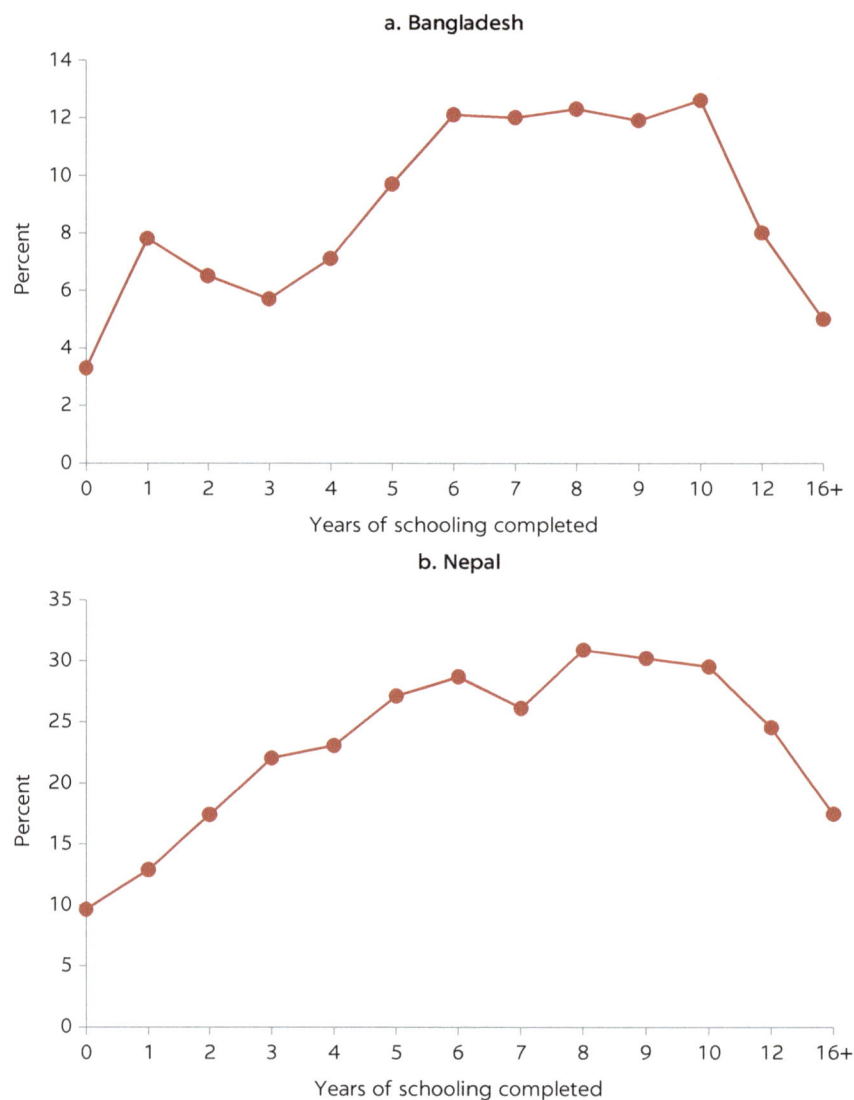

a. Bangladesh

b. Nepal

Sources: World Bank calculations based on the Household Income and Expenditure Survey 2016/17 for Bangladesh and on the Labor Force Survey 2017/18 for Nepal.
Note: Statistics are for males ages 15–64 and account for sampling weights. Individuals are classified as having ever migrated abroad if they are either currently overseas for work or have migrated overseas for work in the past.

The average age of migrants from Bangladesh and Nepal is 34 and 31, respectively, although migrants to Malaysia from these countries tend to be younger. The average ages of Pakistani migrants to Saudi Arabia and the United Arab Emirates are 30 and 29, respectively.

The young age of temporary migrants from South Asia, both in absolute terms and compared with the working-age population, has various explanations. First, the nonmonetary costs of migration tend to be smaller for younger individuals. Second, younger people have a longer time horizon over which to reap the benefits of migration, increasing the overall returns to the migration experience. Finally, employment opportunities for labor migrants from South Asia are

TABLE 1.1 Demographic characteristics of migrants in select corridors

MIGRATION CORRIDOR	NUMBER	PERCENT MALE	PERCENT PRIMARY EDUCATION ONLY	AGE WHEN SURVEYED (YEARS)
India-Qatar	401	99.75	0.75	32
India–Saudi Arabia	409	100	56.72	33
Nepal-Malaysia	165	100	26.83	24
Nepal-Qatar	441	99.32	69.32	30
Nepal–Saudi Arabia	98	100	42.86	29
Pakistan–Saudi Arabia	375	100	44.53	30
Pakistan–United Arab Emirates	259	99.61	40.54	29
Philippines-Qatar	365	54.67	6.15	38
Philippines–Saudi Arabia	484	44.83	4.56	35

Source: KNOMAD-ILO Migration Costs Surveys 2015 and 2016.

FIGURE 1.8

Age distribution of temporary migrants from South Asia compared with the working-age population

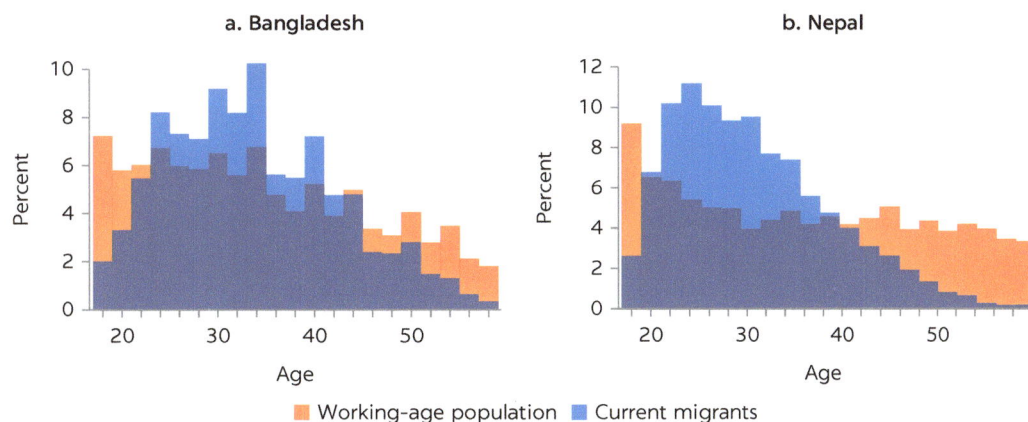

a. Bangladesh

b. Nepal

■ Working-age population ■ Current migrants

Sources: World Bank calculations based on the Labor Force Survey 2017/18 for Nepal and the Household Income and Expenditure Survey 2016/17 for Bangladesh.
Note: Statistics are for males ages 15–64 and account for sampling weights.

primarily in physically intensive blue-collar jobs at destination, which require physical strength and are thus better suited to younger workers.

Females account for a very small minority of temporary migrants from Bangladesh, Nepal, and Pakistan. According to administrative data, females made up only 4 percent of international migrant flows from 1991 to 2014 in Bangladesh, although the proportion increased to 12 percent in 2018, following the bilateral agreement signed in 2015 with Saudi Arabia. The share of female outmigrants in Nepal is about 5 percent (Bossavie and Denisova 2018). It is even lower in Pakistan, consistently less than 1 percent over the past two decades according to administrative data from the Pakistani Bureau of Emigration and Overseas Employment. The very low shares of female international migration from Bangladesh, Nepal, and Pakistan stand in contrast with those of other migrant-sending countries such as the Philippines, where female migrants outnumber males in some corridors (table 1.1).

The very low proportion of female labor migrants can be explained by four main factors common to Bangladesh, Nepal, and Pakistan. First, in all three countries, the labor force participation rate of females is low compared with other countries (Cho and Majoka 2020; Farole et al. 2017; Ruppert Bulmer, Shrestha, and Marshalian 2020). Second, employment in the main destinations is characterized by difficult working conditions and the risk of abuses to which women may be particularly vulnerable. Third, low-skilled temporary migrants are forbidden to migrate with family to the main destinations, in a context in which women bear most of the responsibility for childcare back home (Amir et al. 2018; Farole et al. 2017). Finally, regulations in some of the sending countries contribute to the low rates of female migration from South Asia. The Pakistan Emigration Rules, for example, restrict women's migration to those age 35 and older (with a five-year age exception granted in some cases). Nepal has also adopted a protective policy by prohibiting the migration of females younger than age 25 as domestic workers to the GCC countries, to prevent abuse.

Migrants disproportionately come from certain areas of Bangladesh, Nepal, and Pakistan. The incentives to migrate internationally are affected by the socioeconomic conditions in the region of origin, the so-called migration push factors (World Bank 2018b). International migrants from the most disadvantaged regions at origin can indeed receive greater wage gains by migrating overseas. In Nepal, international migrants disproportionately come from the most the disadvantaged rural areas of the country, as opposed to the Kathmandu Valley (Bossavie and Denisova 2018; Shrestha 2017). Migrants also disproportionately come from specific areas of Bangladesh (Farole et al. 2017). Although less than 20 percent of the population is located in the Chittagong division, it provides about 40 percent of current migrants. In contrast, 11 percent of nonmigrants live in the Rangpur division, but it provides only 2 percent of international migrants (Ahmed et al. 2021; Farole et al. 2017). Punjab and Khyber Pakhtunkhwa province together accounted for 92 percent of the flow of outmigrants from Pakistan in 2016, while their share of the total working-age population (ages 15–64) is 72 percent. In particular, the share of migrants from Khyber Pakhtunkhwa, at 35 percent, far exceeds the province's share of the employed population, at 11 percent (Cho and Majoka 2020).

SOUTH ASIAN LABOR MIGRATION AND THE REGION'S ECONOMIC DEVELOPMENT

Macroeconomic benefits for sending and receiving economies

Migration has large positive effects on South Asian economies overall, with remittances constituting a significant proportion of the GDP of most South Asian economies (figure 1.9). In 2017, Nepal's remittances-to-GDP ratio of almost 28 percent was surpassed, worldwide, only by Haiti, the Kyrgyz Republic, Tajikistan, and Tonga (with ratios greater than 30 percent). The ratio is 11 percent in Bangladesh, 9 percent in Sri Lanka, and 7 percent in Pakistan. The ratios for Afghanistan, Bhutan, and India have always been less than 3 percent.

The inflow of remittances to South Asian countries have also been high in absolute value (figure 1.10). Flows can be either procyclical (moving in the same

FIGURE 1.9

Remittances share of GDP, 2017

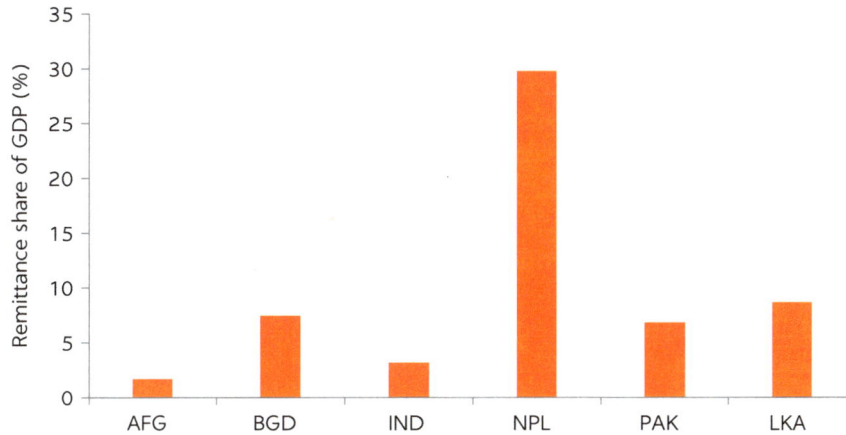

Source: Data from World Development Indicators and KNOMAD Remittances Database.
Note: AFG = Afghanistan; BGD = Bangladesh; IND = India; LKA = Sri Lanka; NPL = Nepal;
PAK = Pakistan.

FIGURE 1.10

Remittances into South Asia, 2017

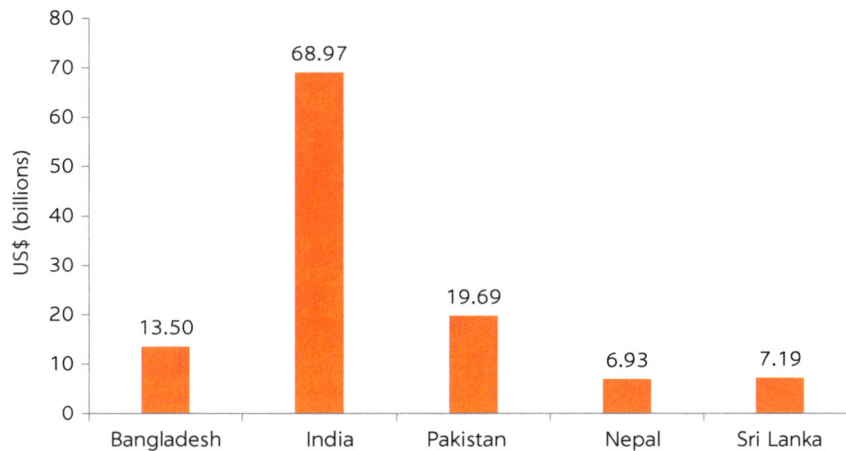

Source: Data from World Development Indicators and KNOMAD Remittances Database.
Note: Afghanistan and Bhutan not shown due to scale. Afghanistan's remittances in 2017
were US$0.38 billion and Nepal's remittances were US$0.04 billion. Average remittances
received by countries globally is US$3.4 billion.

direction as the home country's business cycle), countercyclical (moving in the opposite direction), or acyclical (not correlated with the home country's output) (Frankel 2010; Lueth and Ruiz-Arranz 2006; World Bank 2015). Mughal and Ahmed (2014) show that remittances to India and Pakistan were countercyclical with respect to home output over the period 1975–2011. In contrast, remittance flows for Bangladesh and Sri Lanka were usually procyclical with respect to the economies of the receiving countries.

Although the high dependence on remittances in some economies—such as Nepal—raises the risk of the so-called Dutch disease (see box 1.1), evidence

BOX 1.1

Dutch disease and remittances

Dutch disease is named after a paradoxical effect, that is, when good news in one sector apparently leads to the decline of another (the discovery of large natural gas reserves in the Netherlands heralded the decline of the manufacturing industry there). In the context of migration and remittances, it involves two mechanisms that are triggered when large amounts of remittances increase disposable income, leading to increased spending and demand in the economy (Corden and Neary 1982; Bourdet and Falck 2006). The "spending effect" occurs because of the increased domestic income from the booming sector: public and private sectors increase domestic demand and spending in the nontradable sector. Consequently, prices and output in this sector increase. Rising prices and wages eventually diminish profits in the lagging sector, where prices are fixed in the international market (Corden 1984). The "resource movement effect" occurs because the resource boom leads to a reallocation of factors of production to the booming sector and away from the rest of the economy (Corden 1984). It usually also reduces output in the rest of the economy (Brahmbhatt, Canuto, and Vostroknutova 2010). The increase in household income could also push down labor supply and increase wages, thereby leading to higher production costs and a contraction of the tradable sector (Acosta, Lartey, and Mandelman 2009).

The classic Dutch disease model has been applied to examine the effects of natural resource endowments on the poor economic performance of developing countries. However, various empirical studies find evidence for Dutch disease effects for remittances. A study of 13 Latin American and Caribbean countries suggests that a 100 percent increase in remittances led to real exchange rate appreciation of 22 percent (Amuedo-Dorantes and Pozo 2006). A study on Cabo Verde reveals that remittances lowered the competitiveness of the tradable sector and reduced exports, domestic market shares, and production in the country (Bourdet and Falck 2006). Other evidence indicates that remittances reduced labor force participation in Jamaica, which exacerbated the country's real exchange rate appreciation. Ultimately, the country's export base and small manufacturing import-competing sector deteriorated, which led to a decline in the country's competitiveness (Bussolo and Medvedev 2007). Available data support these results, showing that the growth rates of real exchange rates and remittances were rather volatile and positively correlated over the 1995–2018 period (see figure 1.11).

However, other research suggests that remittances might not always lead to real exchange rate appreciation and could lower an economy's competitiveness. A study for Sub-Saharan African countries demonstrates that remittances do not lead to an appreciation of the real exchange rate in the long run.[a] The real exchange rate might not appreciate because remittances may be used to ease supply constraints or boost productivity in the nontradable sector in the remittances-receiving economy (Mongardini and Rayner 2009).[b] Other evidence suggests that remittances may not lead to a significant loss of competitiveness because they tend to stop if an exchange rate begins to get overvalued. During most of the 1990s, countries with overvalued exchange rates received significantly lower remittances. A plausible reason for the decline in remittances might be that emigrants believed it was cheaper to send goods directly when the exchange rate was overvalued (Rajan and Subramanian 2005).

a. In the estimation, the coefficient for the impact of remittances on the equilibrium real exchange rate is negative, but not statistically significant.
b. The study uses the pooled mean group estimator developed by Pesaran, Shin, and Smith (1999) as the main estimation technique. The data cover the period 1980–2006 in most cases.

suggesting that this is the case in South Asia is limited. It could intuitively be assumed that increased domestic income from remittances would push up domestic prices and migration flows, increasing wages and eventually diminishing the competitiveness of the other sectors. Another implication of Dutch disease would be that it moves labor away from other sectors (such as manufacturing) into overseas labor markets. An often-used indicator of Dutch disease is the movement of real effective exchange rates, and there does not appear to be a statistically significant correlation between remittance flows and interannual changes in real effective exchange rates across countries. Cross-country data suggest that remittance flows follow the same direction as average real effective exchange rates, although once again, there is no statistically significant correlation (figure 1.11).

The short-term nature of South Asian migration is part of the explanation for the persistent flow of remittances to the region. Adams (2009) finds that low-skilled migrants send more remittances home than high-skilled migrants because low-skilled migration is relatively more temporary. In addition, migrants from South Asia typically migrate without other family members. Low-skilled migrants are more concerned about their return home, and therefore their families' economic well-being, than are their high-skilled counterparts. In the past, South Asian migrants might have wanted to compensate for

FIGURE 1.11

Interannual change in real effective exchange rates and remittances

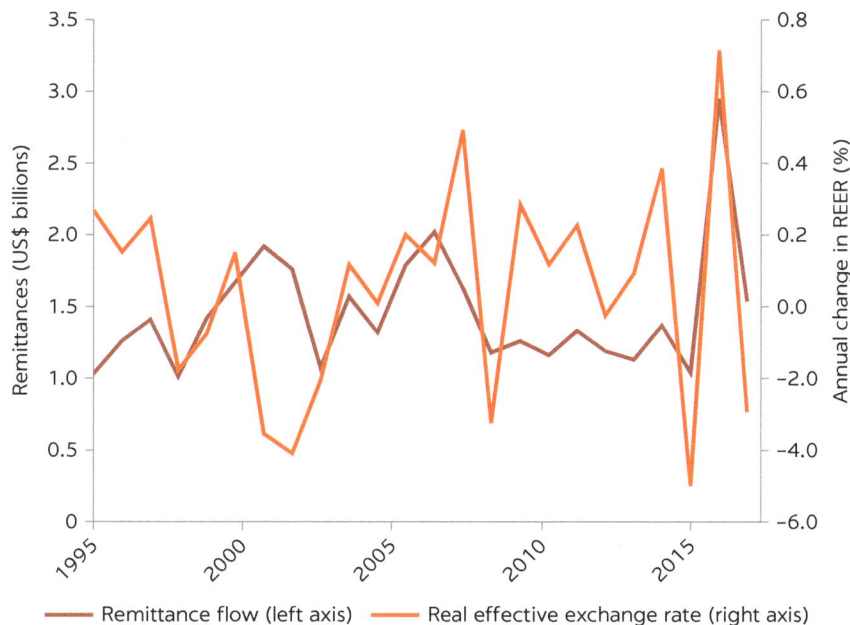

Sources: World Bank estimates using data from the World Development Indicators and Bruegel for 166 countries.
Note: Real effective exchange rate (REER) calculated based on unit labor cost and with 171 trading partners considered for each country.

their families' worsening economic situation during recessions by providing increased remittances. On average, South Asian labor migrants stay two to four years in the host country. The India–Saudi Arabia migration corridor is an exception, with an average stay of only five months (based on data from KNOMAD-ILO Migration Costs Surveys 2015 and 2016). A positive relationship between the expected duration of stay in the host country and the amount of expected monthly remittances can be found in South Asian labor migration (figure 1.12). It must be assumed that if the stay in the receiving country is too short, labor migrants might remit less because they still need to cover their migration-related expenses.

Remittances are an important source of external financing for South Asian countries (figure 1.13). Remittances are directly received by households and therefore much less influenced by political, economic, or geographic characteristics of the home country than official development assistance (ODA), export revenue, and foreign direct investment (FDI). The direct nature of remittances is crucial for South Asian countries that may have other constraints to boosting export revenues or attracting FDI. For example, despite its important geographic location between India and China, Nepal is landlocked and is lagging behind other countries in the region in measures such as the World Bank's Logistics Performance Index. Remittances have been the most important source of external financing for Nepal, followed by export revenue, ODA, and FDI (in that order). In Bangladesh and Pakistan, only export revenue has exceeded the revenue derived from remittances.

Worldwide, remittances have led to a substantial reduction in the proportion of people living in poverty (Adams and Page 2005). Although those who live in

FIGURE 1.12

Correlation between duration of stay overseas and monthly remittances

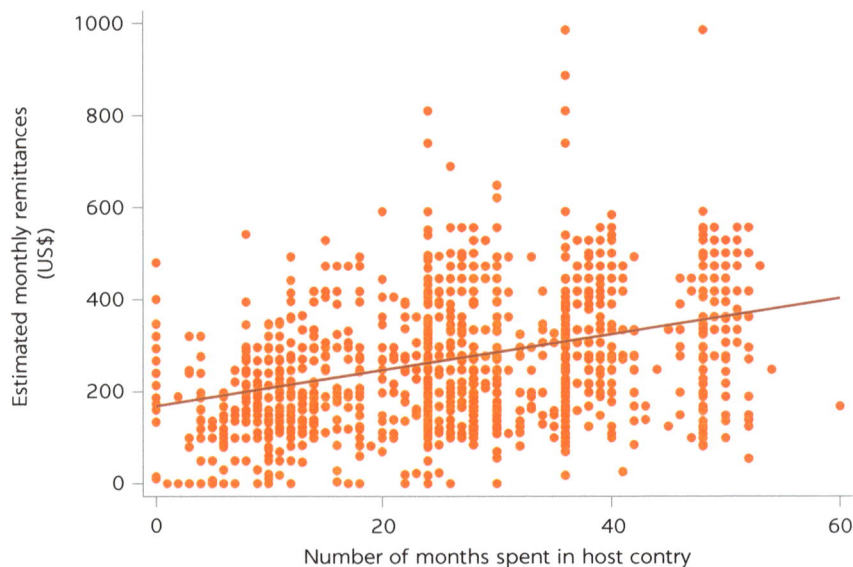

Source: KNOMAD-ILO Migration Costs Surveys 2015 and 2016.
Note: Outliers are omitted (months_expect>1000 and mthremitUSD2016>1500). For the analysis, only migration corridors with South Asian countries as sending countries are included. The Nepal–Saudi Arabia corridor is omitted for lack of data. The red line shows the linear relationship between monthly remittances sent by migrants and duration of stay overseas estimated from the available data points.

FIGURE 1.13

Net remittance inflows into migrant-sending South Asian countries

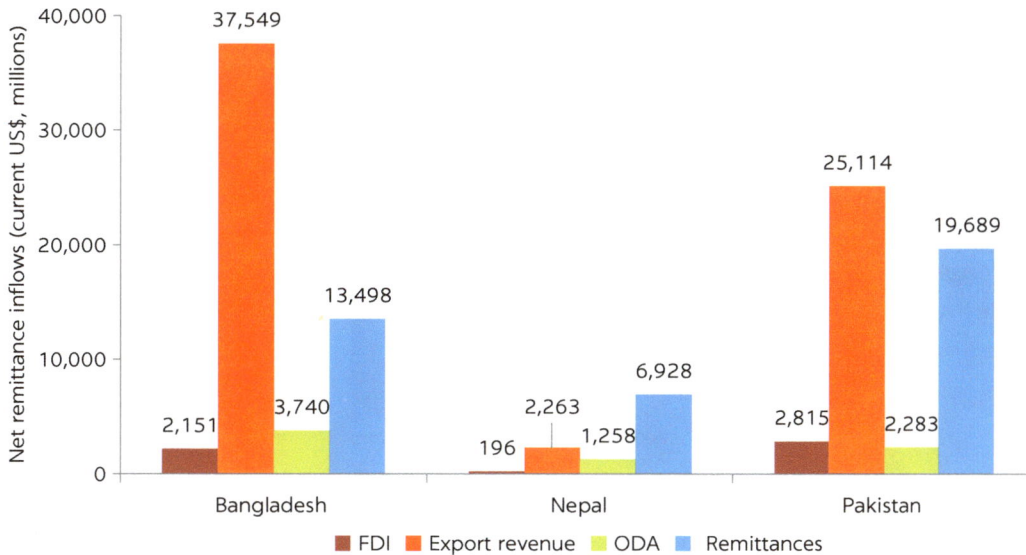

Sources: FDI, ODA, and export revenue data from World Development Indicators 2019; remittance inflow data from KNOMAD Remittances Database.
Note: Remittances = migrant remittance inflows (current US$); ODA = net official development assistance (current US$); export revenue = exports of goods and services (current US$); FDI = foreign direct investment, net inflows (balance of payments, current US$).

extreme poverty in South Asia do not tend to migrate, remittances, overall, have led to a significant decline in poverty across the region. International migration had a positive impact on economic growth and poverty reduction during the 1973–2007 period (Qayyum, Muhammad, and Arif 2008). Lokshin, Bontch-Osmolovski, and Glinskaya (2011) conclude that growth in international migration led to a decline in total poverty by 1.2 percent in Nepal over the 1995–2004 period. Raihan et al. (2009) show that international remittances reduce the probability of a Bangladeshi household becoming poor by 5.9 percent.

Microeconomic benefits to migrants and their households

Migrating individuals benefit directly from international labor migration through higher wages abroad (figure 1.14). South Asian labor migrants earn a large wage premium over earnings at home because of the higher average wages and productivity in receiving countries. On average, monthly earnings of Bangladeshi migrants were, at 35,000 (US$400) Bangladesh taka, almost four times higher in the receiving countries than in their home country (9,000 taka; about US$100).[9] In 2016, labor migrants from India earned an average of US$362 in Saudi Arabia compared with US$112, on average, in their country. Workers from Nepal earned almost five times more in Qatar than at home. Workers from Pakistan earned 3.6 times more when working in the United Arab Emirates and 4.8 times more when working in Saudi Arabia. Higher wages abroad can help improve the welfare of households back home through remittances. In addition to these short-term static effects, this large positive income shock can increase savings and the ability to mitigate any future shocks. It can also help increase lifetime earnings even after migrants have returned home by allowing them to accumulate capital to start up in business back home (Bossavie et al. 2021).

FIGURE 1.14

Migrants' wage gains in destination countries

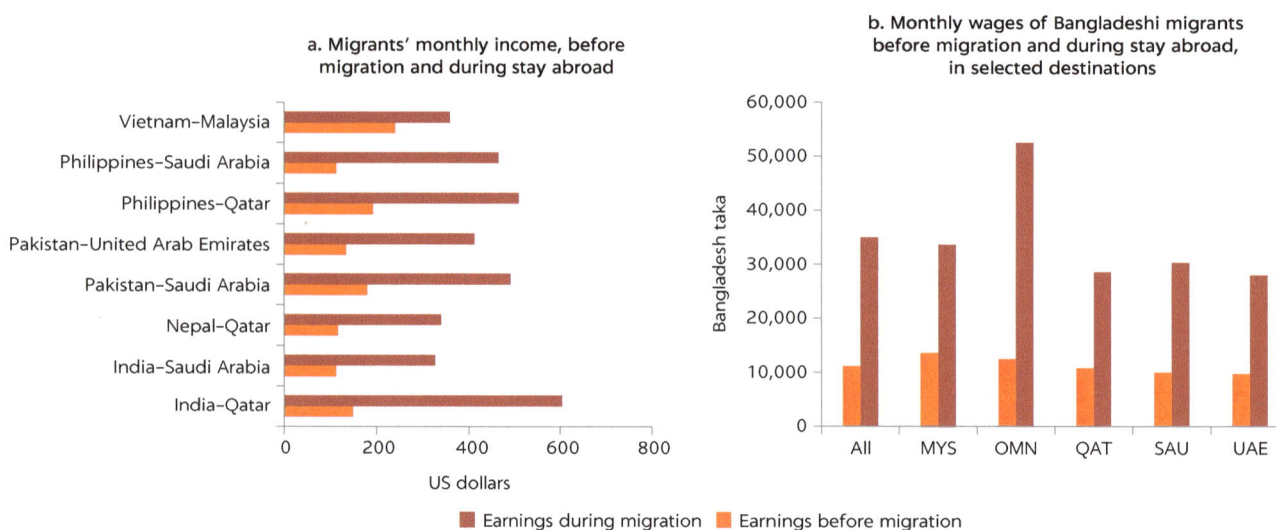

a. Migrants' monthly income, before migration and during stay abroad

b. Monthly wages of Bangladeshi migrants before migration and during stay abroad, in selected destinations

■ Earnings during migration   ■ Earnings before migration

Sources: Data for panel a estimated from KNOMAD-ILO Migration Costs Surveys 2015 and 2016 for select corridors with South and East Asian origin countries. Data for panel b estimated from Bangladesh Return Migrant Survey 2018/19.
Note: All = all destinations; MYS = Malaysia; OMN = Oman; QAT is Qatar; SAU = Saudi Arabia; UAE = United Arab Emirates.

Households left behind in the home country benefit substantially from labor migration through remittances. Low-skilled migrants from South Asia cannot migrate with family to the main destinations in the GCC and Southeast Asia. In addition, because migration is very often a family decision, family members who work as labor migrants are expected to improve their family's economic situation. In South Asia, state-provided social transfers often cannot sufficiently help households cover their basic needs (Chemmencheri 2016). In the absence of state support, remittances can substantially improve the financial well-being of families. Remittance-receiving households can use funds not only to increase and smooth consumption but also for productive and investment purposes, such as working capital for self-employment-related activities or investment in children's schooling (Gupta, Pattillo, and Wagh 2009). In Nepal, remittances have been seen to raise the living standards of migrant families: about 79 percent of remittances are spent on household daily consumption and only 2.4 percent on capital formation (Dhungana 2012). An approximate estimate from Bangladesh suggests that if remittance income were reduced by two-thirds—the estimated share of remittances in migrant households' income—then 41 percent of households with migrants that are currently above the national poverty line would become impoverished, equivalent to about 5.4 million additional poor people (figure 1.15).

Depending on the income level of the remittance-receiving household, funds are spent differently. Poor families tend to spend remittances on consumption, whereas wealthier households are more likely to spend them on productive and investment goods such as health and education (World Bank 2018b). Siddiqui and Abrar (2003) show that remittance-receiving households in Bangladesh use these funds to maintain subsistence, to invest in land, and to finance the migration of other family members. Remittance-receiving households in Nepal spend the funds mostly on consumption and children's education (World Bank 2011).

FIGURE 1.15

Migrant-sending households and their poverty status (percent of all households with at least one international migrant)

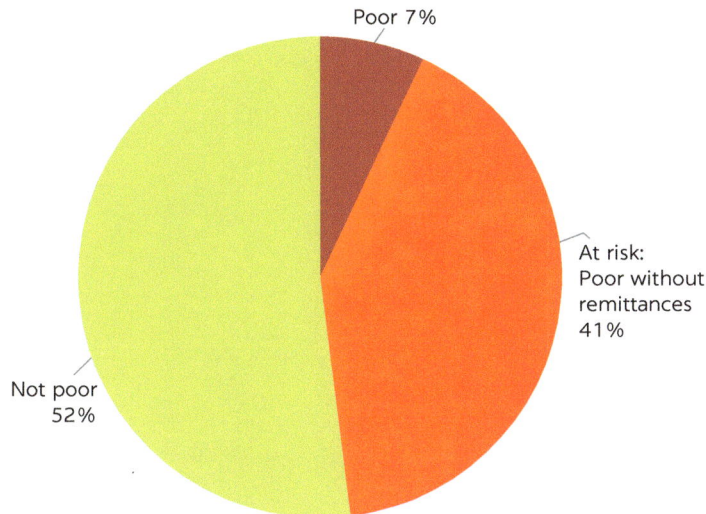

Source: Simulation analysis based on data from the Bangladesh Household Income and Expenditure Survey 2016/17.

Households that receive remittances tend to invest more in human capital, as seen in Bangladesh. Migrants' households have been found to spend more on primary and secondary level education than nonmigrant households (Siddiqui et al. 2019). In Bangladesh, migrant families spend more on education than do families of internal migrants or nonmigrants; their corresponding literacy rates are 79 percent for international migrant family members, 75 percent for internal migrant family members, and 72 percent for nonmigrant family members (Siddiqui 2012). Migrants' families are also likely to spend more on health care and care of the elderly (Fleury 2016).

Estimates from Nepal suggest that, controlling for other characteristics, remittances increase household spending on education and health (table 1.2). This analysis implies that a US$1 increase in remittances is associated with a US$0.008 increase in school expenditure and a US$0.002 increase in health expenditure. It should be noted that the average yearly remittances received by households in this sample is US$1,657, or US$1,922 among those that received nonzero remittances for the previous year. Average expenses on education and health are much smaller, US$157 and US$41, respectively. Thus, the small association between expenditure and remittance amount may make sense, given the difference in magnitudes between the two. The estimates thus suggest that if Nepali migrant workers remitted nothing at all (a US$1,922 decrease in remittances), remittance-receiving Nepali households would reduce spending on education by US$15.4, almost 10 percent of the average expenditure. They would also reduce health spending by US$3.8, again nearly 10 percent of the average expenditure.

TABLE 1.2 Remittances and key components of household expenditure for remittance-receiving households in Nepal

	(1) FOOD EXPENDITURES	(2) NONFOOD EXPENDITURES	(3) SCHOOL EXPENDITURES	(4) HEALTH EXPENDITURES	(5) FARM EXPENDITURES
Remittance amount	0.005	0.006	0.008**	0.002**	0.002
	(0.007)	(0.003)	(0.003)	(0.001)	(0.004)
Household size	122.7***	18.86***	23.55***	3.274***	7.455
	(8.214)	(2.715)	(3.098)	(0.750)	(5.257)
Age of household head	4.467***	0.456	−1.117***	0.152	0.439
	(1.073)	(0.475)	(0.340)	(0.098)	(0.580)
Sector of work of household head	−4.739	−54.68**	10.57	0.375	5.186
	(42.60)	(27.54)	(15.17)	(3.781)	(14.35)
Marital status of household head	84.00**	26.61**	13.71	1.618	12.65
	(40.16)	(12.84)	(13.29)	(4.391)	(14.27)
Value of crops sold	0.149	0.224***	−0.012	−0.008	0.519***
	(0.093)	(0.064)	(0.027)	(0.006)	(0.162)
Value of land owned	−0.000	0.000	0.001*	−0.000***	0.001**
	(0.001)	(0.000)	(0.000)	(0.000)	(0.000)
Constant	73.11	89.12*	8.281	0.892	−35.41
	(85.44)	(47.90)	(29.27)	(7.957)	(32.40)
Destination fixed effects	Yes	Yes	Yes	Yes	Yes
Observations	1,101	1,101	1,101	1,101	1,101
R-squared	0.302	0.209	0.144	0.069	0.140

Source: Nepal Household Risk and Vulnerability Survey 2016.
Note: Robust standard errors are in parentheses. *** $p < 0.01$, ** $p < 0.05$, * $p < 0.1$.

FRAMING SAFER AND MORE PRODUCTIVE MIGRATION THROUGH A LIFE-CYCLE LENS

Whereas previous work has mostly focused on permanent migration and on receiving countries, this book focuses on temporary low-skilled migration from the perspective of low-income sending countries. In that context, migration can be viewed as an engine of development and has been shown to be the most effective poverty-reduction strategy for workers from poor countries (Gibson et al. 2018; McKenzie and Gibson 2014). In addition, temporary migration is generally associated with less political backlash in destination countries than permanent migration.

Given the temporary nature of migration from South Asia, this book treats migration not as a static one-time event, but as part of a migrant's entire life cycle (figure 1.16). The temporary nature of labor mobility from South Asia requires departing from the traditional migration framework that treats migration as a permanent, one-time episode. Instead, migration must be treated as part of a worker's entire life cycle, where all stages are interlinked and are part of the same lifetime decisions (Bossavie et al. 2021; Dustmann and Görlach 2016). For example, premigration

FIGURE 1.16

Temporary migration and the life-cycle framework

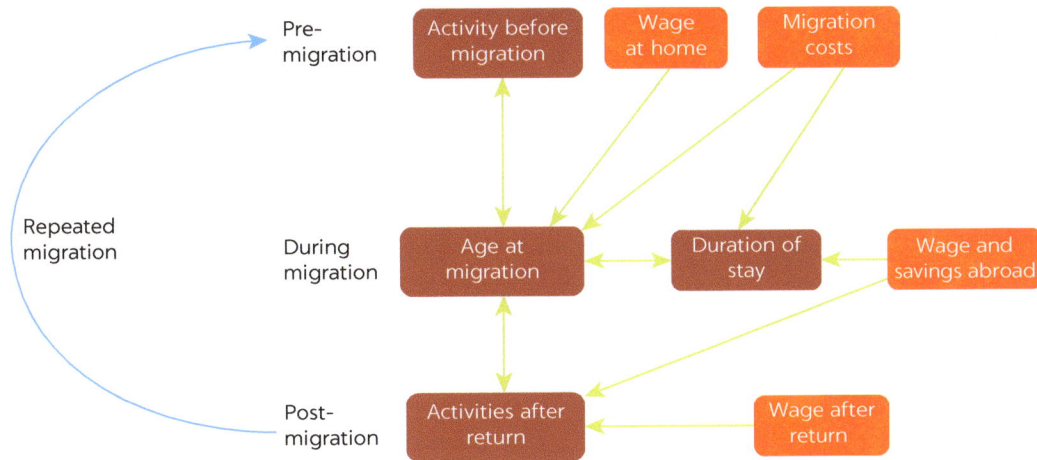

Source: Original compilation.

employment outcomes and age at departure are linked to duration of stay abroad. Duration of stay, in turn, is affected by migration costs and wages abroad, which determine how long migrants need to stay overseas to achieve a given savings target. Closing the full cycle, the ability to finance a self-employment activity after return will be affected by the monetary costs of migration, wages abroad, and duration of stay at destination. Policy interventions that aim to influence any of these decisions or outcomes will thus, by the very nature of these links, also influence the others. It is thus critical for policy makers to consider these links when designing policies related to temporary migration.

Making migration for South Asia safer and more productive requires interventions throughout the migration life cycle (figure 1.17). The migration life cycle is generally described as having four stages (Cho and Majoka 2020). The first stage is predecision, when a worker decides to migrate, having weighed the costs and benefits of migrating. The second stage is predeparture, when, after the worker has decided to pursue an overseas job, he or she can take steps to improve employability, find and secure a job, and obtain the necessary legal documents to migrate (clearances from national authorities, visas, passports, and so forth), and complete the logistical preparations for migration (tickets, financing). The third stage is during migration, when the migrant is employed overseas, and the final stage is after migration, that is, the return home. The recruitment process and access to information are important factors that affect monetary and nonmonetary migration costs specifically in the predecision and predeparture phases. However, migrant costs are also higher for destinations with weaker labor laws and regulations, which is a significant issue during the third stage. At each stage of this process, migrants require information and support from the migration management systems of both their country of origin and the destination country.

FIGURE 1.17

The four illustrative stages of the migration life cycle and common policy issues

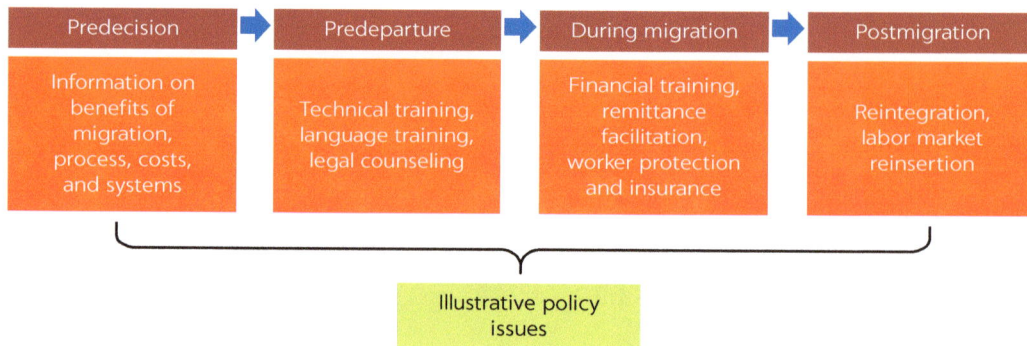

Predecision	Predeparture	During migration	Postmigration
Information on benefits of migration, process, costs, and systems	Technical training, language training, legal counseling	Financial training, remittance facilitation, worker protection and insurance	Reintegration, labor market reinsertion

Illustrative policy issues

Source: Adapted from Cho and Majoka (2020).

THE EFFECTS OF THE COVID-19 PANDEMIC ON MIGRATION AND ITS DEVELOPMENT IMPACT

The COVID-19 (coronavirus) pandemic generated new challenges for South Asian migrants, but mostly exacerbated and brought to light vulnerabilities and migration system insufficiencies that already existed prior to the pandemic. For example, the lack of diversification of migrants' destinations and economic activities overseas greatly exposed them to the negative shocks of COVID-19. Indeed, South Asian migrants are concentrated in markets that have been severely hit by the COVID-19 (coronavirus) pandemic. The GCC countries, the main destinations for South Asian migrant workers, have been severely affected by the pandemic as well as by suppressed global demand for and price of oil (World Bank 2020). A reduction in labor in addition to materials, capital, and intermediate inputs because of disruptions in transport and businesses caused a powerful, immediate cascade of supply contractions (Gopinath 2020).[10] Those restrictions have been having a disproportionate impact on the construction and services sectors, the main employment sectors for low-skilled migrants from South Asia.[11] Many construction sites were closed because of potential infection and spread of the virus, and the risk of infection is high among migrants living in densely populated residential facilities. Moreover, travel bans have restricted international mobility and affected workers in the transport sector (World Bank 2020). The hardest hit sectors include retail and wholesale trade, hospitality and leisure, manufacturing, and food service, where a large share of migrants from the region are also employed.

The sharp slowdown in economic activity and global mobility have strongly reduced the demand for migrants from South Asia. Since the outbreak of the pandemic, demand for South Asian migrant labor has dropped owing to its dependence on the GCC's low-skill-intensive sectors, adversely affecting South Asian migrant workers in several ways. In the short run, many migrant workers already in destination countries have been stranded, often with no jobs, access to health care, or ability to return (Guadagno 2020; Moroz, Shrestha, and Testaverde 2020; World Bank 2020). In addition, aspiring migrants have been unable to depart because of travel restrictions and limited demand for foreign labor in the main destinations: the number of new deployments from the region dropped sharply in 2020 as a result of the global pandemic. In Bangladesh, the number of departures for work overseas dropped from more than 700,000 in 2019 to only 217,000 in 2020. A similar drop in new deployments was observed in Pakistan, from 625,000 in 2019 to 224,705 in 2020. Initial figures for 2021 suggest that new deployments are recovering slightly, though still well below 2019 levels. Remittances, however, stayed at similar levels in 2020, partly because of a diversion of the flow of remittances from informal to formal channels caused by the travel restrictions and the risk of carrying money informally. This effect is also accentuated by incentives provided by governments to channel the flow of remittances through the formal financial system. Although remittance levels were maintained in 2020 compared with prepandemic levels, figures up to March 2021 show a sharp drop in remittances compared with the same period the previous year. Therefore, a sharp drop in remittances may be experienced after a time lag.

Contraction of demand for labor in the main destinations also led to a sharp acceleration in migrant returns. This increased the need for policies to support returning migrants, although home economies' labor markets have been severely hit and thus have limited capacity to absorb them. Before Bangladesh closed its borders in March 2020, about 200,000 migrants returned home, largely because of the impact of COVID-19 in the destination countries. Similarly, the government of Nepal has repatriated about 400,000 displaced workers since the start of the pandemic (IOM 2020). Unanticipated returns are especially challenging for migrants from South Asia, who pay very high upfront costs to migrate overseas, equivalent to six to twelve months of wages at destination (Ratha and Seshan 2018). As a result, migrants who had recently gone overseas and were forced to return prematurely find themselves indebted with high interest rates at a time when labor market opportunities to restart economic activities at home are also quite limited. While the situation of forced returnees has been especially concerning in the context of COVID-19, the pandemic brought to light preexisting vulnerabilities among this population, which need to be addressed beyond the specific context of the pandemic.

Longer-run impacts will depend on the persistence of the pandemic and the pace of labor market recovery once the pandemic is contained. The number of COVID-19 cases in the GCC countries and Malaysia has declined since the beginning of 2021. Deployment of vaccines is expected to bring case numbers down, though the shape of relevant epidemiological curves cannot be predicted with any accuracy. It is thus likely that mobility restrictions will persist for some time. In any case, the global labor market is expected to recover only very gradually from the COVID-19 pandemic. Demand for services, and thus for many types of migrant labor, will probably remain low in the short and medium terms. If and when demand for migrant labor rises again, sending countries will need support to restart managed migration systems, respond quickly, and ensure safe and productive migration.

Structural shifts in the destination economies in response to the pandemic—shifting the type of migrant workers demanded and their volumes—could also have longer-lasting impacts for South Asian migrant workers. Occupations deemed essential, such as frontline health care professionals, have been largely exempt from restrictions on current economic activity or new deployment. For example, health care workers from India (and the Philippines) were exempt from Saudi Arabia's widespread travel ban. More generally, public discussions are under way in higher-income economies about the growing need for more foreign health care personnel. South Asian migrant-sending countries were already investing in the skills of their migrant workers and have been trying to diversify into higher-wage markets such as care services in East Asian economies. More intensively focusing on health care workers as potential migrants may be an additional way for South Asian countries to diversify the opportunities available to prospective migrant workers.[12] In the future, there may also be lower aggregate migrant labor demand in host countries due to both technological change and policy shifts. For example, there may be a greater move toward automation of routine tasks that do not require cognitive thinking, or even labor market nationalization, such as the Saudization policy of Saudi Arabia.

LOOKING AHEAD IN THIS BOOK

The focus of this book is on reducing vulnerability and maximizing productivity throughout all stages of the migration life cycle. Two key objectives in the current context of labor migration from South Asia are to minimize the risks of temporary migration by reducing vulnerability, and to increase its benefits by making migration more productive. Within the life-cycle framework, achieving these two objectives requires interventions to address vulnerability and inefficiencies at each stage of the migration life cycle: predecision, predeparture, during migration, and after return.

The remainder of this book is organized around the perspectives of the life-cycle approach, but also around three sets of policy themes. Chapter 2 examines issues of migrant rights and welfare, and specifically how to reduce migrants' vulnerability at the predecision, predeparture, and migration stages. Chapter 3 examines the factors that may limit the impact of international migration and addresses how to make it more productive. Productivity in this sense is a broad concept, describing not just the returns to the workers themselves, but how migration could be made more inclusive, sustainable, and resilient to shocks. Chapter 4 focuses on enhancing the safety and productivity of return migration through interventions before, during, and after migration. There is a perception that when migrants from Bangladesh, Nepal, and Pakistan return to their countries of origin, they bring back higher human capital as well as greater financial resources (savings). The implication of this perception is that return migrants can be more productive as wage workers or as small-scale entrepreneurs. However, the evidence base to support or contradict these perceptions is limited. In addition, the factors and policy interventions that can make return migrants more productive in their country of origin are not well understood.

As seen throughout the volume, improving the safety and productivity of migration—even after return—will require action and coordination by a range of actors. Governments in both sending and receiving countries are seen to be responsible for developing legal frameworks that meet their economic needs, but that are also consistent with rights-based approaches and that support ethical and fair recruitment. Governments should also shoulder the responsibility to provide services to address market failures, such as information asymmetries. The private sector—primarily recruitment agencies—is seen to have a responsibility to act ethically and within the boundaries of a country's legal framework. The migrants themselves remain responsible for their own decisions, but they need to have access to reliable sources of information.

Unlike unilateral actions or bilateral agreements, multilateral platforms provide a welcome opportunity for countries to openly discuss migration-related issues. Governments of sending and receiving countries have taken unilateral actions by setting up institutions and structures to reduce the negative effects of international labor migration (Thimothy et al. 2016). However, the international dimension of labor mobility means that national arrangements alone cannot efficiently control the outflow or inflow of migrants. As in the past, sending and receiving countries may well enter into bilateral labor agreements or memoranda of understanding to manage and control labor migration in a specific corridor. However, because bilateral labor agreements are mainly designed by host countries, and mostly benefit them, migration-related problems in sending countries may well persist (Sáez 2013). By contrast, multilateral platforms, despite their nonbinding nature, allow diverse groups of migration-affected countries to freely articulate their problems and visions and to learn from each other (table 1.3).

The Abu Dhabi Dialogue Among the Asian Labor Sending and Receiving Countries (ADD)[13] and the Colombo Process (CP) promote intergovernmental cooperation and dialogue on labor migration in Asia. The ADD, established in 2008, is a nonbinding and voluntary consultative process between migrant sending and receiving countries in the Asia region.[14] The ADD aims to protect labor migrants and promote the development of partnerships between member states for adopting best practices. It regularly invites the International Organization for Migration, the International Labour Organization, the private sector, and civil society organizations to contribute to the dialogue as regular observers. Established in 2003, the CP is a member-driven, informal, and nonbinding consultative process on international labor migration in Asia. CP member states are sending countries in the region;[15] receiving countries are invited to cooperate on the implementation of projects at the regional and national levels.[16]

Founded in 2007, the Global Forum on Migration and Development (GFMD) is a nonbinding, informal, and state-led process in which United Nations (UN) member states can discuss topics related to international migration, development, and how they are linked. The platform partners with the private sector, UN agencies, and civil society.[17] The Global Compact for Safe, Orderly, and Regular Migration (GCM) is an intergovernmentally negotiated, nonbinding agreement on all dimensions of international migration that was prepared under the auspices of the UN in 2018.[18] The agreement gives UN member states the flexibility to address the governance of international migration from the standpoint of their lived migration experiences and aspirations (IOM 2020). The activities of the GFMD were an important factor that helped UN member states work toward building consensus on the GCM. The GCM explicitly foresees its continuing role to be as a platform for member states to exchange experiences on the implementation of its recommendations.[19]

TABLE 1.3 Multilateral platforms on international migration

PLATFORM	COMMON FEATURE	DISTINCTIVE FEATURES
Abu Dhabi Dialogue	Nonbinding, informal, and member-driven consultation process or agreement	Focus on international labor migration in Asia with receiving and sending countries as member states
Colombo Process		Focus on international labor migration in Asia with sending countries as member states
Global Forum on Migration and Development		Focus on all aspects of international migration and development globally with UN member states
Global Compact for Migration		Focus on all aspects of international migration globally with UN member states

Source: Original work for this publication.

ANNEX 1A: MINCERIAN REGRESSIONS

TABLE 1A.1 Mincerian regressions for determinants of wages at destination for migrants from multiple corridors

	(1)	(2)	(3)
	BASE SPECIFICATION	COUNTRY-SECTOR INTERACTIONS	DESTINATION COUNTRY FIXED EFFECTS
Age (in years)	0.024**	0.0240**	0.026***
	(0.010)	(0.010)	(0.010)
Age squared	−0.000*	−0.000**	−0.000**
	(0.000)	(0.000)	(0.000)
Low education	−0.248***	−0.247***	−0.213***
	(0.031)	(0.031)	(0.031)
Female	−0.220***	−0.145**	−0.189***
	(0.053)	(0.064)	(0.065)
Country of origin: India	−0.059	−0.093**	−0.087**
	(0.036)	(0.040)	(0.039)
Country of origin: Nepal	−0.268***	−0.302***	−0.384***
	(0.047)	(0.052)	(0.051)
Country of origin: Pakistan	−0.230***	−0.295***	−0.111*
	(0.045)	(0.051)	(0.058)
Agriculture	0.087	0.292*	0.401**
	(0.058)	(0.165)	(0.167)
Household services	−0.263***	−0.378***	−0.283***
	(0.043)	(0.069)	(0.072)
Industry	0.210***	0.0446	0.105
	(0.037)	(0.133)	(0.140)
Services	0.008	−0.092*	−0.015
	(0.041)	(0.049)	(0.053)
India × Industry		−0.332**	−0.289**
		(0.136)	(0.141)
Nepal × Agriculture		−0.527**	−0.604***
		(0.211)	(0.218)
Nepal × Household		0.216***	0.121
		(0.075)	(0.077)
Nepal × Industry		−0.052	−0.109
		(0.145)	(0.150)
Nepal × Services		0.372***	0.283***
		(0.051)	(0.053)
Pakistan × Agriculture		−0.198	−0.364**
		(0.176)	(0.176)
Pakistan × Household		0.068	−0.006
		(0.083)	(0.136)
Pakistan × Industry		0.236*	0.194
		(0.141)	(0.147)
Pakistan × Services		0.336***	0.304***
		(0.090)	(0.097)
Country of destination: Saudi Arabia			−0.163***
			(0.028)
Country of destination: United Arab Emirates			−0.401***
			(0.046)
Constant	5.809***	5.855***	5.896***
	(0.174)	(0.174)	(0.173)
Observations	2,502	2,502	2,502
R^2	0.169	0.177	0.200

Note: Estimates using data from KNOMAD-ILO Migration Costs Surveys 2015 and 2016. The dependent variable is the logarithm of monthly earnings in the destination country. Coefficients were estimated by ordinary least squares with heteroscedasticity-robust standard errors. The omitted comparison sector is construction. * $p < .10$, ** $p < .05$, *** $p < .01$

NOTES

1. World Bank (2019) provides a detailed description of the differences between the groups that are often collectively referred to as "migrants"—international migrants, refugees, irregular migrants, and temporary migrants. This book focuses almost exclusively on temporary, international, regular migrant workers. They are engaged in remunerated activities in countries of which they are not nationals.

2. Estimated using data from the UN World Population Prospects 2017 (UN DESA 2017).

3. Estimated using administrative data on clearances provided for migrant workers from the Bureau of Manpower Employment and Training (Bangladesh), Department of Foreign Employment (Nepal), and Bureau of Emigration and Overseas Employment (Pakistan).

4. Estimates based on data from 71 low- and middle-income countries over a 20-year period (1980–99). There is a rich literature on the development implications of migration. Murrugarra, Larisson, and Sasin (2011) offers one such synthesis of this literature, as does World Bank (2018b).

5. The threshold of US$1 per day was the international poverty line set in *World Development Report 1990: Poverty* (World Bank 1990), and it remained in use until the update to US$1.25 per day in Ravallion, Chen, and Sangraula (2009).

6. The implications of this concentration are explored in chapter 3.

7. The sample from KNOMAD-ILO Migration Costs Surveys 2015 and 2016 might not be representative of all migrants in the corridor.

8. The nature of selection in labor migration—whether migrants are more skilled or less skilled than nonmigrants—has been shown to depend on labor market conditions at home and destination (Borjas and Bratsberg 1994). Global evidence indicates that international labor migrants tend to be positively selected overall, meaning that migrants have higher skill levels than nonmigrants of working age in their home countries (World Bank 2018a).

9. These data are from the Bangladesh Return Migrant Survey 2018/19 conducted for this book and described in Ahmed et al. (2021).

10. Annex A of Gopinath (2020) summarizes the current state of the outbreak in the major sending and receiving countries discussed in this book. It also provides a list of mobility restrictions and other measures taken by GCC countries to address COVID-19 transmission.

11. Cross-country evidence suggests that the construction and finance sectors expand the most during a boom period and contract the most during a recession (Dell'Ariccia et al. 2020).

12. Although there are valid misgivings about the possibility of resulting shortages of health care workers in sending countries ("brain drain"), recent papers in the "brain gain" literature suggest that workers invest in human capital in response to migration opportunities, thus leading to a net domestic increase in skilled workers, despite labor outflow. See, for example, Khanna and Morales (2019) on the net increase in computer scientists in India and Abarcar and Theoharides (2018) on the net increase of health care professionals in the Philippines.

13. Abu Dhabi Dialogue Among the Asian Labor Sending and Receiving Countries (http://abudhabidialogue.org.ae).

14. Member states are seven migrant-receiving countries (Bahrain, Kuwait, Malaysia, Oman, Qatar, Saudi Arabia, and the United Arab Emirates) and 11 migrant-sending countries (Afghanistan, Bangladesh, China, India, Indonesia, Nepal, Pakistan, the Philippines, Sri Lanka, Thailand, and Vietnam). The United Arab Emirates provides the permanent secretariat.

15. The 12 CP member states are Afghanistan, Bangladesh, Cambodia, China, India, Indonesia, Nepal, Pakistan, the Philippines, Sri Lanka, Thailand, and Vietnam (Colombo Process, https://www.colomboprocess.org).

16. The CP also cooperates with the International Organization for Migration, United Nations agencies, and development partners (https://www.colomboprocess.org).

17. Global Forum on Migration & Development (https://www.gfmd.org).

18. The negotiation of the GCM followed the New York Declaration for Refugees and Migrants, which was unanimously adopted by the UN General Assembly in 2016.

19. Global Forum on Migration & Development (https://www.gfmd.org).

REFERENCES

Abarcar, Paolo, and Caroline Theoharides. 2018. "The International Migration of Healthcare Professionals and the Supply of Educated Individuals Left Behind." Unpublished. https://economics.nd.edu/assets/289077/theoharides_amherst_intl_migration_of_healthcare_pros.pdf.

Acosta, Pablo A., Emmanuel K. K. Lartey, and Federico S. Mandelman. 2009. "Remittances and the Dutch Disease." *Journal of International Economics* 79 (1): 102–16.

Adams, Richard H., Jr. 2009. "The Determinants of International Remittances in Developing Countries." *World Development* 37 (1): 93–103.

Adams, Richard H., Jr., and John Page. 2005. "Do International Migration and Remittances Reduce Poverty in Developing Countries?" *World Development* 33 (10): 1645–69.

Ahmed, S. Amer, Faiz Ahmed, Laurent Bossavie, Çağlar Özden, and He Wang. 2021. "Temporary Migration and Development: A New Dataset from Bangladesh." Background paper for *Toward Safer and More Productive Migration for South Asia*, World Bank, Washington, DC.

Ahmed, S. Amer, Delfin Go, and Dirk Willenbockel. 2016. "Global Migration Revisited: Short-Term Pains, Long-Term Gains, and the Potential of South-South Migration." Policy Research Working Paper 7628, World Bank, Washington, DC.

Amir, Saman, Aphichoke Kotikula, Rohini P. Pande, Laurent Bossavie, and Upasana Khadka. 2018. *Female Labor Force Participation in Pakistan: What Do We Know?* World Bank, Washington, DC.

Amuedo-Dorantes, Catalina, and Susan Pozo. 2006. "Migration, Remittances, and Male and Female Employment Patterns." *American Economic Review* 96 (2): 222–26.

Borjas, George J., and Bernt Bratsberg. 1994. "Who Leaves? The Outmigration of the Foreign-Born." Working Paper 4913, National Bureau of Economic Research, Cambridge, MA.

Bossavie, Laurent, and Anastasiya Denisova. 2018. "Youth Labor Migration in Nepal." Jobs Working Paper 13, World Bank, Washington, DC.

Bossavie, Laurent, Joseph Simon Görlach, Çağlar Özden, and He Wang. 2021. "Temporary Migration for Long-Term Investment." Background paper for *Toward Safer and More Productive Migration for South Asia*, World Bank, Washington, DC.

Bourdet, Yves, and Hans Falck. 2006. "Emigrants' Remittances and Dutch Disease in Cape Verde." *International Economic Journal* 20 (3): 267–84.

Brahmbhatt, Milan, Otaviano Canuto, and Ekaterina Vostroknutova. 2010. "Dealing with Dutch Disease." Economic Premise 16, World Bank, Washington, DC.

Budina, Nina, Gaobo Pang, and Sweder van Wijnbergen. 2007. "Nigeria's Growth Record: Dutch Disease or Debt Overhang?" Policy Research Working Paper 4256, World Bank, Washington, DC.

Bussolo, Maurizio, and Denis Medvedev. 2007. "Do Remittances Have a Flip Side? A General Equilibrium Analysis of Remittances, Labor Supply Responses, and Policy Options for Jamaica." Policy Research Working Paper 4143, World Bank, Washington, DC.

Chemmencheri, Sudheesh Ramapurath. 2016. "Social Protection as a Human Right in South Asia." *Indian Journal of Human Development* 10 (2): 236–52.

Cho, Yoonyoung, Anastasiya Denisova, Soonhwa Yi, and Upasana Khadka. 2018. "Lessons from Korea's Employment Permit System: Bilateral Arrangement of Temporary Labor Migration." World Bank, Washington, DC.

Cho, Yoonyoung, and Zaineb Majoka. 2020. *Pakistan Jobs Diagnostic: Promoting Access to Quality Jobs for All.* Jobs Series 20, World Bank, Washington, DC.

Corden, W. Max. 1984. "Booming Sector and Dutch Disease Economics: Survey and Consolidation." *Oxford Economic Papers* 36 (3): 359–80.

Corden, W. Max, and J. Peter Neary. 1982. "Booming Sector and De-Industrialization in a Small Open Economy." *Economic Journal* 92 (368): 825–48.

Dell'Ariccia, Giovanni, Ehsan Ebrahimy, Deniz O. Igan, and Damien Puy. 2020. "Discerning Good from Bad Credit Booms: The Role of Construction." Staff Discussion Note 20/02, International Monetary Fund, Washington, DC.

Dhungana, Bharat Ram. 2012. "Remittance and Nepalese Economy." Unpublished, Pokhara University.

Dustmann, Christian, and Joseph-Simon Görlach. 2016. "The Economics of Temporary Migrations." *Journal of Economic Literature* 54 (1): 98–136.

Farole, Thomas, Yoonyoung Cho, Laurent Bossavie, and Reyes Aterido. 2017. "Bangladesh Jobs Diagnostic." Jobs Series 9, World Bank, Washington, DC.

Fleury, Anjali. 2016. "Understanding Women and Migration: A Literature Review." World Bank, Washington, DC.

Frankel, Jeffrey. 2010. "Are Bilateral Remittances Countercyclical?" Faculty Research Working Paper Series, Harvard Kennedy School, Cambridge, MA.

Gibson, John, David McKenzie, Halahingano Rohorua, and Steven Stillman. 2018. "The Long-Term Impacts of International Migration: Evidence from a Lottery." *World Bank Economic Review* 32 (1): 127–47.

Gopinath, G. 2020. "Limiting the Economic Fallout of the Coronavirus with Large Targeted Policies." In *Mitigating the COVID Economic Crisis: Act Fast and Do Whatever It Takes*, edited by Richard Baldwin and Beatrice Weder di Mauro, 41–48. London: CEPR Press.

Guadagno, Lorenzo. 2020. "Migrants and the COVID-19 Pandemic: An Initial Analysis." International Organization for Migration, Geneva.

Gupta, Sanjeev, Catherine A. Pattillo, and Smita Wagh. 2009. "Effect of Remittances on Poverty and Financial Development in Sub-Saharan Africa." *World Development* 37 (1): 104–15.

Hertog, Steffen. 2012. "A Comparative Assessment of Labor Market Nationalization Policies in the GC." In *National Employment, Migration and Education in the GCC: Economic Development and Diversification*, edited by Steffen Hertog, 65–106. Berlin: Gerlach Press.

IOM (International Organization for Migration). 2020. "Global Compact for Migration." https://www.iom.int/global-compact-migration.

Khanna, Gaurav, and Nicolas Morales. 2019. "The IT Boom and Other Unintended Consequences of Chasing the American Dream." Unpublished. http://dx.doi.org/10.2139/ssrn.2968147.

Lokshin, Michael, Mikhail Bontch-Osmolovski, and Elena Glinskaya. 2011. "Work-Related Migration and Poverty Reduction in Nepal." In *Migration and Poverty: Toward Better Opportunities for the Poor*, edited by Edmundo Murrugarra, Jennica Larisson, and Marcin Sasin, 35–62. World Bank, Washington, DC.

Lueth, Eric, and Marta Ruiz-Arranz. 2006. "A Gravity Model of Workers' Remittances." Working Paper 06/290, International Monetary Fund, Washington, DC.

McKenzie, David, and John Gibson. 2014. "The Development Impact of a Best Practice Seasonal Worker Policy." *Review of Economics and Statistics* 96 (2): 229–43.

Mongardini, Joannes, and Brett Rayner. 2009. "Grants, Remittances, and the Equilibrium Real Exchange Rate in Sub-Saharan African Countries." Working Paper 09/75, International Monetary Fund, Washington, DC.

Moroz, Harry, Maheshwor Shrestha, and Mauro Testaverde. 2020. "Potential Responses to the COVID-19 Outbreak in Support of Migrant Workers." World Bank, Washington, DC.

Mughal, Mazhar Y., and Junaid Ahmed. 2014. "Remittances and Business Cycles: Comparison of South Asian Countries." *International Economic Journal* 28 (4): 513–41.

Murrugarra, Edmundo, Jennica Larisson, and Marcin Sasin. 2011. "Migration and Poverty: Toward Better Opportunities for the Poor." World Bank, Washington, DC.

Pesaran, M. Hashem, Yongcheol Shin, and Richard J. Smith. 1999. "Pooled Mean Group Estimation of Dynamic Heterogeneous Panels." *Journal of the American Statistical Association* 94 (446): 621–34.

Qayyum, Abdul, Javid Muhammad, and Umaima Arif. 2008. "Impact of Remittances on Economic Growth and Poverty: Evidence from Pakistan." MPRA Paper 22941, University Library of Munich.

Raihan, Selim, Bazlul H. Khondker, Guntur Sugiyarto, and Shikha Jha. 2009. "Remittances and Household Welfare: A Case Study of Bangladesh." Economics Working Paper 189, Asian Development Bank, Manila.

Rajan, Rughuram G., and Arvind Subramanian. 2005. "What Undermines Aid's Impact on Growth?" Working Paper 05/126, International Monetary Fund, Washington, DC.

Ratha, Dilip, and Ganesh Seshan. 2018. "Worker-Paid Recruitment Costs." In *Global Labour and the Migrant Premium: The Cost of Working Abroad*, edited by Tugba Basaran and Elspeth Guild. London: Routledge.

Ruppert Bulmer, Elizabeth, Ami Shrestha, and Michelle Marshalian. 2020. *Nepal Jobs Diagnostic*. Jobs Series 22, World Bank, Washington, DC.

Ravallion, Martin, Shaohua Chen, and Prem Sangraula. 2009. "Dollar a Day Revisited." *World Bank Economic Review* 23 (2): 163–84.

Sáez, Sebastián. 2013. "Trade in Services and Bilateral Labor Agreements: Overview." In *Let Workers Move. Using Bilateral Labor Agreements to Increase Trade in Services*, edited by Sebastián Sáez, 1–15. Washington, DC: World Bank.

Shediac, Richard, Chucrallah Haddad, and Moncef Klouche. 2010. "The Case for Flexible Employment in GCC Countries." Booz & Company.

Shrestha, Maheshwor. 2017. *Push and Pull: A Study of International Migration from Nepal*. Policy Research Working Paper 7965, World Bank, Washington, DC.

Siddiqui, Tasneem. 2012. "Impact of Migration on Poverty and Development." University of Sussex, Brighton.

Siddiqui, Tasneem, and Chowdhury R. Abrar. 2003. "Migrant Worker Remittances and Micro-Finance in Bangladesh." Working Paper 38, Social Finance Programme, International Labour Office, Geneva.

Siddiqui, Tasneem, Mariana Sultana, Rabeya Sultana, and Sanjida Akhter. 2019. "Labour Migration from Bangladesh 2018." Refugee and Migratory Movements Research Unit, Dhaka.

Thimothy, Rakkee, S. K. Sasikumar, Padmini Ratnayake, and Alvin P. Ang. 2016. "Labour Migration Structures and Financing in Asia." International Labour Organization, Geneva.

Treviño, Juan Pedro. 2011. "Oil-Price Boom and Real Exchange Rate Appreciation: Is There Dutch Disease in the CEMAC?" Working Paper 11/268, International Monetary Fund, Washington, DC.

UN DESA (United Nations Department of Economic and Social Affairs). 2017. *World Population Prospects: The 2017 Revision*. New York: UN DESA.

World Bank. 1990. *World Development Report 1990: Poverty*. Washington, DC: World Bank.

World Bank. 2011. "Large-Scale Migration and Remittance in Nepal: Issues, Challenges, and Opportunities." World Bank, Washington, DC.

World Bank. 2013. *Bangladesh Poverty Assessment: Assessing a Decade of Progress in Reducing Poverty, 2000–2010*. Washington, DC: World Bank.

World Bank. 2015. *Global Economic Prospects, January 2015: Having Fiscal Space and Using It*. Washington, DC: World Bank.

World Bank. 2018a. "A Migrant's Journey for Better Opportunities: The Case of Pakistan." World Bank, Washington, DC.

World Bank. 2018b. *Moving for Prosperity: Global Migration and Labor Markets*. Washington, DC: World Bank.

World Bank. 2019. "Leveraging Economic Migration for Development." World Bank, Washington, DC.

World Bank. 2020. "COVID-19 Crisis through a Migration Lens." Migration and Development Brief 32, World Bank, Washington, DC.

2 Supporting Development Comes at a Cost for Migrants

INTRODUCTION

International migration clearly offers substantial benefits for migrants, their households, and their wider families, but there are costs to their welfare and safety. This chapter examines these costs—both monetary and nonmonetary. It also endeavors to track down underlying institutional contributory factors before suggesting some possible policy solutions.

MONETARY AND NONMONETARY MIGRATION COSTS

Migrant workers from South Asia pay some of the highest migration costs in the world, and it takes them several months to recoup this outlay in some cases. Total migration costs vary substantially across migration corridors (figure 2.1). Pakistani migrants in Saudi Arabia incur the largest overall costs: almost US$5,000 on average. In comparison, migrants from Nepal spend less than US$1,000 to migrate to Malaysia, Qatar, or Saudi Arabia. When Filipinos migrate to Saudi Arabia they pay only a very small fraction of the costs incurred by their Pakistani counterparts. Similarly, migrants from India pay less than a third of the expenditure incurred by Pakistani labor migrants when moving to the Gulf Cooperation Council (GCC) countries. On average, Bangladeshi workers spend more than US$3,000 on migration costs on average.[1] Total migration costs are greatest for the Bangladesh-Qatar corridor at almost US$4,000 and least for the Bangladesh-Malaysia corridor, at roughly US$2,900. Regardless of the complexity of the overall picture, and intriguing discrepancies, migration costs are invariably higher for workers from South Asia than for migrants from other countries of origin going to those same GCC countries, suggesting that features of the migrant recruitment market at home play an important systemic role in determining costs. The excess demand from South Asian workers for migrant-labor jobs in the GCC countries and the visa-trading practices allowed by some of the destination countries are probably also contributing factors.

FIGURE 2.1

Migration and recruitment costs in select corridors

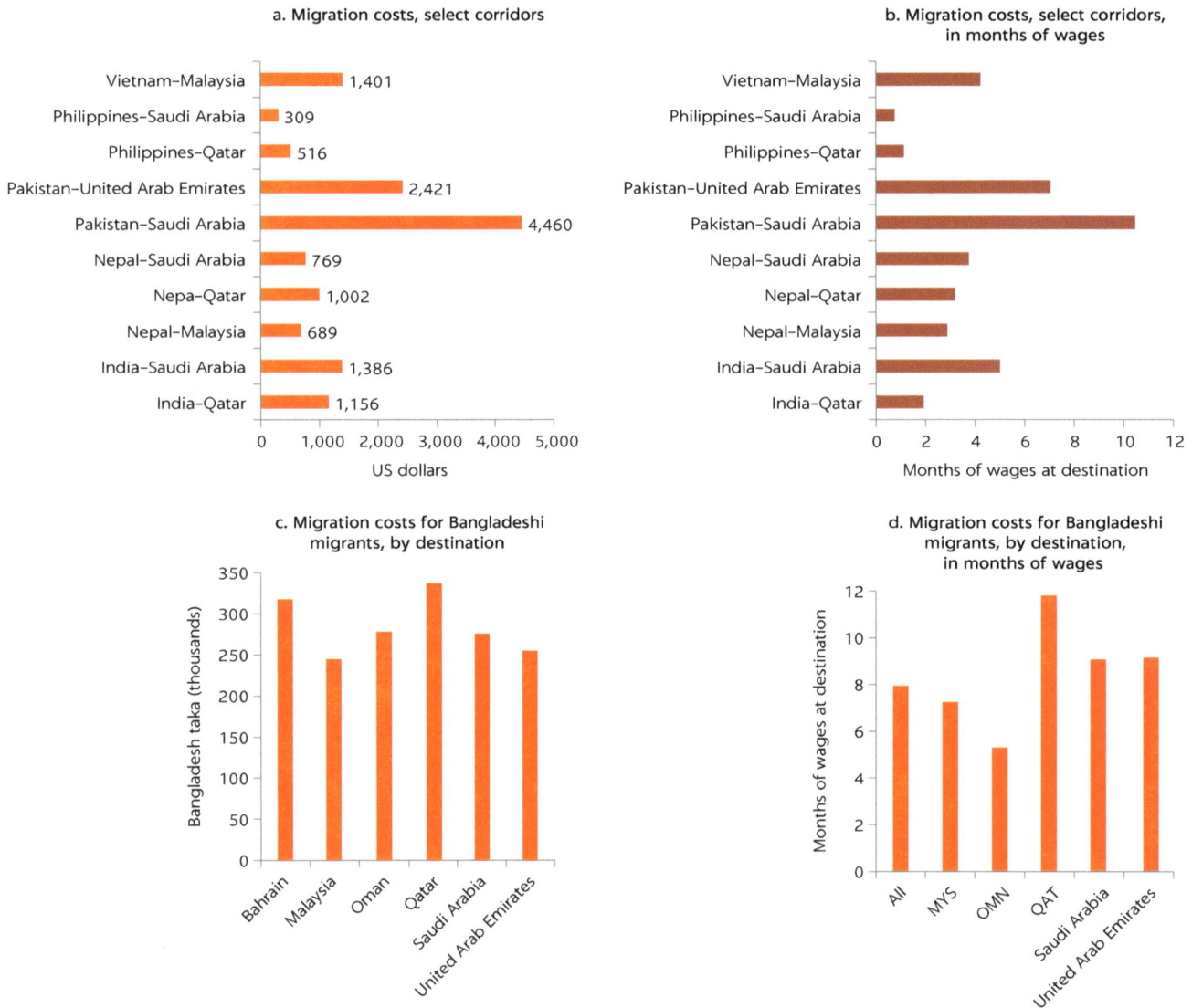

a. Migration costs, select corridors

b. Migration costs, select corridors, in months of wages

c. Migration costs for Bangladeshi migrants, by destination

d. Migration costs for Bangladeshi migrants, by destination, in months of wages

Sources: For panels a and b, KNOMAD-ILO Migration Costs Surveys 2015 and 2016. For panels c and d, Bangladesh Return Migrant Survey 2018/19.
Note: For panels b and d, the migration cost indicator (MCI) is calculated as the average worker-incurred migration costs in 2016 US dollars as a multiple of the migrant's monthly foreign earnings in 2016 US dollars (KNOMAD-ILO Migration Costs Surveys 2015 and 2016). Migration costs include fees paid to recruitment agents, costs for documents (passport, visa, medical certificates, language test, security clearance), and transportation cost (KNOMAD-ILO Migration Costs Surveys 2015 and 2016). All = all destinations; MYS = Malaysia; OMN = Oman; QAT is Qatar; SAU = Saudi Arabia; UAE = United Arab Emirates.

The migration costs for workers from Bangladesh, Nepal, and Pakistan are not just high in absolute terms, but also relative to their wages at destination. The recruitment costs for Pakistani labor migrants are more than 10 times their monthly earnings upon arrival. They are also extremely high compared with wages and household income at home. For Bangladesh, total migration costs have been estimated to equate to roughly 30 months of migrant household income before departure (Ahmed et al. 2021). In this situation, brokers (recruitment agents) have the leverage to set extremely high prices for their services (KNOMAD 2017).

Intermediation costs account for large differences in total expenditures for South Asian labor migrants (figures 2.2 and 2.3). Pakistani migrants to Saudi Arabia and the United Arab Emirates spend more than 60 percent of their direct migration costs on visa fees. Without these high visa costs, the total expenditure would most likely be on par with the migration-related costs of their

FIGURE 2.2

Migration cost breakdown for select corridors

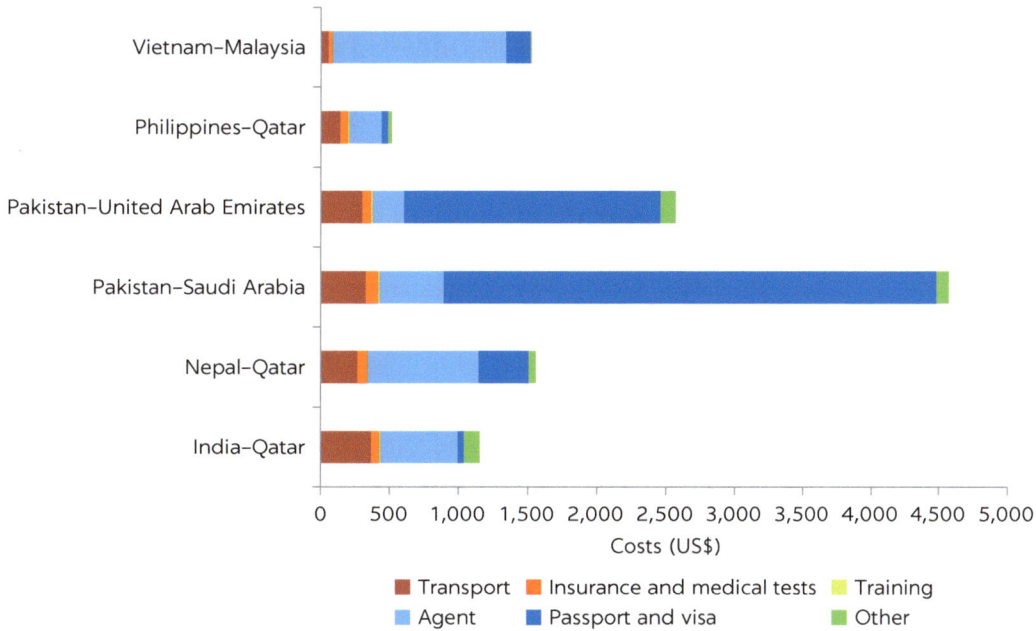

Source: KNOMAD-ILO Migration Costs Surveys 2015 and 2016.
Note: Costs that constitute less than 1 percent of total expenditures are dropped.

FIGURE 2.3

Intermediation costs by component

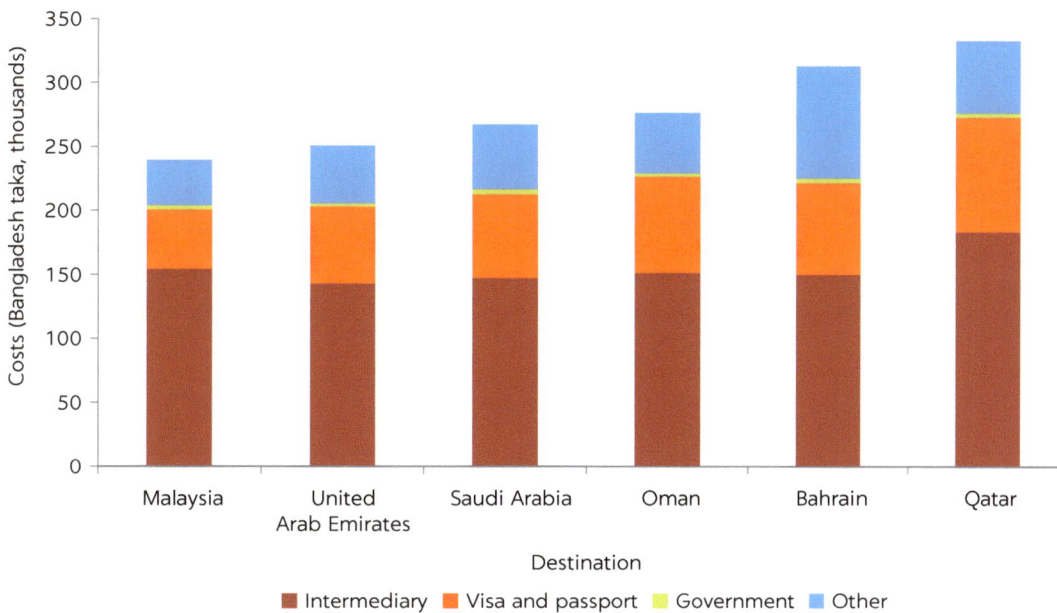

Source: Bangladesh Return Migrants Survey 2018/19.

counterparts from other countries. Nepali migrants to Saudi Arabia and Malaysia spend about 60 percent and 40 percent, respectively, of their total migration outlay on fees for brokers (agents). Agents' fees account for about 40 percent of the total expenditure of Nepali migrants in Qatar. Bangladeshi labor migrants spend, on average, more than 50 percent of the total migration cost on these intermediaries. On average, more than 20 percent of their total migration expenditure is used to obtain a passport and procure the visa of the relevant destination country.

Over and above the financial costs, costs associated with deficiencies in the working conditions of migrants in host countries also increase the overall costs of South Asian labor migration. These nonpecuniary costs are usually only revealed after arrival in the receiving country. Such costs not only affect the overall well-being of migrants (Aleksynska, Aoul, and Petrencu 2017), but can also affect their decision to return home. The overall success or failure of the migration experience can thus hinge on these aspects.

High migration costs contribute to high vulnerability in the host country. Given the very high total costs of migration, migrants from South Asia have to stay abroad for a minimum of about a year merely to break even on their initial investment. In addition, migration costs are high compared with household incomes at origin (figure 2.4). As a result, a large share of migrants borrow to finance their migration episode, which further inflates costs and creates the additional pressure of loan repayment (figure 2.5). Once they have repaid these very large fixed costs, migrants also need to stay at destination long enough to generate an adequate return on their initial investment while they simultaneously accumulate savings and send remittances back home for consumption. These very large upfront costs greatly reduce the bargaining power of migrants, whose stay at destination is entirely tied to their sponsoring employer. In the absence of alternative options, migrants are legally bound to continue working for their employer, irrespective of their conditions of employment, leaving them

FIGURE 2.4

Migration costs and annual income before migration among Bangladeshi households with an international migrant

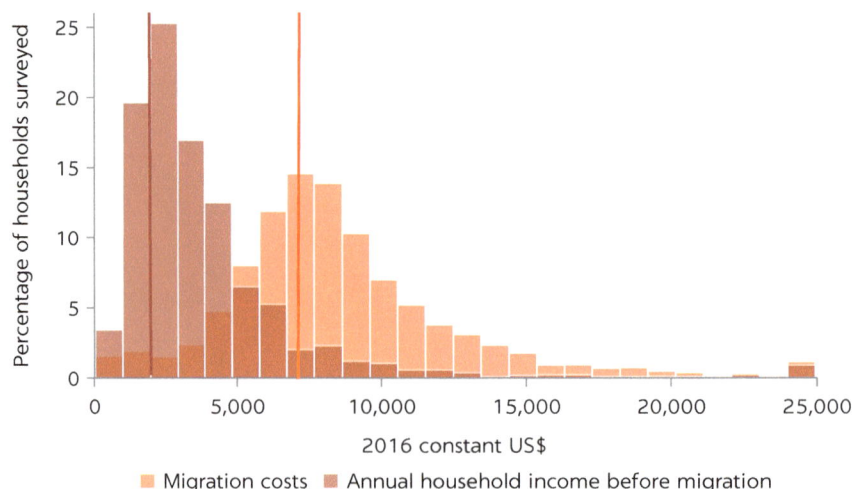

Sources: Bossavie et al. (2021), based on the Bangladesh Return Migrant Survey 2018/2019.
Note: Statistics are for males ages 15–64. Vertical lines indicate median values.

FIGURE 2.5

Borrow to finance temporary economic migration

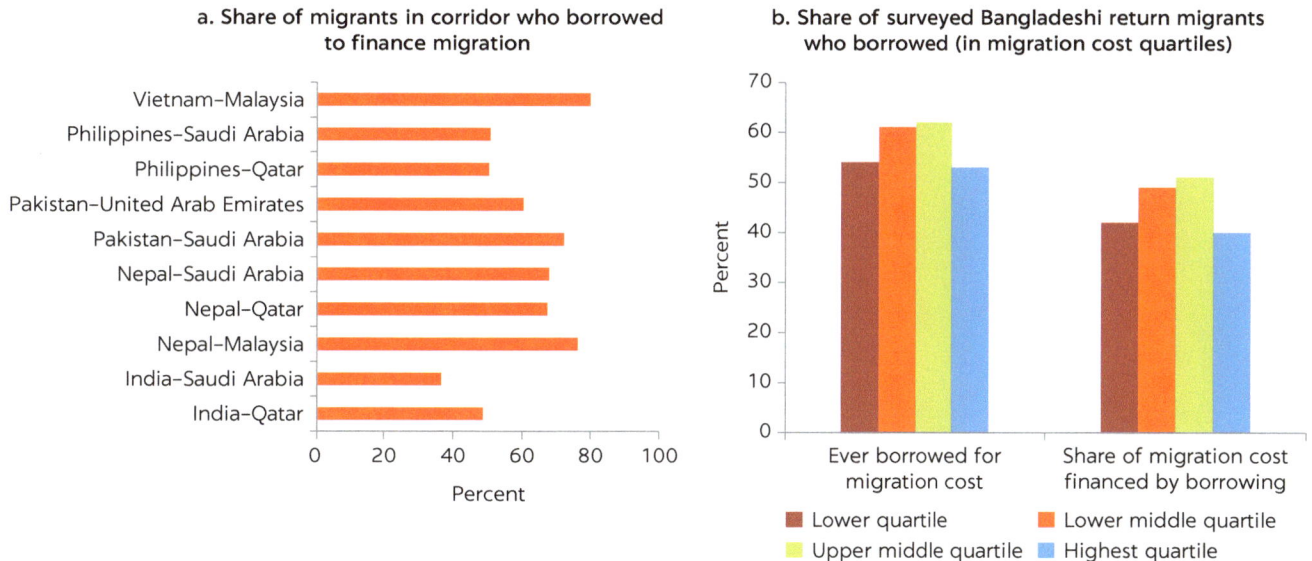

a. Share of migrants in corridor who borrowed to finance migration

b. Share of surveyed Bangladeshi return migrants who borrowed (in migration cost quartiles)

Sources: Panel a is from the KNOMAD-ILO Migration Costs Surveys 2015 and 2016. Panel b is from the Bangladesh Return Migrant Survey 2018/19.

exposed to abuse by the employer (Khan and Harroff-Tavel 2011). In addition, the high costs of migration also serve as an incentive for migrants (who originally migrated legally) to overstay illegally at destination if their employment contract and work permit are not renewed. In Bangladesh, for example, 12 percent of return migrants report expulsion from the destination country owing to issues with visas and work permits as the main reason for returning.[2]

As a result, migrants from Bangladesh, Nepal, and Pakistan have strong incentives to stay and continue remitting, even when faced with rights violations or unsafe work conditions. More than 90 percent of Pakistani labor migrants report being deprived of their rights in Saudi Arabia and the United Arab Emirates (figure 2.6). These rights include, for example, the ability to express their views, join unions, engage in industrial action, change employers, freely remit earnings, retain their own travel documents (passports are still commonly withheld), or be remunerated without suffering wage discrimination relative to native-born workers. By contrast, almost no Indian labor migrant reports being deprived of his or her rights in Qatar and Saudi Arabia. About half of all Nepali migrants report violations of their rights in Qatar. Violated rights are numerous, ranging from restrictions on political and economic rights to the lack of ability to communicate with people (figure 2.7). The top three human rights violations that Bangladeshi labor workers suffer abroad are prolonged exposure to extreme heat, that is, to temperatures above 45°C (37 percent of respondents); the inability to change employers (30 percent); and withholding of travel or identity documents by the employer (24 percent). Oman and Qatar are the two destination countries where Bangladeshi labor migrants report facing the most issues (table 2.1).

It has been suggested that outmigration—and thus the absence of an adult household member—may have adverse effects on the educational and nutritional outcomes of children. Global evidence is ambiguous, and effects tend to

FIGURE 2.6

Share of migrants reporting they had been deprived of rights in the host country

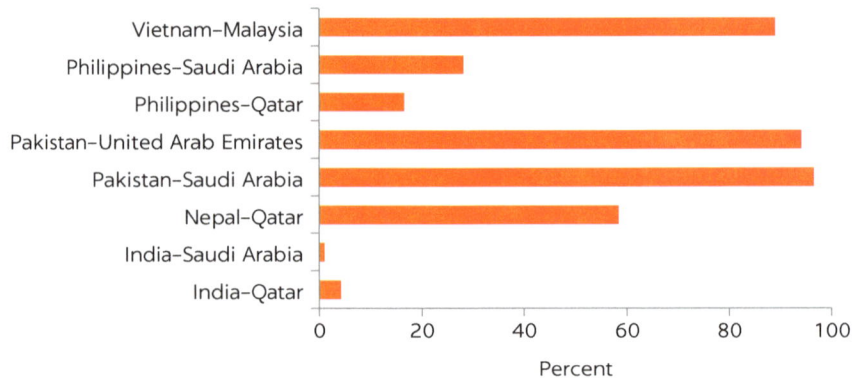

Source: KNOMAD-ILO Migration Costs Surveys 2015 and 2016.
Note: Data based on answers to this survey question: "Have you been deprived of any rights during your employment in [current country]?"

FIGURE 2.7

Distribution of complaints by corridor for type of rights violated

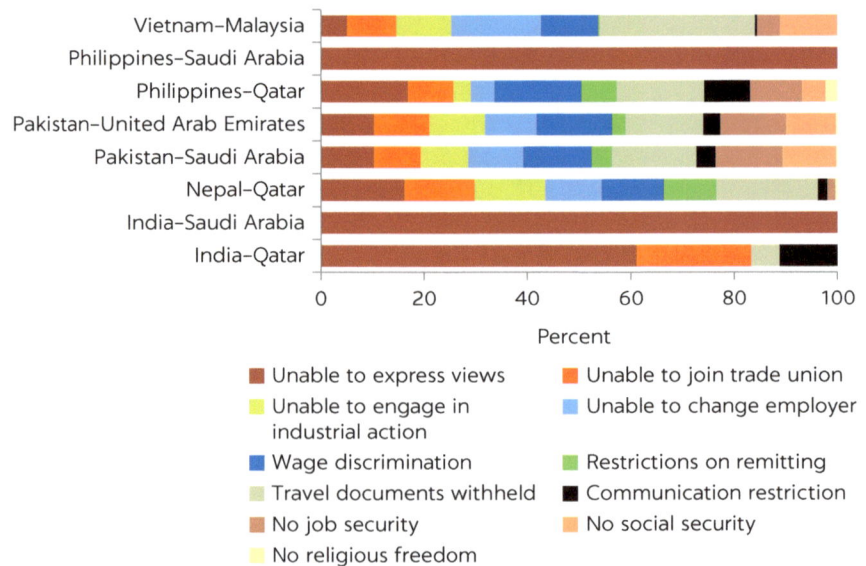

Source: KNOMAD Cost of Migration Survey 2015 & 2016.

differ depending on the gender, age, and sibling birth order of the children left behind (Antman 2012). In South Asia, evidence so far suggests some positive effects on children's development and human capital. In Nepal, estimated effects are heterogeneous, but overall effects on school enrollment are positive (Bossavie and Denisova 2018; Shrestha 2017b). In Bangladesh, the effects of outmigration on children's educational and nutritional outcomes through the Malaysia-Bangladesh government-to-government (G2G) program have also been positive overall (Mobarak, Sharif, and Shrestha 2020).

Receiving remittances from overseas may reduce the labor supply of other household members at home, particularly of females, through an income

TABLE 2.1 **Share of Bangladeshi migrants at destination who report being deprived of a right**

Percent

	DID YOU PERSONALLY FACE THE FOLLOWING ISSUES WHILE IN EMPLOYMENT ABROAD? (SHARE OF TEMPORARY MIGRANTS ANSWERING YES)	SAUDI ARABIA	UNITED ARAB EMIRATES	OMAN	MALAYSIA	QATAR	BAHRAIN	AVERAGE
1	Unable to change employers	26	31	37	29	37	28	30
2	Travel documents or identification documents withheld by employer	20	25	30	22	30	24	24
3	Excluded from social security	16	17	21	14	21	19	17
4	Threatened with deportation or denouncement to authorities	17	19	25	15	24	19	19
5	Problem with authorities	20	23	27	19	30	23	22
6	Physical abuse at workplace	6	7	11	6	9	4	7
7	Verbal abuse at workplace	17	16	24	19	25	20	19
8	Unsafe working conditions	11	14	18	13	16	15	14
9	Discrimination and xenophobic attitudes	11	10	12	12	11	07	11
10	Sexual harassment at workplace	2	2	3	2	2	0	2
11	During work, were you continually exposed to extreme heat (temperatures above 45°C)?	34	39	43	34	39	32	37

Source: Bangladesh Return Migrant Survey 2018/19.
Note: Columns do not sum to 100 because some migrants report being deprived of multiple rights.

effect. Global evidence on this question tends to find no effect of labor migration on the labor supply of males staying behind, but negative effects on the labor supply of females (Acosta 2006; Amuedo-Dorantes and Pozo 2006; Bossavie and Ozden 2022; Mendola and Carletto 2012). In Bangladesh, no adverse effects on the labor supply of other household members, including females, has been shown in the context of the G2G program with Malaysia (Mobarak, Sharif, and Shrestha 2020). In addition, positive effects on female involvement in decision-making have been found. In Nepal, evidence on this question is mixed: Shrestha (2017a) finds that outmigration increases female participation in nonagricultural activities in communities with higher outmigration rates, whereas Lokshin and Glinskaya (2009) and Bossavie and Denisova (2018) find that female labor supply declines in households that receive remittances from international outmigrants.

Institutional factors contributing to high costs and vulnerability

A key driver of high migration costs is the high demand for jobs in foreign markets, given the substantial wage and welfare gains that temporary migration brings. There are typically many more aspiring migrants than there are positions available, as illustrated by the case of Nepalis interested in going to the Republic of Korea through the Korean Employment Permit System. Under the Employment Permit System, selected migrants must meet rigorous qualifications, including Korean language proficiency and other skills, and must come from a preselected list of destinations through a process that is completely managed by Human Resources Development Service of Korea (Cho et al. 2018). The number of migrants is also subject to a quota set by the Korean government. For Nepal, there were more than 92,000 applications for 7,100 jobs in 2019 (Ruppert Bulmer, Shresta, and Marshalian 2020). The excess demand is unsurprising, given that the monthly minimum wage for Employment Permit System workers was US$1,307 as of 2017, compared with Nepal's minimum wage of US$93. Similarly, in 2012, when the Bangladesh-Malaysia G2G memorandum of understanding was signed, the objective was to recruit 30,000 male workers to work in the Malaysian palm oil sector. In early 2013, Bangladesh's Bureau of Manpower Employment and Training began nationwide registration of interested applicants and received responses from 1.43 million applicants (Shrestha, Mobarak, and Sharif 2019). This excess demand—combined with the tolerance in some host countries of practices such as visa trading—contributes to the high costs for migrants from South Asia.

In all three countries, private recruitment agencies are the dominant mechanism for overseas job intermediation for most aspiring migrants. Bangladesh, Nepal, and Pakistan have dedicated government agencies that are responsible for vetting and receiving job demands from foreign employers, providing the necessary clearances to outbound migrant workers, and regulating recruitment agencies (known in Pakistan as overseas employment promoters). These government agencies are the Bureau of Manpower Employment and Training in Bangladesh, the Bureau of Emigration and Overseas Employment in Pakistan, and the Department of Foreign Employment in Nepal.[3] However, the main tasks of intermediation—finding interested and qualified applicants for overseas jobs and matching them to the positions—are undertaken by private recruitment agencies.

In some cases, recruitment agencies and aspiring migrants alike rely on additional intermediaries, referred to by different names, such as middlemen, subagents, or *dalals* (in Bangladesh). These additional—and generally unlicensed—intermediaries are embedded in the local communities and serve the important function of linking migrants with recruitment agents. These individual recruitment agents go to villages, disseminate job information, and scout out workers for recruitment companies in main cities.[4] Subagents typically support them by disseminating information, mobilizing potential applicants, and collecting documentation at all stages of the migration process. Migrants tend to work through individual intermediaries because of trust, proximity, and access to support services. In both Nepal and Bangladesh, middlemen also help migrants with services such as acquiring documentation, arranging interviews, preparing for interviews, and accompanying them to various places (for medical tests; to the airport) as needed.[5] Use of this support is highly prevalent among workers from rural areas who have limited, if any, access to information.

Geographic dispersion also leads to the use of intermediaries.[6] A sizable share of migrants come from remote areas within the origin country, and formal recruitment agencies cannot afford to maintain a physical presence in many areas. Intermediaries also support with follow-up. The formal recruitment process requires several documents and persistent follow-up, which can be challenging, given that many migrants have low literacy levels and are geographically dispersed. It is difficult and costly for formal recruitment agency staff to administer and monitor the process from the capital or urban areas where they are located, not only because of distance, but frequently also because of linguistic or cultural differences. These tasks are thus often outsourced to intermediaries, at a commission. From a logistical perspective, recruitment firms are often located in urban areas, whereas subagents, being decentralized, have easier access to migrants in rural areas. Manpower companies can rely on them to persuade the migrant to stick to the decision about migrating. Subagents from Nepal also report that a formal recruitment agency will generally prefer that migrants communicate through the subagent, thereby deferring responsibility and delaying calls or visits from the migrants or their families if circumstances abroad fail to turn out as planned.[7] In sum, the various legal and cultural contexts in the countries under consideration all tend—at present—to leave formal recruitment agencies dependent on the various services provided by local agents.

Information asymmetries about migration opportunities leave potential migrants vulnerable to exploitation. Intermediaries are often the primary source of information, even in instances in which migrants have friends and neighbors who are migrants and have already experienced the process. This exposes the prospective migrant to a higher risk of fraud (in 3 percent of the cases). Because of insufficient information, a third of migration attempts from Bangladesh end in failure, with significant financial losses for already poor households (Das et al. 2019). Failures impose a huge cost on failed migrants, with a median loss of US$250. Migrants also spend a substantial amount of time and resources in the attempt, with only 25 percent of those trying to migrate succeeding within six months. After a year, a further 35 percent have succeeded, while the remaining 40 percent are still trying after 36 months. Among return migrants to Bangladesh, 10 percent report having come home because their wages were lower than expected. Among individuals still trying to migrate, the main difficulties are lack of information, difficulty with the paperwork involved, and financial constraints.

In Pakistan in particular, issues around visas are particularly important drivers of costs for major destinations (Cho and Majoka 2020). Pakistani migrant workers pay more than US$3,500, on average, to migrate to GCC countries, with visa fees accounting for more than four-fifths of the cost. These fees are much higher than the official cost of a visa to Saudi Arabia or the United Arab Emirates (less than US$100). Much of the excess charge is due to the popularity of a category of work arrangement referred to informally as the *azad* ("freedom") visa, often arranged by social networks or subagents. The attractiveness of the azad visa is that it is seemingly not tied to one employer. Instead, for a certain monthly fee, the *kafeel* (sponsor) provides the visa to a migrant, ostensibly in conjunction with a broad set of employment options. However, the visa tends to be misunderstood—or misrepresented—with visa holders generally still tied to a single kafeel.

The regulatory environment for temporary economic migration in the main destinations contributes to migrants' vulnerability. In the 1950s, all the Gulf states adopted a new approach to procuring foreign labor, the so-called *kafala* (sponsorship) system, which requires foreign labor migrants to obtain the sponsorship, including visa and work permit, of a citizen or a government entity in the destination country.[8] As a result, a migrant's stay at destination is entirely dependent on being employed by a given public or private entity at destination. This system also greatly limits the ability of migrants to change employers while at destination. The system used to grant employers the right to withhold workers' passports and to send them back to their home countries at will, at any time, although reforms in recent years have sought to reduce the prevalence of these abuses (Malit and Naufal 2016). Compared with financial costs, these costs are hard to quantify and therefore are often overlooked or underestimated by individuals considering migration to the GCC.

INSTITUTIONAL STRENGTHENING TO REDUCE MIGRATION COSTS AND VULNERABILITY

Four broad areas of action emerge as common priorities for Bangladesh, Nepal, and Pakistan to reduce the vulnerability of their labor migrants. The first is to improve the institutional and regulatory framework to directly address information asymmetries. The second is to prepare migrants adequately for working overseas—not just technically, to improve employability, but also cultural and language knowledge and soft skills. The third is to enhance public sector intermediation to complement private sector recruitment agencies, or even as an alternative. The fourth is to enhance the capacity of governments to support migrants while they are overseas. The exact formulation of a government response in these areas will depend on the country-specific institutional context (illustrations are provided in box 2.1).

BOX 2.1

Recommendations for safer migration from Bangladesh, Pakistan, and Nepal

In Pakistan, international labor migration needs to be managed more systematically. Cho and Majoka (2020) highlight several areas that need to be strengthened throughout the process, including predecision and predeparture support, services in destination countries, and support of return migration. In the short term, immediate support for workers and better regulation of middlemen should be prioritized. Given that many workers rely on a relatively narrow set of personal networks and middlemen for information, the government can provide a wide range of informational interventions, which have been shown in the Philippines to be effective in increasing workers' chances of getting a job in the formal sector (Beam 2016). Various mechanisms can be used, such as job fairs, media, migration resource centers, local government offices, and religious centers. In addition, mandatory predeparture orientation and training could be made far more practical and helpful. Further, regulations regarding overseas employment promoters and their use of subagents can be better monitored and enforced by introducing robust grievance redressal mechanisms.

Bangladesh could improve information services and systems by, for example, mainstreaming improvements to the quality of information services to aspiring migrants (building on the Safe Migration Pilot interventions) given that the Bureau of Manpower Employment and Training currently maintains multiple unconnected databases of prospective migrants seeking information, trying to match with employers, and seeking financing. The bureau currently has no way to track unique beneficiaries of its various services and provide appropriate services or referrals for other services. Given that rights and conditions of work are not uniformly provided or protected in receiving countries, strengthening the implementation capacity of the Overseas Employment and Migrants Act 2013 and of the Expatriates' Welfare and Overseas Employment Policies 2016 will also be important. The texts of agreements could also be published to provide transparency, following international best practices.

Nepal could provide prospective employers at destination with information on prospective labor migrants. In addition, Nepal's management of the foreign employment process could also benefit from efforts—using available documentation, data, and analysis—to (1) improve the performance of formal grievance redressal systems for workers, (2) make the agent market more open and competitive, (3) provide crucial information to prospective workers on the migration process and related costs, and (4) detect, punish, and debar agents and agencies that engage in fraudulent or exploitative transactions with workers. Finally, safe female migration for domestic work could be facilitated through bilateral labor agreements with the main destination countries, as is done for domestic workers from Sri Lanka and the Philippines.

Strengthening institutions and interventions to support information structures about migration opportunities

A lack of structured regulation of information leads to an absence of formal sources of information about migration opportunities. Though many South Asian governments have set up migration information centers, these centers do not have the capacity to reach the masses, especially in rural areas. Communication campaigns are presently being run by various organizations, although often on too modest a scale to reach the relevant rural areas. For example, manpower agents in Pakistan are required to advertise jobs on media, especially newspapers (such as *Daily Jang, Daily Din, Express, Daily Ausaf*), but are mostly present in urban areas and do not cover rural areas. Laws in both Nepal and Pakistan do require recruitment agencies to publish foreign job vacancies in daily newspapers with a national circulation. However, in Bangladesh, the government permits recruitment agencies to advertise vacancies in the newspapers (subject to the government's prior approval) only if they do not find qualified workers from the government's job-seeker pool.

As a result, prospective migrants rely heavily on informal intermediaries when making their migration decisions, which exposes them to potential fraud. Aspiring migrants tend to rely heavily on job information from individual recruitment agents (so-called middlemen) or their social networks, mainly because middlemen (or other intermediaries between formal recruitment firms and aspiring migrants) have a far wider reach, including into remote areas. A 2017 International Organization for Migration survey in Bangladesh revealed that 60 percent of migrants had never been exposed to information about safe migration. Of those who had learned about safe channels, 58 percent said their source of information was their friends rather than any official channel (IOM 2018). About 60 percent of aspiring migrants and 72 percent of return migrants were assisted by brokers (agents) in preparing travel documents. Workers from rural areas, who have limited access to information, are most likely to use such middlemen.

The Philippines has established a robust system that provides not only standardization but also accountability for the recruitment agents that post job advertisements. The Philippines Overseas Employment Agency (POEA) posts job advertisements to multiple sources to facilitate coordination and heighten visibility. The information circulated through the advertisement links the relevant migrants to the recruitment agents. Philippine regulations prevent foreign agencies from directly recruiting Filipinos. An agency based abroad that would like to tap into the Filipino labor market has to work with an accredited agency based in the Philippines that acts as the intermediary or representative, providing information on the job opening and other relevant details. To avoid illegal recruitment and human trafficking, potential migrants are required to obtain confirmation from the POEA that the employer offering overseas employment is POEA accredited, that the recruitment agency advertising the job is POEA licensed, and that the job in question is supported by a POEA-approved job order. The authenticity of a recruitment agency can also be confirmed by a recruitment advisor (POEA 2016).

Information may need to be provided through mechanisms that most effectively reach the target group of aspiring migrants, including through community-focused approaches. In Nepal, migrants have been shown to systematically overestimate risks at destination, such as mortality rates

(Shresta 2020). In Bangladesh, the Safe Migration for Bangladeshi Workers pilot program—supported by the World Bank and implemented by BRAC (formerly named the Bangladesh Rural Advancement Committee)—used an intensive approach to provide information to and orient potential migrants and their families on how to navigate the migration process safely, the social and economic costs and benefits of migration, and how to finance migration and manage remittances effectively.[9] It used community-level volunteers, community radio programs, and interactive popular traditional theater. Among its outcomes, the intervention was found to reduce the rate of migration among poor households, which now had better information about the costs and benefits of migration (Das et al. 2019). As a result, the rates of migration failure declined: the proportion of poor households whose chosen migrant either did not depart or had to return prematurely dropped significantly.

In Bangladesh, BRAC's migration program leverages this intensive community-based approach (box 2.2). BRAC relies heavily on local nongovernmental organizations and community-based organizations to reach potential migrants and provide them with information and training. Their voluntary members are from the local community, including return migrants who are respected by migrant workers (Sarker 2018). At the same time, BRAC partners with international organizations such as the World Bank to implement

BOX 2.2

Life-cycle approaches to migration programs at BRAC

BRAC's migration program is intended to alleviate poverty and improve the well-being of society's vulnerable groups. Since its establishment in Bangladesh in 1972, BRAC has reached 110 million people with its service delivery programs. Its primary goal is to alleviate poverty and support people's livelihoods in Bangladesh and other developing countries.[a] BRAC programs target especially vulnerable groups in society, that is, the poor and poorest, as well as women and children (Smillie 2009). Services offered range from primary and secondary education programs to the provision of microfinance products and migration services (Smillie 2009). Since 2006, BRAC has provided 937,000 potential migrants with information regarding safe migration and reintegration.[b]

BRAC's migration program offers a full "360-degree" service to ensure the safe, regular, and responsive migration of Bangladeshi workers. Bangladeshi migrants face a multitude of risks before, during, and after migration, all of which BRAC tries to mitigate. The majority of Bangladesh's migrants are low skilled and only have a few years of schooling, which fuels poor understanding of potential unfair practices by recruitment agencies and exploitation at the workplace in host countries (Das et al. 2019). BRAC's migration program aims to improve knowledge about migration, reduce criminal activities by recruitment agencies, and improve contact between relevant agencies in the receiving countries and those in Bangladesh (Sarker 2018). Before workers leave the country, BRAC offers awareness activities, capacity building through skills development, and information sharing to prevent trafficking. During migration, BRAC provides support to migrants through embassies in the receiving countries and shares information on how to make the best use of remittances. Emergency support for vulnerable migrants in host countries is also offered. Finally, BRAC provides psychological services, training, and financial support to facilitate the socioeconomic reintegration of return migrants into Bangladeshi society.[c]

a. BRAC, "Who We Are" (http://www.brac.net/).
b. BRAC, "Migration" (http://www.brac.net/program/migration/).
c. BRAC, "Migration" (http://www.brac.net/program/migration/).

and manage migration projects across Bangladesh. For instance, BRAC, together with the World Bank, implemented a pilot project supported by UN Women that offered income-generating activities and skills development training sessions for return migrant workers, especially women, in Bangladesh (Sarker 2018).

Similar community-level approaches are taken even in countries with more mature systems, such as Indonesia. Indonesia's Ministry of Manpower delivers migration-related services to migrant workers and families at the village level. Village heads in Indonesia have traditionally served as gatekeepers who ensure that a worker migrates through official channels. They are involved in the implementation of the Desmigratif program (Desa Migran Produktif, or Productive Migrant Village, a safe migration program), which provides information services, data collection, education services tailored to villagers' needs, and economic activities for returnees and their families. This program includes information dissemination activities that directly target prospective migrants through both door-to-door outreach activities and brochures available in Desmigratif village service centers. The brochures explain the official placement procedures as well as potential difficulties in destination countries (but are only handed out on request because of budget constraints). The ministry plans to allocate funds to keep these brochures up to date in compliance with Law No. 18/2017. The 2017 law also tasks village governments with the additional responsibility of monitoring the return of migrant workers; the law's implementing regulation will need to clarify the scope of this monitoring (World Bank 2019).

Predeparture orientation and training programs

Migrants are insufficiently prepared for employment at destination. Predeparture orientation is an important part of the predeparture phase of migration and should address the basic needs of migrants but not overload them with too much information. The predeparture orientation session should be designed to reduce the risks of abuse and contractual violations and raise awareness of the support available. However, current orientations typically provide simple logistical information to migrants on life abroad, including rules, employment, resources available in times of difficulty, culture, and finances. They typically deliver basic information in a much too perfunctory manner, and sometimes omit essential information, such as how to obtain necessary paperwork. In addition, these orientation programs are often very generic and do not consider the specific contexts of migrants' destinations or the relevant sector of employment (Khadka 2018a).

Predecision and predeparture training and orientations in the Philippines and Sri Lanka offer some examples of what else could be done. The predeparture program for migrant workers in the Philippines is comprehensive—as is its counterpart in Sri Lanka—and it concentrates on the requirements of migrants at the various stages along the migration process. The program is highly customized, with a focus on specific sectors and destination countries. The duration of the Predeparture Orientation Program in the Philippines is between two and eight hours for all overseas Filipino workers (OFWs) and permanent emigrants. Predeparture orientation typically consists of modules on the following topics:

- Employment contract familiarization
- A profile of the destination country
- Stages of the overseas worker's life

- Health and safety
- Airport procedures
- Government programs and services
- Employment contracts

India also has a detailed predeparture orientation program. The Predeparture Orientation Training Program is the first project of its kind project in India. Its 12 modules cover basic features of international migration, including the costs and benefits associated with migration and how prospective migrants could prepare for the experience. The program's training manual was conceived of as a week-long training course; however, it can be reduced or extended as required by the complexity of the context. The electronic platform e-Migrate also provides a detailed account of foreign employers' and registered recruiting agents' recruitment processes. The issues covered include entry formalities, labor laws in host countries, sociocultural and religious aspects, and language (IOM 2016).

Stronger public sector intermediation

The Bangladesh-Malaysia G2G program offers some insights into how a publicly intermediated system can enhance information, reduce costs, and improve welfare (Shreshtha, Mobarak, and Sharif 2019). Overall, a quarter of the migration from Bangladesh happens through arrangements initiated by family, relatives, and friends. Those without such a social network are less likely to successfully migrate abroad. The G2G program offers access to migration opportunities to those without social network contacts abroad. Among private channel migrants, 45 percent knew someone in the destination country. The rate was only 7 percent for G2G migrants. Whereas migrants from Bangladesh pay an average of about US$4,500 to migrate to Malaysia, under the program they paid only US$520. This reduction amounts to a very significant expansion of access to less well-off households, lowering the burden of debt. The G2G program reduced borrowing by 19 percent, reduced the average amount borrowed by 72 percent, and reduced average interest rates by 40 percent. Compared with private channel migrants, G2G migrants were also more likely to migrate with necessary clearances, training, orientation, and employment contracts and with proper insurance.

That G2G program is just one example of the institutional agreements between countries to manage temporary flows of workers; others include bilateral labor agreements (BLAs) and memoranda of understanding (MOU). A BLA is essentially a legal agreement between countries to ensure that migration takes place in accordance with agreed-on principles and procedures. A BLA sets out each side's commitments and may provide for quotas. BLAs are popular between countries in the Middle East (receiving) and South Asia (sending). Between 2012 and 2016, 2.5 million to 3 million workers migrated temporarily from Bangladesh, India, Nepal, Pakistan, and Sri Lanka every year under such temporary labor agreements. Less formal is an MOU, which is a nonbinding agreement that is easier to negotiate, implement, and modify according to changing economic and labor market conditions. For the destination countries, bilateral labor agreements help achieve a flow of labor that meets the needs of employers and industrial sectors while providing for better management of that flow and promoting cultural ties and exchanges. For the countries of origin, these agreements ensure continued access to overseas labor markets and opportunities to promote the protection and welfare of their workers. These agreements require special administration to ensure their smooth operation—including the recruitment, testing, and certification of applicants and timely data flow between the two countries.

Incorporating rights-based considerations could support safer migration through BLAs and MOUs. International normative frameworks, such as those supported by the International Labor Organization, provide guidance to countries on rights-based labor migration governance. However, these frameworks are frequently ignored. The BLAs and MOUs signed by South Asian countries often fail to reflect national laws, let alone relevant international human rights and labor rights treaties. As a result, they overlook fundamental issues in the protection of the rights of migrant workers and members of their families (Migrant Forum in Asia 2014).

BLA enforcement mechanisms also remain weak, leading to gaps between de jure and de facto agreements. There is currently a lack of transparency in the bilateral negotiation process and secrecy around the agreements, which makes it difficult to work with the destination country on issues affecting migrants while in their jurisdiction.[10] In instances in which intergovernmental and interagency cooperation alike should be fundamental to the bilateral negotiation process, little interaction is seen between relevant international organizations such as the United Nations and the International Labor Organization. Coordination between the standards-setting agencies is crucial because they are in a strong position to advise all stakeholders in the development of bilateral instruments that serve the common interests of states parties and the protection of the rights of migrant workers. Lack of mechanisms for implementation, monitoring, and evaluation hinder proper enforcement of BLAs (Migrant Forum in Asia 2014).

Enforcement of conditions with publicly provided intermediation—such as through BLAs and MOUs— requires greater administrative capacity. Although Bangladesh, Nepal, and Pakistan are starting to establish databases to monitor migration flows, the databases are far from comprehensive. In destination countries, there is no trace of government action to implement agreed-on provisions of the MOUs, such as strengthened workplace inspection procedures and increased awareness of workers' rights on the part of employers. The general and vague objectives set out in bilateral instruments make it difficult to follow up on state obligations, and the secrecy of negotiations prevent parliaments and people from holding their governments to account. The implementation, monitoring, and evaluation of BLAs and MOUs are feasible only if the process is open and inclusive of relevant stakeholders.

Expanding services at destination

Labor attachés (LAs) are one common mode by which Bangladesh, Nepal, and Pakistan provide on-site support services to their migrant workers within the laws and regulations of the receiving country.[11] LAs have been entrusted with the responsibility of dealing with host country authorities, employers, and recruiting agencies to protect migrants. Practically, the functions of the LA include authentication and verification; approval of documents pertaining to recruitment; counseling and assistance to workers in settling disputes related to work contracts; market exploration; assistance to workers in claiming termination benefits to which they are legally entitled; registration of death and assistance in follow-up work with sponsors and local authorities, including local burial or transportation of the body; assistance to family members in claiming compensation for death due to accidental or other unnatural causes; and assistance in taking up problems of a personal nature faced by migrants or their kin in countries of origin (Abrar et al. 2014).

LAs' offices are often understaffed and underresourced, and employees have insufficient training. Migrants reported a perceived lack of capacity at LA offices, as well as differential treatment for low-skilled migrants, and limited opening times, which made accessing services difficult. The challenges faced by LAs in rendering effective services include physical distance, which makes it difficult for centrally located LAs to reach out to migrants working in remote rural areas of destination countries (Abrar et al. 2014). If LAs are not fluent in the local language of the destination country, they typically also need the assistance of interpreters and legal advisers to bring migrant worker issues to the attention of local authorities, making cumbersome processes even lengthier.

For corridors with female migrants, as in those starting in Bangladesh and Nepal, there is also a need to enhance gender-sensitivity training for LAs, or to hire more female LAs. Since the early 2000s, traditional female-labor-sending countries, such as the Philippines and Sri Lanka, have discouraged female migration to the Arab states because of the poor treatment received there. The government of Bangladesh saw this development as an economic opportunity and began sending female migrants, despite the precarious situation. These female migrants are extremely vulnerable, although they are arguably in some ways better off than they would otherwise be, perhaps escaping abusive situations at home, and now able to contribute to their household income. Problems that LAs could help address include irregular payment of wages; physical, verbal, and sexual abuse; runaways (so-called absconders); and escapes. LAs then need to help these migrants engage in informal negotiations with their employers to change sponsorship (that is, obtain permission to work for somebody else) or return home (RMMRU 2016).

Another mechanism for supporting migrant workers is through the services provided by migrant welfare funds, although these funds are financed by migrant worker fees and are currently limited. To finance migrant protection services, countries of origin in South Asia have established such migrant welfare funds. The scope of protection services is, however, limited to extreme cases of distress such as sickness, disability, or death. Services cover repatriation of the migrant worker or the body of the worker, and compensation and financial assistance to migrant workers for disability or to their families for occupational death. In Bangladesh, the Wage Earner's Welfare Fund is also used to provide predeparture briefings and legal support to migrant workers. Pakistan has also established a Worker Welfare Fund for migrant workers and their families. The services of the Nepali Foreign Employment Welfare Fund are somewhat more extensive. This fund is mandated to protect migrants throughout the migration cycle—that is, to conduct foreign employment promotion, provide skill-oriented training to aspiring migrants, and to run employment programs for returnees. The coverage does not, however, include mental health issues. Thus, when compensation is awarded for abuse of migrant workers, it is only a portion of the money due to them in unpaid wages, without compensation for harm suffered (United Nations Children's Fund and Global Migration Group 2014).

Migrants often face major obstacles to lodging grievances and resolving complaints. Barriers to accessing formal assistance leave migrant workers vulnerable to labor rights violations during recruitment and employment

(Harkins and Åhlberg 2017). Weaknesses in the rights enforcement system mean that abuses may go undetected and unaddressed. Migrants typically prefer informal mediation methods to formal mechanisms and are willing to settle cases before they reach official channels. This preference may occur partially because the scales of justice tend to be biased against migrants regardless of the merits of their cases. The willingness to settle is also often simply a matter of time and cost, given that all the grievance services are centralized and migrants are in need of quick payments to repay loans. The lack of information about these grievance services also plays a role, but the overriding consideration is the view that manpower companies are very powerful and can buy themselves out of any awkward situation. There is also very little trust that a government regulatory agency will conduct a thorough investigation (essential when documentation is weak) or follow up on cases to ensure that victims are genuinely compensated. The risk from the migrant's perspective is, therefore, that considerable effort (and associated delays) will only ultimately yield the refund of recorded recruitment costs, which are significantly lower than actual costs.[12]

Impact evaluations of interventions aimed at reducing migrants' vulnerabilities suggest that such interventions can be effective. Interventions that improve the accuracy of information provided to prospective migrants regarding the benefits of migration and risks has been shown to significantly influence migration decisions in Nepal (Shrestha 2020). Job fairs on employment overseas have also been shown to be effective in changing individual perceptions about the overseas labor market (Beam 2016). Well-managed G2G migration programs, such as the seasonal migration between Tonga and New Zealand and the Bangladesh-Malaysia G2G program, have been shown to have very large positive effects on the welfare of migrants and their households (McKenzie and Gibson 2014; Mobarak, Sharif, and Shrestha 2020). Financial literacy programs, when targeted to both migrants and their household members, have been found to be effective in increasing savings from migration (Doi, McKenzie, and Zia 2014). Impact evaluations of predeparture orientation training, however, have been few (McKenzie and Yang 2015).

Reducing vulnerability can require the coordination of numerous actors involved in the migration process. By its very nature, migration involves a multiplicity of actors, including government entities in countries of destination and origin, private entities at origin such as recruitment agencies, employers at destination, migrants themselves and their households, and in some cases other migrant-sending countries in the region. Some of the policy actions to reduce vulnerability can be taken unilaterally and require the involvement and coordination of actors in the country of origin only, such as providing systematic information on employment opportunities abroad. It will require regulatory action from the government combined with verifiable and monitored compliance by recruitment agencies, and the use of formal information channels by prospective migrants. In contrast, policy tools such as BLAs would require close partnerships between governments both at origin and at destination, and may even require regional collaboration to ensure uniformity and avoid a "race to the bottom" (whereby less scrupulous operators corner newly created economic opportunities). Reducing migration costs will primarily depend on actions taken in origin countries to regulate the fees of brokers (middlemen) and the recruitment market. However, altering practices allowed by some destination countries, such as visa trading, would also contribute to driving down costs.

To reduce vulnerability, the tracking of and data collection on migrants abroad need to be strengthened, together with mechanisms for monitoring and evaluation. Bangladesh, Nepal, and Pakistan have made substantial progress in recent years in improving administrative databases to track outbound and returning migrants—an area of weakness in the past. However, detailed data on vulnerable migrants are often unavailable, unclear, or dispersed, even though such data are universally regarded as essential to providing proper services to migrants, to informing policy makers, and to monitoring safe migration. It is thus essential that national databases be created and maintained to pull together and manage data (currently scattered across different organizations and agencies) in the interests of national and transnational cooperation built on information exchange. If a country seeks to provide genuinely safe avenues for migration and mobility, it must analyze the intentions—and monitor the effects—of policies and procedures such as labor migration programs study visas, family reunification, and humanitarian visas. The use of standardized registration data systems in different countries could improve the quality of the data collected and thus enable better comparison activities (IOM, GMDAC, and UKAID 2016).

NOTES

1. Current exchange rate used for conversion.
2. Bangladesh Return Migrant Survey 2018/2019.
3. Institutional details can be found in Luthria and Smith (2018) and Khadka (2018a) for Bangladesh; Khadka (2018b) and Bossavie and Denisova (2018) for Nepal; and Cho and Majoka (2020) for Pakistan.
4. Focus group discussions and key informant interviews (Khadka 2018a, 2018b).
5. Key informant interviews and focus group discussions documented in Khadka (2018a, 2018b).
6. Key informant interviews and focus group discussions documented in Khadka (2018a, 2018b).
7. Key informant interviews and focus group discussions documented in Khadka (2018a, 2018b).
8. The kafala system was originally used for migrant workers employed primarily in construction and domestic service activities. It was in use in GCC countries, and a few other economies in the Middle East and North Africa, such as Iraq, Jordan, and Lebanon. Several studies have examined the structure of the kafala system and its political economy, such as Khan and Harroff-Tavel (2016), Malit and Naufal (2016), and Murray (2013), among others.
9. The program also provided links to services at centers to increase employability, and an innovation fund was set up to enable small local organizations to test innovative services and support for migrants.
10. Based on focus group discussions and key informant interviews, as documented in Khadka (2018a, 2018b).
11. The specific nomenclature may vary (for example, within a diplomatic mission for Pakistan they are referred to as community welfare attachés).
12. Focus group discussions and key informant interviews (Khadka 2018a, 2018b).

REFERENCES

Abrar, C. R., S. Irudaya Rajan, L. K. Ruhunage, and Tasneem Siddiqui. 2014. "Institutional Strengthening of the Office of Labour Attaché: Research Findings from Bangladesh, India and Sri Lanka." Migrating Out of Poverty Research Programme Consortium, University of Sussex, Brighton.

Acosta, Pablo. 2006. "Labor Supply, School Attendance, and Remittances from International Migration: The Case of El Salvador." Policy Research Working Paper 3903, World Bank, Washington, DC.

Acosta, Pablo A., Emmanuel K. K. Lartey, and Federico S. Mandelman. 2007. "Remittances and the Dutch Disease." Working Paper 2007–8a, Federal Reserve Bank of Atlanta.

Ahmed, S. Amer, Faiz Ahmed, Laurent Bossavie, Çağlar Özden, and He Wang. 2021. "Temporary Migration and Development: A New Dataset from Bangladesh." Background paper for *Toward Safer and More Productive Migration for South Asia*, World Bank, Washington, DC.

Aleksynska, Mariya, Samia Kazi Aoul, and Veronica Petrencu (Preotu). 2017. "Deficiencies in Conditions of Work as a Cost to Labor Migration: Concepts, Extent, and Implications." KNOMAD Working Paper 28, World Bank, Washington, DC.

Amuedo-Dorantes, Catalina, and Susan Pozo. 2006. "Migration, Remittances, and Male and Female Employment Patterns." *American Economic Review* 96 (2): 222–26.

Antman, Francisca M. 2012. "The Impact of Migration on Family Left Behind." Discussion Paper 6374, Institute of Labor Economics (IZA), Bonn.

Beam, E. Andrew. 2016. "Do Job Fairs Matter? Experimental Evidence on the Impact of Job-Fair Attendance." *Journal of Development Economics* 120 (C): 32–40.

Bossavie, Laurent, and Anastasiya Denisova. 2018. "Youth Labor Migration in Nepal." Jobs Working Paper 13, World Bank, Washington, DC.

Bossavie, Laurent, Joseph-Simon Görlach, Çağlar Özden, and He Wang. 2021. "Temporary Migration for Long-Term Investment." Background paper for *Toward Safer and More Productive Migration for South Asia*, World Bank, Washington, DC.

Bossavie, Laurent, and Çağlar Özden. 2022. "Impacts of Temporary Migration on Development in Origin Countries." World Bank, Washington DC.

Cho, Yoonyoung, Anastasiya Denisova, Soonhwa Yi, and Upasana Khadka. 2018. "Lessons from Korea's Employment Permit System: Bilateral Arrangement of Temporary Labor Migration." World Bank, Washington, DC.

Cho, Yoonyoung, and Zaineb Majoka. 2020. *Pakistan Jobs Diagnostic: Promoting Access to Quality Jobs for All*. Jobs Series 20, World Bank, Washington, DC.

Das, Narayan, Alain de Janvry, Sakib Mahmood, and Elisabeth Sadoulet. 2019. "Migration as a Risky Enterprise: A Diagnostic for Bangladesh." *International Migration Review* 53 (3): 900–29.

Doi, Yoko, David McKenzie, and Bilal Zia. 2014. "Who You Train Matters: Identifying Combined Effects of Financial Education on Migrant Households." *Journal of Development Economics* 109 (2): 33–55.

Harkins, Ben, and Meri Åhlberg. 2017. "Access to Justice for Migrant Workers in South-East Asia." International Labor Organization, Geneva.

IOM (International Organization for Migration). 2018. "Safe Migration in Bangladesh: Media Profile & Communication Channels." IOM, Brussels.

IOM (International Organization for Migration), GMDAC (Global Migration Data Analysis Centre), and UKAID. 2016. "Understanding and Measuring 'Safe' Migration." Final Report for Workshop, Nuremberg, June 21–22.

Khadka, Upasana. 2018a. "The Migrant's Journey—Bangladesh." Unpublished.

Khadka, Upasana. 2018b. "The Migrant's Journey—Nepal." Unpublished.

Khan, Azfar, and Helene Harroff-Tavel. 2011. "Reforming the Kafala: Challenges and Opportunities in Moving Forward." *Asian and Pacific Migration Journal* 20 (3–4): 293–313.

KNOMAD (Global Knowledge Partnership on Migration and Development). 2017. "Migration and Remittances: Recent Developments and Outlook." Special Topic: Global Impact on Migration, Migration and Development Brief 27, World Bank, Washington, DC.

Lokshin, Michael, and Elena Glinskaya. 2009. "The Effect of Male Migration on Employment Patterns of Women in Nepal." *World Bank Economic Review* 23 (3): 481–507.

Luthria, Manjula, and Rebekah Smith. 2018. "Institutional Assessment of Migration Systems in Bangladesh." Unpublished.

Malit, Froilan, T., Jr., and George Naufal. 2016. "Asymmetric Information under the Kafala Sponsorship System: Impacts on Foreign Domestic Workers' Income and Employment Status in the GCC Countries." *International Migration* 54 (5): 76–90.

McKenzie, David, and John Gibson. 2014. "The Development Impact of a Best Practice Seasonal Worker Policy." *Review of Economics and Statistics* 96 (2): 229–43.

McKenzie, David, and Dean Yang. 2015. "Evidence on Policies to Increase the Development Impact of International Migration." *World Bank Research Observer* 30 (2): 155–92.

Mendola, Mariapia, and Calogero Carletto. 2012. "Migration and Gender Differences in the Home Labour Market: Evidence from Albania." *Labour Economics* 19 (6): 870–80.

Migrant Forum in Asia. 2014. "Bilateral Agreements and Memoranda of Understanding for the Promotion and Protection of the Rights of Migrant Workers and Members of Their Families." Policy Brief 10, Migrant Forum in Asia, Quezon City, Philippines.

Mobarak, Mushfiq, Iffath Sharif, and Maheshwor Shrestha. 2020. *Returns to Low-Skilled International Migration: Evidence from the Bangladesh-Malaysia Migration Lottery Program.* Policy Research Working Paper 9165, World Bank, Washington, DC.

Murray, Heather E. 2013. "Hope for Reform Springs Eternal: How the Sponsorship System, Domestic Laws and Traditional Customs Fail to Protect Migrant Domestic Workers in GCC Countries." *Cornell International Law Journal* 45 (2): 461–86.

POEA (Philippine Overseas Employment Administration). 2016. "Revised POEA Rules and Regulations Governing the Recruitment and Employment of Land-Based Overseas Filipino Workers." POEA, Mandaluyong, Philippines.

RMMRU (Refugee and Migratory Movements Research Unit). 2016. "Rendering Services to Female Migrants by Labor Attachés of Bangladesh." Policy Brief 18, RMMRU, Dhaka.

Ruppert Bulmer, Elizabeth, Ami Shresta, and Michelle Marshalian. 2020. *Nepal Jobs Diagnostic.* Jobs Series 22, World Bank, Washington, DC.

Sarker, Bonosree. 2018. "BRAC Migration Program: A Lighthouse for Migrants." In *Human Rights Education in Asia-Pacific*, Volume 8, 147–66. Asia-Pacific Human Rights Information Center, Osaka.

Shrestha, Maheshwor. 2017a. "The Impact of Large-Scale Migration on Poverty, Expenditures, and Labor Market Outcomes in Nepal." Policy Research Working Paper 8232, World Bank, Washington, DC.

Shrestha, Maheshwor. 2017b. *Push and Pull: A Study of International Migration from Nepal.* Policy Research Working Paper 7965, World Bank, Washington, DC.

Shrestha, Maheshwor. 2020. "Get Rich or Die Tryin': Perceived Earnings, Perceived Mortality Rates, and Migration Decisions of Potential Work Migrants from Nepal." *World Bank Economic Review* 34 (1): 1–27.

Shrestha, Maheshwor, Ahmed Mushfiq Mobarak, and Iffath Anwar Sharif. 2019. *Migration and Remittances: The Impacts of a Government Intermediated International Migration Program.* Washington, DC: World Bank.

Smillie, Ian. 2009. *Freedom from Want: The Remarkable Success Story of BRAC, the Global Grassroots Organization That's Winning the Fight against Poverty.* Sterling, VA: Kumarian Press.

United Nations Children's Fund and Global Migration Group. 2014. *Migration and Youth: Challenges and Opportunities.* New York: United Nations Children's Fund.

World Bank. 2019. "Leveraging Economic Migration for Development: A Briefing for the World Bank Board." Washington, DC: World Bank.

3 Increasing the Gains from Migration

Even though international migration has made important contributions to economic development in South Asia, this chapter addresses how some of the benefits of international migration could be enhanced to make it more productive. Increased productivity in this context refers to two aims. The first is to increase the development impact of international migration, both by making it more accessible to the poor and by increasing the returns from migration at the individual and household levels. The second aim is to address the sustainability at the national level of international migration from South Asia, given its exposure to global and regional shocks as well as to structural shifts in the global economy.

THE HIGH COSTS OF MIGRATION

Reduced access to migration for poorer households

Migration expenditure reduces access to migration for the poor in South Asia. For workers from South Asia, migration costs are high relative to the comparatively low wages in their home countries. As chapter 1 notes, the poorest households in South Asia have fewer international migrants than higher-income households. The high migration costs usually restrict access to international labor migration for aspiring migrants from lower-income households. Those households that nevertheless decide to send a migrant often have insufficient savings with which to do so and therefore need to borrow to cover their migration-related expenses. More than 60 percent of Pakistani and Nepali labor migrants (but fewer than 40 percent of Indian labor migrants) borrow money to finance their move (figure 3.1); 57 percent of Bangladeshi labor migrants indicate that they have had to borrow money in the past to move abroad. On average, Bangladeshi labor migrants finance 45 percent of their total migration costs by borrowing. As expected from simple migration theory, reducing the costs of migration increases access to migration for the poorest

FIGURE 3.1

Composition of migration costs by source, by corridor

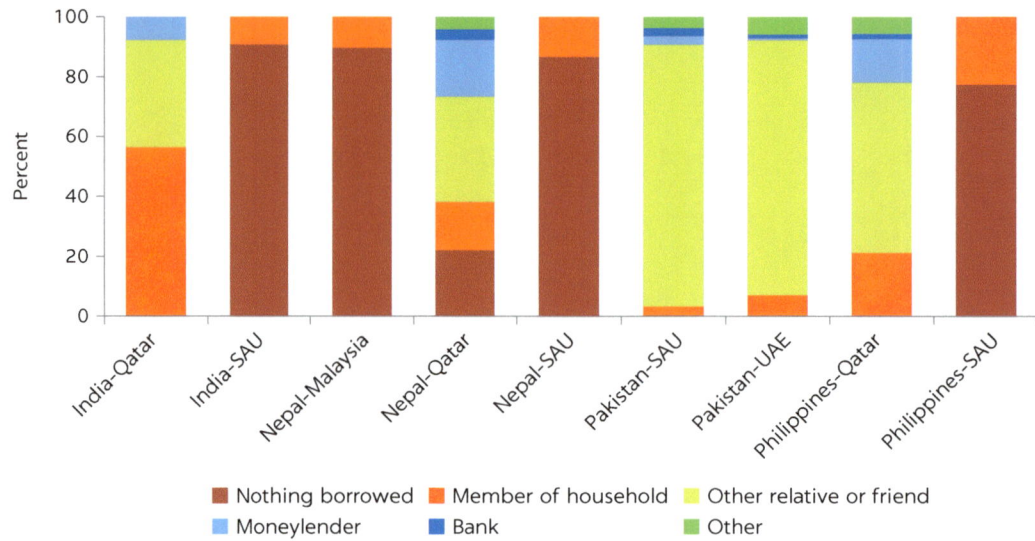

Source: Data from KNOMAD-ILO Migration Costs Surveys 2015 and 2016.
Note: SAU = Saudi Arabia; UAE = United Arab Emirates.

FIGURE 3.2

International migrants in poorer and richer households in Bangladesh and Nepal

a. Share of Bangladeshi households with an international migrant (left axis) and remittance share of income in households with at least one migrant (right axis), by consumption decile

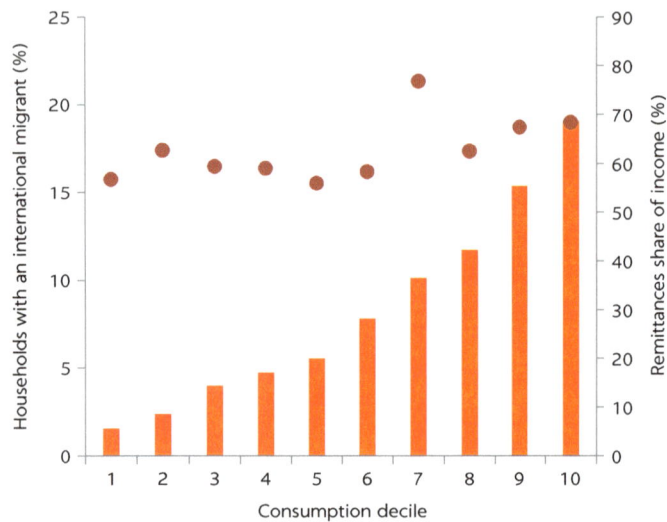

b. Share of Nepali households receiving remittances from an international migrant, by consumption quintile

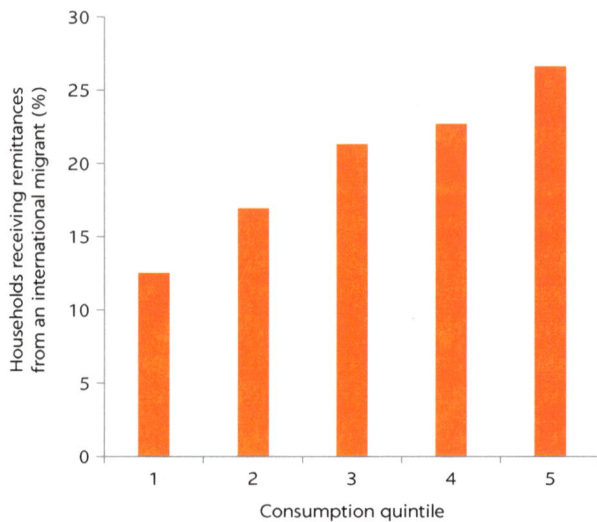

Share of households with an international migrant (left scale)

Remittance share of income in households with at least one migrant (right scale)

Sources: Estimated from Household Income and Expenditure Survey Bangladesh 2016/17 and the Nepal Household Risk and Vulnerability Survey 2016.

and increases the propensity to migrate (Angelucci 2015; Bryan, Chowdhury, and Mobarak 2014).

Household income affects the ability to migrate as well as the incidence and amount of remittances in South Asia. South Asia has the second-highest percentage of extreme poverty in the world after Sub-Saharan Africa, but the extreme poor are not generally the people who migrate. In Bangladesh, only 2 percent of households in the first and second consumption deciles have one or more migrating family members (figure 3.2). The richer the household in Bangladesh and Nepal, the higher the likelihood that a family member works as a migrant in another country (figure 3.2).[1] The consumption level of the migrating household is also associated with the incidence and amount of remittances. In Nepal, poorer households receive remittances more frequently than wealthier households. However, richer households receive larger amounts (Lokshin, Bontch-Osmolovski, and Glinskaya 2011).

Reduced propensity to remit and decreased remittance volume

Even though remittances into South Asia are high in both absolute and relative terms, the costs of migration may affect the amount remitted. The Nepali and Pakistani migrants in the KNOMAD-ILO Migration Costs Surveys 2015 and 2016 sample have a very high propensity to remit, with 100 percent of Nepali and 94 percent of Pakistani migrants sending money back to their households. High recruitment costs may affect the amount of remittances received by households in one of two ways. Households may receive less because migrants use their labor earnings first to pay off their recruitment costs. Alternatively, if migrants borrowed from the household or from near relatives to pay the recruitment costs, then remittances may be used to pay back this informal loan, resulting in higher remittances. In the Nepal-Qatar, Pakistan–Saudi Arabia, and Pakistan–United Arab Emirates corridors, many of those who borrowed to finance their migration obtained loans from relatives (figure 3.1).

Pakistani labor migrants going to Saudi Arabia and the United Arab Emirates, and facing higher recruitment costs, are significantly less likely to remit (table 3.1). The dummy for whether the migrant has borrowed money to migrate takes on a statistically significant negative coefficient, suggesting that migrants who borrow tend to borrow outside the household, so remittances to pay these debts are diverted from the household. Two other variables—duration of stay abroad and marital status—both have a statistically significant positive coefficient.

Along with having a negative association with the propensity to remit, high recruitment costs appear to have negative effects on the amount of remittances sent (table 3.2).[2] Across the corridors studied, a 1 percent increase in recruitment cost is associated with a 0.05 percent to 0.15 percent decrease in monthly remittances.[3] Although remittances may appear to be inelastic with respect to recruitment cost, remittance amounts are repeated monthly; that is, the impact of the one-time migration cost is multiplied over the period of migration. For example, if migrants expect to remit in excess of their recruitment

TABLE 3.1 Probit regressions predicting propensity to remit, Pakistan–Saudi Arabia and Pakistan–United Arab Emirates corridors

	(1)	(2)
	PROBIT	**AME**
ln(migration costs)	−0.581**	−0.044**
	(0.281)	(0.021)
ln(income)	1.336***	0.101***
	(0.321)	(0.022)
Age	−0.306*	−0.023*
	(0.160)	(0.012)
Age²	0.004	0.000
	(0.002)	(0.000)
Borrowed money	−0.689***	−0.052***
	(0.263)	(0.020)
Months in host country	0.079***	0.006***
	(0.017)	(0.001)
Married	1.210***	0.091***
	(0.331)	(0.023)
Low education	0.167	0.013
	(0.204)	(0.016)
Destination country: United Arab Emirates	−0.009	−0.000
	(0.245)	(0.019)
Constant	2.606	
	(3.627)	
Observations	631	631

Source: KNOMAD-ILO Migration Costs Surveys 2015 and 2016.
Note: Pooled probit regression including the Pakistan–Saudi Arabia and Pakistan–United Arab Emirates migration corridors. The omitted comparison corridor is Pakistan–Saudi Arabia. The dependent variable is a remittance dummy (0 = no remittance, 1 = remittance) and the independent variable is the recruitment cost in log form. AME = average marginal effects. Robust standard errors in parentheses. *** $p < 0.01$, ** $p < 0.05$, * $p < 0.1$.

costs, then in absolute terms, 0.05 percent of the total remittances may be large, perhaps even larger than 1 percent of recruitment costs. These findings imply that even a small reduction in recruitment cost could have substantial impacts on remittance behavior.

Migration costs thus significantly lower the disposable income of the migrant. Instead of transferring remittances to the household, the migrant uses the money to pay back migration-related expenses or money that was borrowed from individuals beyond the household. These effects are most pronounced in Pakistan, where recruitment costs are higher. For corridors originating in Pakistan, a 1 percent increase in recruitment costs could lead to a 0.11 percent to 0.16 percent decrease in remittances.[4] Other than reflecting differences in statistical power, the fact that the negative effect of recruitment costs is larger in the Pakistani corridors may imply the existence of a threshold effect: where recruitment costs are relatively lower (as in Nepal), they may be less important in determining remittance

TABLE 3.2 Recruitment costs and remittances for select corridors, ordinary least squares regressions

	(1) BASIC SPECIFICATION	(2) CORRIDOR FIXED EFFECTS	(3) NEPAL-MALAYSIA	(4) NEPAL-QATAR	(5) NEPAL-SAUDI ARABIA	(6) PAKISTAN-SAUDI ARABIA	(7) PAKISTAN-UNITED ARAB EMIRATES
ln(migration costs)	−0.146***	−0.046**	0.012	−0.064*	0.056	−0.159***	−0.113***
	(0.020)	(0.022)	(0.044)	(0.038)	(0.053)	(0.043)	(0.035)
ln(income)	0.728***	0.766***	0.295	0.402***	0.007	0.999***	1.101***
	(0.073)	(0.077)	(0.268)	(0.119)	(0.064)	(0.045)	(0.106)
Age	−0.046***	−0.023*	0.043	−0.026	−0.166**	−0.031	0.021
	(0.013)	(0.012)	(0.051)	(0.020)	(0.064)	(0.036)	(0.029)
Age²	0.001***	0.000	−0.001	0.000	0.002**	0.000	−0.000
	(0.000)	(0.000)	(0.001)	(0.000)	(0.001)	(0.000)	(0.000)
Borrowed money	0.041	−0.004	−0.057	−0.0189	−0.048	0.010	0.011
	(0.027)	(0.026)	(0.045)	(0.041)	(0.076)	(0.060)	(0.068)
Married	0.079***	0.031	0.029	0.106**	0.139	−0.053	−0.011
	(0.029)	(0.028)	(0.040)	(0.047)	(0.129)	(0.056)	(0.062)
Low education	−0.150***	−0.128***	−0.147**	−0.092**	−0.197**	−0.070	−0.082
	(0.025)	(0.026)	(0.061)	(0.039)	(0.078)	(0.045)	(0.063)
Female	−0.156	−0.173	n.a.	−0.460***	n.a.	n.a.	0.113
	(0.206)	(0.226)		(0.118)			(0.081)
Nepal-Malaysia		0.260***					
		(0.042)					
Nepal–Saudi Arabia		0.177***					
		(0.050)					
Pakistan–Saudi Arabia		−0.122***					
		(0.043)					
Pakistan–United Arab Emirates		−0.214***					
		(0.040)					
Constant	2.955***	1.681***	3.291***	3.874***	7.595***	1.203*	−0.715
	(0.382)	(0.483)	(1.199)	(0.751)	(1.080)	(0.721)	(0.591)
Observations	1,282	1,282	157	436	97	357	235
R-squared	0.317	0.360	0.100	0.107	0.162	0.543	0.591

Source: KNOMAD-ILO Migration Costs Surveys 2015 and 2016.
Note: The dependent variable for all regressions is ln(remittance) sent and includes migration corridor fixed effects. The total sample contains the following migration corridors: Nepal-Malaysia, Nepal-Qatar, Nepal-Saudi Arabia, Pakistan–Saudi Arabia, Pakistan–United Arab Emirates; the omitted comparison corridor is Nepal-Qatar. n.a. = not applicable. Robust standard errors in parentheses.*** $p < 0.01$, ** $p < 0.05$, * $p < 0.1$.

decisions, or their effect may be small relative to the total amount of remittances. It may be only at high levels that recruitment costs have a detectable impact on total remittances.

In addition to these short-term static effects, migration costs have dynamic effects on a migrant's entire life cycle. Decisions about when and where to migrate, how long to stay at destination, and what to do after return are all interdependent and part of the same process of life-cycle optimization undertaken by migrants (Dustmann and Görlach 2016; Dustmann and

Kirchkamp 2002). All these decisions are affected by both the costs and the benefits of temporary migration. Migration costs thus have an impact on when migrants leave (because they need to accumulate enough savings to finance costs), on how long they need to stay at destination (to generate sufficient net returns from migrating), and on their economic activity after returning home. In particular, temporary migration can allow workers to accumulate savings relatively quickly, overcome credit constraints back home, and then start up in self-employment after return (Bossavie et al. 2021; Dustmann and Kirchkamp 2002; Wahba 2015). In this scenario, higher migration costs increase the duration of stay overseas required to achieved targeted savings, or, if migrants cannot stay longer at destination, total net savings are reduced. As a result, for lack of start-up capital, migrants may upon their return be unable to start self-employment or may have to postpone it. These challenges and delays due to higher migration costs can thereby affect total lifetime earnings.

RESILIENT AND SUSTAINABLE MIGRATION FOR DEVELOPMENT AT RISK FROM CURRENT PATTERNS

As noted, South Asian labor migration is regionally concentrated in Gulf Cooperation Council (GCC) countries, and in Malaysia. After intraregional migration is excluded, the stock of migrants from South Asia is heavily concentrated in a handful of economies. Just five economies host 81.5 percent of migrants from Bangladesh, 72.8 percent of those from Nepal, and 66 percent of those from Pakistan. This regional concentration increases the sending countries' exposure to shocks in the receiving countries. In 2017, 2.7 million Bangladeshis worked as labor migrants abroad. Roughly 1 million of them worked in Saudi Arabia and an additional million in the United Arab Emirates. Among the 2.5 million Pakistani labor migrants abroad, 1.3 million worked in Saudi Arabia, and roughly another million in the United Arab Emirates. Half of all Nepali temporary migrant workers are in Saudi Arabia.

South Asia sends high volumes of temporary migrant workers to many economies, but the flows are highly volatile, and demand growth for low-skilled South Asian labor migrants in major destinations could continue to decline (as seen in chapter 1). Nepal can be illustrative (Ruppert Bulmer, Shresta, and Marshalian 2020). As of 2018/19, Nepal was sending labor migrants to 136 countries, but five countries—Kuwait, Qatar, Saudi Arabia, the United Arab Emirates, and Malaysia—accounted for 89 percent of total permitted outmigration. The outflows of migrants to these major destinations were disrupted by several incidents, such as the crisis in Qatar in 2017 and Nepal's government ban on Malaysia-bound migrants in mid-2018 following a crackdown on agencies levying excess charges on Nepali migrants. Weaker oil prices have in general dampened the demand for foreign labor in the oil-producing economies of the Middle East, notably in the GCC countries. Saudi Arabia has also imposed higher fees on foreigners, increasing the cost of migration for Nepalis. Together, these external shocks could have contributed to a 50 percent reduction in the number of labor permits issued since the peak in 2015.

In recent years, Gulf region economies dependent on oil exports have experienced slower growth because volatile oil prices have led to a reduction in government revenues and a decline in spending on new construction projects (Deloitte 2018). To sustain economic growth in the future, GCC countries will need to invest more heavily in new services and industries, and these sectors usually require a more sophisticated skill set from workers than does the construction sector (Callen et al. 2014). South Asian labor migrants, who are mostly low skilled and work in the construction sector, will be negatively affected by the ongoing economic changes in the GCC. Changing economic structures in the GCC, and associated uncertainties, could thus contribute to macroeconomic vulnerability in major migrant-sending South Asian countries.

Factors that influence volatility can be divided into demand shocks in the destination country economy, policy shocks in the destination economy, and policy shocks that influence both the sending and receiving countries. The first category could include economic shocks such as a financial crisis (global or national) or contractionary episodes (like recessions), whereby labor demand in the destination country economy may fall. The second category includes policy decisions in the destination country that make hiring foreign-born workers more expensive, make foreign-born workers less employable (for example, not recognizing certifications and skills), or impose outright restrictions that prohibit their employment (such as controlling legal work authorizations, or bans on employing workers from specific countries). The final category includes legal frameworks such as bilateral labor agreements (BLAs) and memoranda of understanding (MOUs) that may facilitate market access and reduce volatility.[5] Multilateral agreements that foster mobility of workers could also be considered, such as the European Union's freedom of movement of workers (one of the four freedoms enshrined in the Treaty of Rome).

Beyond volatility, policy shocks could also have long-term implications for demand for migrant workers from South Asia. Policy reform in the destination country or in bilateral and multilateral frameworks could shift long-term demand for workers. For example, Japan is a highly desirable option for South Asian economies to scale up flows to a new destination (even though they currently are very small). The government of Japan passed a law in April 2019 that allows for the recruitment of 500,000 migrant workers by 2025. This number is equivalent to a third of Japan's current 1.46 million person foreign workforce. Workers on the "Specified Skill Worker" visa would include the kind of temporary, lower-skilled foreign workers that Japan's immigration policy has long excluded, traditionally restricting labor migration only to the highly skilled. Under the new visa, "Type 1" (less-skilled) visa holders would be allowed to stay up to five years.

Structural shifts, such as demographics, can also play a role in the changing demand for migrant workers, especially given that many higher-income economies are aging faster than many lower-middle-income countries in South Asia. Bangladesh, Nepal, and Pakistan (along with other South Asian economies) are expected to have relatively large working-age population shares for a few more decades, while the labor supply of several higher-income economies in East and Southeast Asia is expected to decline because of aging. Temporary economic migration can help rebalance demographics in destination countries and mitigate the impact of the potentially slower labor supply growth. Simulation analyses suggest that allowing migrants to move freely in response to differences in wages (driven in part by demographic changes) occurring in East and Southeast Asia over the next 50 years would be beneficial to real incomes and real GDP in most economies in South Asia over the 2007–50 period (Walmsley, Aguiar, and Ahmed 2017). The scale of that benefit would also depend on other developments within the destination country, such as demand for services that cannot be automated or delivered through arm's-length services trade (such as care of the elderly) and, conversely, the adoption of labor-substituting and labor-augmenting technologies.

Demand for migrant workers affected by global and host-country economic shocks

Events such as the global financial crisis or commodity price booms that accelerate growth for commodity exporters are good examples of covariate shocks that affect migrant labor demand across several major destination economies. In the GCC countries, the main destination for low-skilled migrants from South Asia, migration outflows are closely synchronized with fluctuations in oil prices, an important determinant of labor demand. Bangladesh, where departures overseas clearly coincide with periods of higher oil prices (figure 3.3), illustrates this point. The oil price boom in oil-rich countries between 2003 and 2008 substantially increased their demand for foreign labor migrants. Before the crisis, the average annual growth rate of 6.6 percent and high oil prices had boosted economic activity in GCC countries (Saif 2009). In 2006, oil revenue generated 51 percent of GDP in Saudi Arabia, 42 percent in Oman, and 25 percent in the United Arab Emirates. In comparison, oil rents constituted only a small portion of the total revenue of high-income Asian countries. In 2006, Malaysia had the largest share of oil rent in high-income Asia, at almost 7 percent.

FIGURE 3.3

Year of departure of labor migrants from Bangladesh and global oil prices

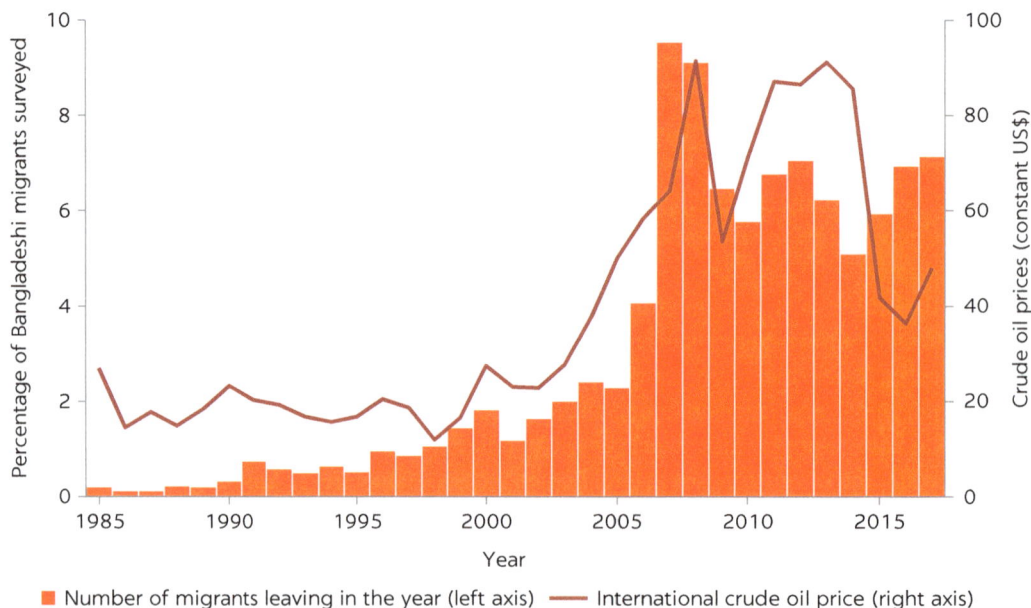

■ Number of migrants leaving in the year (left axis)　—— International crude oil price (right axis)

Sources: Bossavie et al. (2021) based on data from the Bangladesh Return Migrant Survey 2018/19.

To meet demand in the booming construction sector, governments of oil-dependent economies substantially increased the annual inflow of South Asian labor migrants in the years before the global financial crisis. The annual inflow of Pakistani labor migrants to Saudi Arabia increased from about 35,000 in 2005 to almost 140,000 in 2008. The inflow of Pakistani workers to the United Arab Emirates approximately tripled during this period, from about 74,000 in 2005 to 222,000 in 2008. In 2005 the inflow of Bangladeshi migrants to Oman was less than 5,000—it was almost 53,000 in 2008. The demand for foreign labor also increased in East Asia during this period. The inflow of Bangladeshi labor migrants to Malaysia increased from only 3,000 in 2005 to almost 60,000 in 2008.

However, the boom left oil–export dependent economies increasingly vulnerable to shocks. Despite attempts by GCC governments to launch policies to diversify their economies, reduce unemployment, and increase labor productivity, their economies came to increasingly depend on oil (Saif 2009). The average GCC headline inflation rate increased from 1.7 percent in 2004 to 10.7 percent in 2008 (Khamis and Senhadji 2010). Because of the economic slowdown in 2007, the United States started reducing interest rates, forcing GCC countries to do likewise because their exchange rates were pegged to the US dollar (except for Kuwait). The resulting negative real interest rates, combined with the inflationary pressure, led to rapid credit growth and an expansion of domestic demand (Saif 2009).

The global financial crisis led to a contraction in oil-producing economies. The crisis led to a substantial reduction of the flow of foreign investment in real estate, bringing to a halt the rise in real estate prices in the GCC region. In Dubai, which had experienced the largest and fastest real estate boom in the region, developers rapidly halted many construction projects (Habibi 2009). Simultaneously, the crisis caused a steep drop in demand for crude oil, leading to a 70 percent price drop between July 2008 and February 2009. During that period, oil revenues of migrant-receiving countries declined substantially: Saudi Arabia saw a 37 percent decline in oil revenue expressed as a share of GDP; the United Arab Emirates saw a 34 percent decline; and Oman a 21 percent decline. Elsewhere, oil revenues of oil-reliant high-income Asian countries declined as well. In Malaysia, the oil sector's share of GDP fell by 44 percent.

The subsequent recession caused a drop in demand for foreign migrant labor in GCC countries and high-income Asia. An event study (see annex 3B) clearly demonstrates the impact of the crisis on migrant demand, where $t = 0$ is set for 2009, when the global financial crisis hit Asia (figure 3.4). The global financial crisis is chosen as the main event because GDP, oil prices, and the demand for foreign migrant labor dropped across all migration corridors under consideration. Migrant workers in the GCC and other economies in recession were thus among those that felt the impact of the global financial crisis and its aftermath most acutely (Buckley et al. 2016). The number of South Asian labor migrants flowing into GCC countries and high-income oil-producing countries in Asia dropped significantly. From 2008 to 2009, the number of Bangladeshi labor migrants flowing into Malaysia decreased by 91 percent, but to Oman only by 21 percent. From 2009 to 2010, the inflow of Pakistani labor migrants to Saudi Arabia declined by 6 percent, and to the United Arab Emirates by 20 percent. There was a more severe decline in the number of labor migrants in high-income Asian countries than in South Asian countries, given that they were more affected by the economic crisis

FIGURE 3.4

Indicators of host country demand and sending country migration and remittances

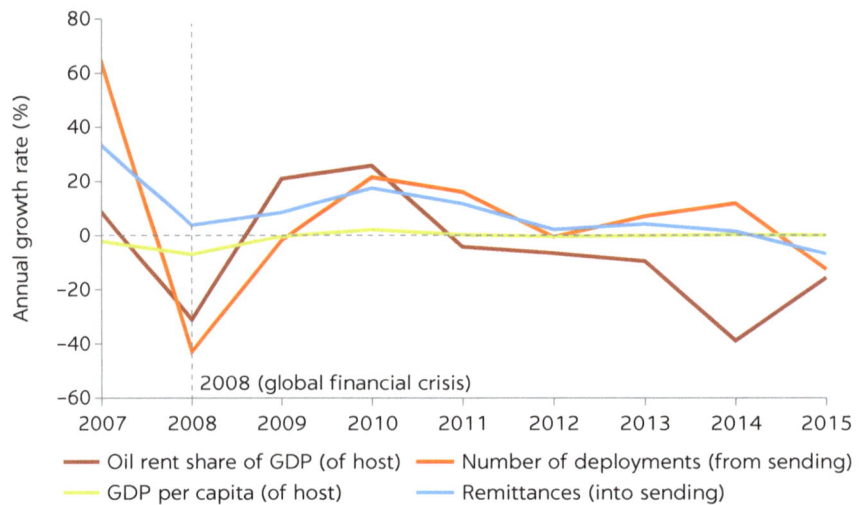

Sources: For data on oil rent share of GDP and GDP per capita, World Development Indicators; for data on remittances, KNOMAD Remittances Database; for deployments, Bangladeshi Bureau of Manpower Employment and Training; Sri Lankan Bureau of Foreign Employment; Pakistan Bureau of Emigration and Overseas Employment; Nepali Department of Foreign Employment; Indian Ministry of External Affairs.
Note: The figure shows annual growth rates during the period 2008–17. Number of deployments is calculated as average for Bangladeshi, Indian, Nepali, Pakistani, and Sri Lankan labor migrants in their respective top five destination countries. Data for Nepal's migration corridors are only available for the period 2009–17. Oil rent share of GDP is calculated as average for Bahrain, Kuwait, Malaysia, Oman, Qatar, Saudi Arabia, and the United Arab Emirates. Hong Kong SAR, China; and Singapore are excluded for lack of available data. GDP per capita is calculated as the average for the host countries with the largest shares of South Asian labor migrants (Bahrain, Kuwait, Malaysia, Oman, Qatar, Saudi Arabia, and the United Arab Emirates); remittances are defined as total amount of remittances that flow into Bangladesh, India, Nepal, and Pakistan.

because of their more open economies. The sharp drop in exports of manufactures, foreign investment, and tourist arrivals, combined with a decline in prices of major export crops such as palm oil, led to the severe drop in the number of labor migrants in Malaysia (Abella and Ducanes 2009).

In the aftermath of the economic crisis, demand for South Asian labor migrants picked up. Despite the severity of the recession, many affected economies recovered fairly quickly. Oil revenue and GDP of GCC and high-income Asian countries increased substantially in 2010, and again in 2011. Consequently, most host countries began receiving labor migrants at scale once again in 2011. The inflow of Bangladeshi labor migrants to Oman increased by more than 200 percent, from 42,000 in 2010 to more than 135,000 in 2011. In the same year, the number of Pakistani labor migrants to the United Arab Emirates increased by 38 percent. In some receiving countries, the increased inflow of South Asian labor migrants was more delayed. The number of Pakistani labor migrants to Saudi Arabia increased by only 17 percent from 2010 to 2011, but by 61 percent from 2011 to 2012. The inflow of Bangladeshi migrants to Malaysia increased substantially in 2013, from about 800 to almost 4,000.

Effect of labor market policies in host countries on migrant labor demand

In the 1990s, policies in GCC countries to nationalize the domestic labor force did not lead to reduced demand for low-skilled labor migrants. At that time a priority for GCC economies was the nationalization of their labor markets, that is, the adoption of policies to encourage local industries to hire local citizens instead of foreign workers, following specific quotas. In theory, a halt to their customary overreliance on foreign labor would lead to higher employment rates of nationals and higher productivity (Randeree 2012). As part of these nationalization policies, governments banned foreigners, taxed the employment of foreigners by domestic companies, and provided financial incentives to hire nationals. GCC countries also provided training to nationals to develop skills necessary for the labor market (Hertog 2012). Before the economic crisis, the nationalization policies of GCC countries had had limited success. The most significant hurdles in all GCC countries to any substantial reduction in demand for labor migrants were the small size of the national labor force, the cultural bias of locals against manual jobs, and women's low levels of participation in the labor force (Randeree 2012). There may have also been shortages of native-born workers with the skills in demand by firms (Al-Lamki 2000; De Bel-Air 2018).

After recovering from the 2008 economic crisis, GCC countries became more cautious about low-skilled labor entry. In 2011, the Saudi government launched a new nationalization program called Nitaqat to effectively reduce the country's reliance on foreign labor migrants. This program, which is one of the most coherent nationalization strategies in the GCC, classified private sector companies into three categories. Companies in the first two categories were considered to have excessively high shares of foreign workers and were therefore restricted regarding the hiring of foreigners. Companies in the third category were those that were compliant with the government's quota requirements on foreign workers, and were allowed to hire additional foreign workers from among those that were already hired by the companies in the first two categories (Randeree 2012). In line with the nationalization efforts, in 2013 the Saudi government launched nationwide large-scale deportations of undocumented migrants (Carey 2013). These actions were triggered by an amendment to the labor law empowering authorities to enforce labor code provisions against undocumented labor migrants who did not work for their designated employers. The measures included detentions and deportations (Coogle 2015). In comparison, in the years after the economic crisis, the Emirati government did not launch any policies, but promoted various individual measures to reduce domestic demand for foreign labor migrants. In 2011, the salaries of federal employees were increased by 35 percent to 45 percent (Dajani 2011). In 2012, the government suspended the issuance of new visas to labor migrants from Bangladesh (Malit and Al Youha 2013). In 2015, the Abu Dhabi Human Resource Authority was created as the principal agency for guiding the nationalization policy and to direct learning and training programs toward local workers to fulfill labor market demand (*Khaleej Times* 2015).

Nationalization policies in GCC countries implemented after the 2008 economic crisis may have led to reduced intake of labor migrants from various South Asian countries. The introduction of Saudization did not lead to an immediate reduction of undocumented South Asian labor migrants in the country. It was only in 2013, when the national labor law was amended, that the number of South Asian migrants in Saudi Arabia declined. Between 2015 and 2017, because of Saudi Arabia's newly adopted nationalization strategy and large-scale deportations, the number of visas for foreign workers dropped by more than half (De Bel-Air 2018). In 2016, the inflow of Indian labor migrants to Saudi Arabia dropped by 46 percent compared with the previous year, and again by more than 52 percent in 2017. Between 2016 and 2017, the intake of Nepali and Pakistani labor migrants to Saudi Arabia dropped by 46 percent and 69 percent, respectively. In the aftermath of the suspension of new visas to Bangladeshi labor migrants to the United Arab Emirates, their intake dropped by fully 93 percent, from more than 215,000 in 2012 to only about 14,000 in the following year. From 2015 to 2016, about the time the Abu Dhabi Human Resource Authority was created, the inflow of Bangladeshi labor migrants to Abu Dhabi declined from about 25,000 to 8,000.

The reduced intake of migrants negatively affected the flow of remittances back to South Asia. Nepal faced the largest negative impact, with a contraction of almost 2 percent from 2015 to 2016 compared with growth of 14 percent in the previous year. In Bangladesh, remittances fell by 11 percent in 2016, compared with 2 percent growth the previous year. Remittances to Pakistani households grew by less than 3 percent from 2015 to 2016, compared with 12 percent in the previous year. Growth rates for remittances to India were negative in 2015 (a drop of 2.1 percent) and in 2016 (a drop of 8.9 percent).

Nevertheless, overall reliance on South Asian labor migration remains high in the GCC region. Similar to GCC nationalization policies in the 1990s, nationalization strategies in the aftermath of the economic crisis do not appear to have substantially reduced this reliance. Overall, the only noticeable change was in the composition of migrants' countries of origin. The number of Bangladeshi labor migrants flowing into Saudi Arabia increased rapidly over the 2016–17 period (see the section "The impact of bilateral agreements between sending and receiving countries"). The intake of Nepali labor migrants to the United Arab Emirates increased as well: it was roughly 58,000 in 2017, compared with 52,000 in the previous year. There is some evidence that the number of labor visas issued to foreign domestic workers never substantially declined in Saudi Arabia (De Bel-Air 2018).

The nationalization policies in the GCC have not substantially reduced demand for migrant workers for a number of reasons. There are persistent social norms in the GCC countries that contribute to low female labor force participation by the native-born population, as well as a reluctance to take on low-skilled work (Forstenlechner and Rutledge 2011). Firms also did not seem interested in reducing the number of foreign workers to achieve the nationalization quotas. Despite training programs for local workers, mismatches between the skills of the local labor supply and those demanded by employers remained unresolved. The low cost of migrant workers has persistently guaranteed large benefits to companies and ultimately suppressed the prices of goods and services in the host economies, thereby supporting the real incomes of residents (Forstenlechner and Rutledge 2011; Peck 2017).

The impact of bilateral agreements between sending and receiving countries

In recent decades, South Asian countries have signed various BLAs and MOUs with GCC and other destination countries. Countries sign BLAs to regulate the recruitment and employment of foreign workers. In contrast to BLAs, which are legally binding, governments often prefer signing MOUs, whose effectiveness is determined by subsequent implementation and enforcement (IOM 2011). Bangladesh and Pakistan signed MOUs with the United Arab Emirates in 2007 and 2006, respectively. With these memoranda, the parties aim to regulate employment of the relevant temporary contractual workers, reduce the role of illegal recruitment agencies, and diminish labor abuse, among other issues (UAE Ministry of Labour 2007). The BLA signed by India and Qatar in 2007 aims to protect the rights of Indian labor migrants and guarantees full wages as per the contract if a worker returns to India prematurely through no fault of his or her own. The BLA also ensures the welfare of Indian workers in the informal sector, who have been especially vulnerable to abuse (*Economic Times* 2007). In 2015, Bangladesh signed an MOU with Saudi Arabia on the recruitment of female domestic workers, lifting the ban Saudi Arabia had imposed in 2008 on Bangladeshi migrants. In the MOU, the Saudi government set quotas for the recruitment of female Bangladeshi labor migrants by agencies (World Bank 2018a).

BLAs and MOUs have had positive implications for the inflow of South Asian labor migrants to GCC countries. In 2007, when Bangladesh signed the MOU with the United Arab Emirates, the inflow of Bangladeshi labor migrants to the United Arab Emirates was roughly 226,000, a 74 percent increase over the previous year's total of about 130,000. In 2008, the inflow increased again by 85 percent to about 419,000. When Pakistan signed the MOU with the United Arab Emirates in 2006, the inflow of Pakistani labor migrants to the United Arab Emirates was about 100,000, a 36 percent increase over the previous year's total of approximately 73,000. In 2007, the intake increased by another 39 percent to about 139,000. When Bangladesh signed the MOU with Saudi Arabia in 2015, the number of Bangladeshi labor migrants was approximately 58,000, more than four times higher than in the previous year (roughly 11,000); in 2016, the inflow further increased to about 144,000.

Labor agreements have also had various positive implications for South Asian migrant workers and employers in receiving countries. In the years since Qatar signed the BLA with India, it has adopted various programs to regulate the intake of Indian and other labor migrants (Abraham 2018). It could be assumed that the 2022 FIFA World Cup and, in this context, the international pressure on the Qatari government to comply with international human rights standards, has forced the country to further regulate labor migration. Labor migration programs in high-income Asia led to various positive impacts for all involved parties. The Republic of Korea's Employment Permit System (EPS) has led to significant benefits for employees and employers by reducing reliance on informal brokers and sharpening respect for the rights of labor migrants overall (box 3.1). The MOU between Malaysia and Bangladesh implemented a migration program in the palm oil sector solely regulated by the two governments (box 3.2). The program reduced the costs for Malaysian employers when hiring Bangladeshi labor migrants and guaranteed a minimum wage for the workers.

Different shocks interact to drive volatility in migration flows

The earlier sections describe three distinct sets of economic and policy shocks that could affect migration flows in a given year, but volatility is often due to multiple shocks occurring over time, as illustrated by Bangladesh and some of its major destinations. Between 2000 and 2017, migration flows from Bangladesh to

BOX 3.1

Republic of Korea's Employment Permit System

In 2004, the Republic of Korea adopted the Employment Permit System (EPS) to help small domestic companies meet their demand for low-skilled workers. The EPS aims to address structural and immediate demand for low-skilled labor in manufacturing, agriculture, livestock, fisheries, and construction (ADBI, OECD, and ILO 2019). The system functions through bilateral agreements: various South Asian countries have signed memoranda of understanding with the Korean government, including Sri Lanka (2004), Pakistan (2006), Nepal (2007), and Bangladesh (2007) (Cho et al. 2018). Hiring follows a strict step-by-step process. Candidates are eligible if they are ages 18 to 39 and pass a basic Korean language exam. A home country agency (a public employment body) assesses their qualifications, then holds their profiles in the application pool for one year. The information is then sent to the respective department of the Korean government, which checks the qualifications of foreign job applicants. The Korean government also ensures that the small and medium enterprises that want to hire foreign labor migrants receive prior authorization (ADBI, OECD, and ILO 2019).

The EPS has led to significant benefits for employees and employers. The governments of Korea and South Asian countries have supervised the recruitment process to ensure that the skills that labor migrants offer meet the requirements of Korean small and medium enterprises. Thus, compared with other destination countries, companies in Korea no longer need to rely on informal brokers to find workers (who could well turn out not to meet Korea's labor standards). Within the EPS, Korea provides various services for the foreign workers, such as the resolution of workplace conflicts, integration in the national community, and assistance finding new jobs (Cho et al. 2018). The EPS is also attractive for the workers, who pay much lower fees than they did previously for recruitment and thus can remit a larger share of their earnings, which are substantial given the much higher wages in Korea than in other destinations (ADBI, OECD, and ILO 2019).

BOX 3.2

Historical development of labor agreements between Malaysia and Bangladesh

In 1994, Malaysia, whose economy was growing steadily at that time, signed an agreement with Bangladesh to recruit 50,000 workers, mostly for the construction sector (Ahmed 1998). However, in the aftermath of the 1998 Asian financial crisis, the program came to an end when the Malaysian government adopted a new migration policy and conducted large-scale deportations of foreign labor migrants (Pillai 1999). In 2001, Malaysia's government announced a complete ban on Bangladeshi migrants after social tensions arose resulting from intermarriage between Bangladeshi workers and local women (Netto 2001). Consequently, the number of labor migrants flowing into the country dropped from almost 5,000 in 2001 to only 85 in 2002.

In 2005, the Malaysian government reopened its doors to Bangladeshi labor migrants. The intake of labor migrants from the South Asian country rose from 224 in 2004 to approximately 3,000 in 2005 to about 20,500 in 2006. However, in 2009, Malaysia's government froze the intake again, in an effort to reduce the country's reliance on foreign labor and to end the exploitation of migrant workers by agents (Amnesty International 2010; Kibira 2011). In various incidents, informal agents, who were in charge of the migration process from Bangladesh to Malaysia at that time, exploited migrants by, for instance, overcharging them (Sarker 2016). As a consequence of the tightening of the migration policy, the number of migrants from Bangladesh dropped by 93 percent, from more than 12,000 in 2009 to fewer than 1,000 in 2010.

In 2012, Malaysia signed a memorandum of understanding with Bangladesh to avoid the exploitation of migrants by agents. After a four-year ban on migration

continued

Box 3.2, *continued*

from Bangladesh, the government of Malaysia planned to recruit 30,000 Bangladeshi men to work in the palm oil sector through the so-called government-to-government (G2G) migration lottery program. The minimum wage was guaranteed, and migration costs were fixed under this program (Shrestha, Mobarak, and Sharif 2019). The intention behind the collaboration was to take complete responsibility for the recruitment of labor migrants, given that private employment agencies had eroded the benefits of labor migration in the past. The intake of Bangladeshi labor migrants increased significantly, from 804 in 2012, to 3,853 in 2013, to more than 30,000 in 2015.

The G2G program contributed to substantially lowering migration costs and further demonstrated the ability of agencies under the Ministry of Expatriates' Welfare and Overseas Employment to efficiently manage recruitment and placement. However, the program has come under increasing criticism in recent years. Private employment agencies started putting increased pressure on the program to open it up to the private sector (Wickramasekara 2016). By 2018, fewer than 10,000 winners of visas—via a program lottery—had migrated from Bangladesh to Malaysia (Shrestha, Mobarak, and Sharif 2019). After the perceived limited success of the G2G mechanism, a "G2G plus" program was launched, whereby the Malaysian government would provide oversight of private sector recruitment. But this new program eventually came under criticism because fewer than 10 recruitment agencies were involved in the migration process (Shrestha, Mobarak, and Sharif 2019). In 2018, the government of Malaysia suspended the G2G plus program altogether amid allegations that it functioned as a trafficking scheme exploiting Bangladeshi labor workers, imposing exorbitant migration costs on them (Bhuyan 2018).

destinations such as the United Arab Emirates and Malaysia fluctuated dramatically. Bangladesh sent as many as 419,000 workers to the United Arab Emirates in 2008, preceded by similar numbers in the previous years. However, in 2009, after the global financial crisis, the number fell by half (figure 3.5). Then in 2012, the United Arab Emirates imposed an outright ban on recruitment of Bangladeshi workers. Bangladesh has experienced several similar boom-bust cycles of migration flows to Malaysia, usually punctuated by the signing of agreements such as an MOU or BLA.

The direct shocks to a corridor may have real or perceived externalities to other corridors. If different South Asian economies send workers with similar skills profiles to the same destination, there is suspected competition for the positions available. It follows that policy measures in some countries to increase the safety and protection of migrant workers may be thought to reduce the competitiveness of workers from that country. There are some perceptions in Nepal that labor migrants are easily replaced by other unskilled workers, whether from Nepal or other countries.[6] For example, after India implemented its e-Migrate system in 2015 to manage its labor migrants better and enhance their protection, the flow of migrants from India to the GCC dropped. Through the e-Migrate platform, the Indian Protector of Emigrants issues clearances for workers to leave the country after various conditions have been met, including the issuance of a contract that specifies that the worker will receive at least a minimum wage set by the Indian government. In the same year, Saudi Arabia signed MOUs for workers from Bangladesh, including for female domestic workers. What was observed then was that the flows of migrant workers from India to Saudi Arabia collapsed in 2015, while flows from Bangladesh soared (figure 3.6).

FIGURE 3.5

Migration flows from Bangladesh to United Arab Emirates (thousands of migrants)

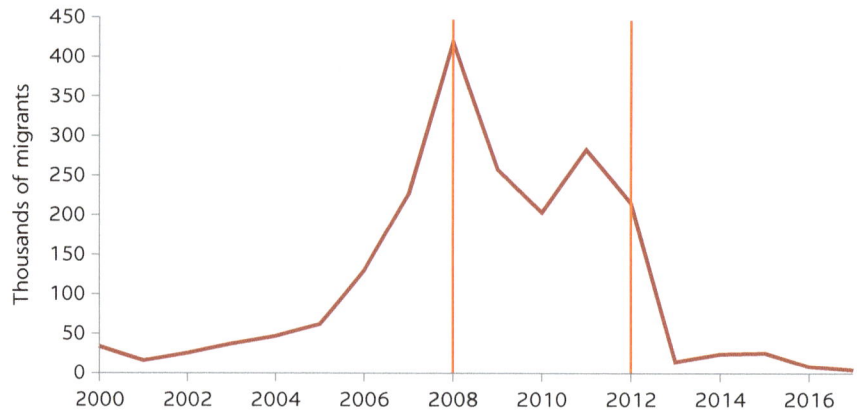

Source: World Bank estimates.
Note: Data are clearances for new deployments from the Bureau of Manpower Employment and Training (Bangladesh).

FIGURE 3.6

Migration flows to Saudi Arabia, by origin (thousands of migrants)

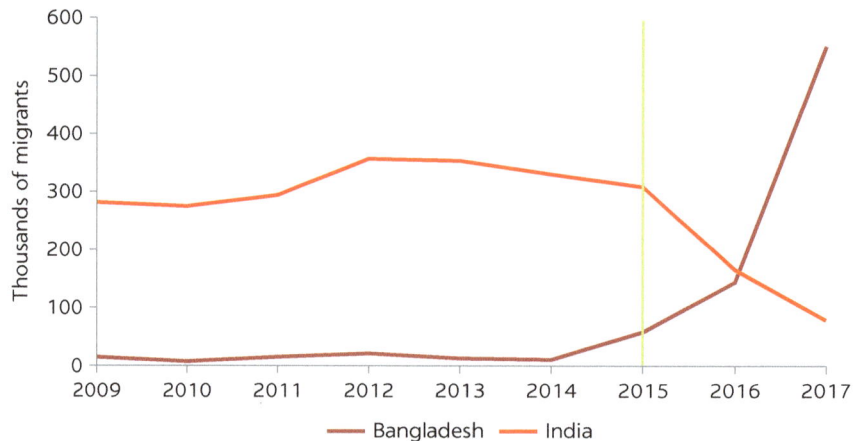

Source: World Bank estimates.
Note: Data are clearances for new deployments from the Bureau of Manpower Employment and Training (Bangladesh); and Ministry of External Affairs (India).

Market diversification

Economic gains for South Asian economies from diversifying toward higher-income East and Southeast Asia might be substantial, but how the trajectories will unfold and what their impact will be on the sending economies is uncertain. Four different scenarios are considered in this book. The first three scenarios break down and analyze the effects of diversifying destinations: more flows to East Asian countries, and fewer to the GCC and other Middle East and North African countries. A fourth scenario is also considered, in which South Asian migrants replace the declining working populations in various high-income countries to keep the labor force constant. The analysis is based on a computable general equilibrium model extended to account for bilateral migration flows. The implications for various economic agents as well as various macroeconomic variables are quantified in annex 3C, including the aggregation of the various economies of the world into 20 countries and regional blocs.

The results of the simulations are reported relative to a hypothetical business-as-usual or baseline scenario in 2027. This baseline scenario is constructed in multiple steps. In the first step, the database underlying the simulations is updated from 2011 to 2017 using historical data on GDP growth from the World Bank's Global Economic Prospects and bilateral migrant stocks and population growth from the United Nations Population Division. In the second step, the baseline database is extrapolated to capture the world economy in 2027, using average historical growth and migration rates as well as population projections for each region. It is assumed that the total number of South Asian migrants will grow by an average 2.8 percent per year, from 38.4 million in 2017 to 50.6 million in 2027 (figure 3.7). The estimated outcome of each counterfactual scenario is then compared with the 2027 baseline scenario to capture the marginal impacts of each alternative.

The four different scenarios represent possible trajectories for migrant labor flows from South Asia:

- *Scenario 1* assumes accelerated growth of South Asian migration to East Asian economies—Hong Kong SAR, China; Japan; Korea; Malaysia; and elsewhere in East Asia. In this scenario, there is no change in South Asian region migration to GCC and other Middle East and North African economies. The exact rate of growth in each migrant destination is inferred from the maximum rate of historical growth rate over the past decade. Overall, the number of South

FIGURE 3.7

Projected labor outmigration from South Asia

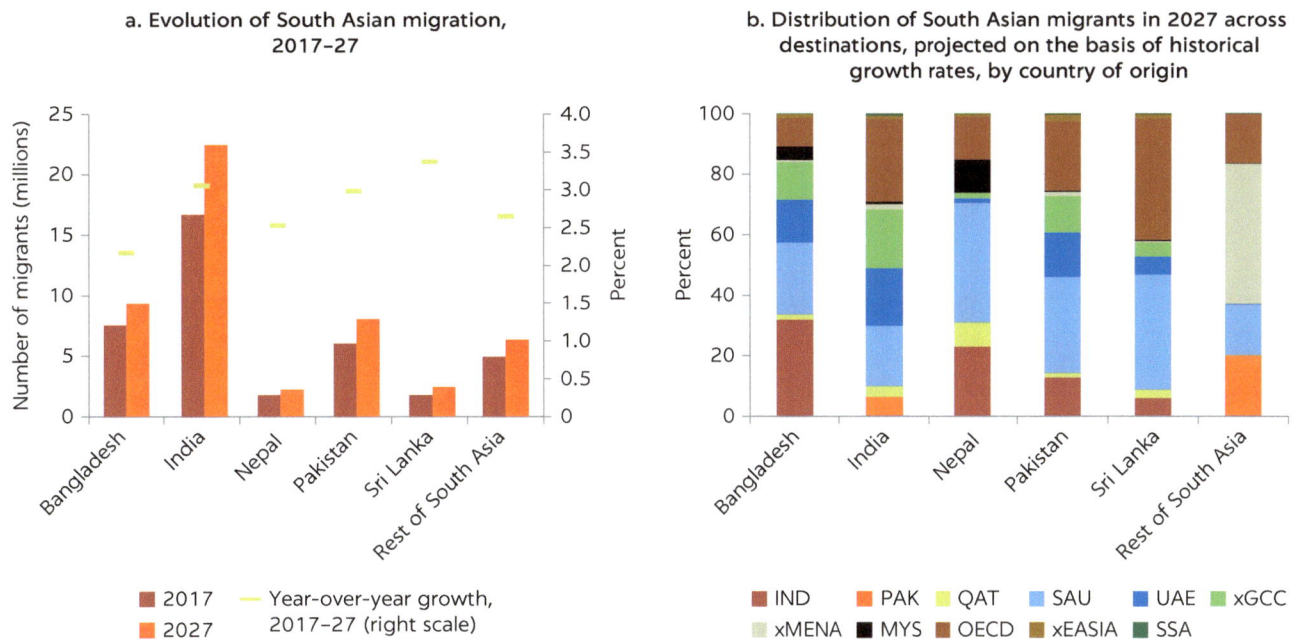

a. Evolution of South Asian migration, 2017–27

b. Distribution of South Asian migrants in 2027 across destinations, projected on the basis of historical growth rates, by country of origin

Legend (panel a): 2017; 2027; Year-over-year growth, 2017–27 (right scale)

Legend (panel b): IND; PAK; QAT; SAU; UAE; xGCC; xMENA; MYS; OECD; xEASIA; SSA

Source: World Bank estimates.
Note: Data from UN DESA International Migrant Stocks 2017 for panel a. Panel b presents projections based on historical trends.
IND = India; MYS = Malaysia; PAK = Pakistan; QAT = Qatar; SAU = Saudi Arabia; UAE = United Arab Emirates; xGCC = rest of Gulf Cooperation Council; xMENA = rest of the Middle East and North Africa; xEASIA = rest of East Asia; SSA = Sub-Saharan Africa.

Asian migrants to East Asia is assumed to increase by 12 percent, or 196,000 additional migrants, relative to the 2027 baseline scenario (table 3.3). The rate of increase of migration from Pakistan and Sri Lanka is more pronounced, at about 23 percent, but the absolute increase in migration from Bangladesh and India accounts for more than half of the total.

- *Scenario 2* depicts the reversion of South Asian migrant labor stocks in East Asia, GCC, and other Middle East and North African countries to their 2010 levels. The total number of South Asian migrants to GCC and other Middle East and North African countries declines by close to 50 percent, or 13.5 million people, relative to the 2027 baseline scenario. The decrease in South Asian migrants to East Asia would be less pronounced, at 21 percent, or 330,000 migrants. Overall, total outward South Asian migration is assumed to decline by 27 percent.

- *Scenario 3* combines the earlier two scenarios and assumes the accelerated growth of South Asian migrants to East Asia from scenario 1 (an increase of 12 percent, or 196,000 additional migrants) and the decline of migrant stocks in GCC and other Middle East and North African countries to their 2010 levels. Overall, this scenario translates into a decline of South Asian migration of 13.2 million people, that is, more than 26 percent.

- *Scenario 4* assumes that South Asian migrants fully replace the shrinking unskilled labor force in Hong Kong SAR, China; Japan; Korea; the Rest of East Asia (covering all economies in Southeast Asia not individually modeled); Europe and Central Asia; and Organisation for Economic Co-operation and Development (OECD) economies to keep labor forces in those economies constant at their 2017 levels. International Labor Organization estimates show that over the 2017–23 period, the combined unskilled labor forces in these economies will decline by more than 44 million people. Most of this drop is accounted for by the decline in employment in the Rest of East Asia region (31.6 million), followed by Europe and Central Asia (5.5 million), Western OECD (4.9 million), Japan (1.3 million), and Korea (0.7 million). South Asian migrants are assumed to replace this shrinking labor force in accordance with their current shares of migration. In addition, it is also assumed that South Asian migrant labor stocks in GCC and other Middle East and North African economies revert to their 2010 levels. Overall, South Asian migration would increase by close to 60 percent, from 50 million in 2017 to 80 million in 2027.

TABLE 3.3 Number of migrants, assumptions by scenarios

Thousands of people

	MIDDLE EAST AND NORTH AFRICA						EAST ASIA				
	2017	2027	S1	S2	S3	S4	2017	2027	S1 S3	S2	S4
Bangladesh	3,120	4,767	4,767		2,606		487	545	591	445	6,851
India	8,919	13,401	13,401		5,724		414	471	534	356	14,829
Nepal	666	1,101	1,101		369		249	276	289	235	1,622
Pakistan	3,103	4,821	4,821		2,644		212	243	299	176	9,868
Sri Lanka	743	1,227	1,227		718		65	73	90	66	2,126
Rest of South Asia	2,793	3,075	3,075		2,853		2	4	4	4	72
South Asia	**19,343**	**28,393**	**28,393**		**14,913**		**1,428**	**1,612**	**1,808**	**1,282**	**35,369**

Source: World Bank data.

Note: S1 = Scenario 1; S2 = Scenario 2; S3 = Scenario 3; S4 = Scenario 4.

Although the aggregate effects of accelerated growth of South Asian migration to East Asian countries on both migration sending and receiving countries are estimated to be modest, new migrants are significant winners.[7] Overall, new migrants benefit from an increase in their income of US$2.7 billion—nearly US$13,700 per capita (table 3.4).[8] The highest increase in income per capita accrues to new migrants from Pakistan and Bangladesh, by US$18,400 and US$15,300, respectively, over the period 2017–27. As the expanding labor force in migrant-receiving countries exerts downward pressure on wages, migrants who had arrived earlier are found to lose, but only modestly, by an overall decline in their income of US$0.3 billion, or US$5.3 per capita, over the period 2017–27. Overall, South Asian remittances sent to home countries are estimated to increase by US$2.1 billion, or 1.5 percent (table 3.5). Even though migrant-sending countries experience an overall contraction of activity and a slight decrease in GDP (table 3.6), these countries also benefit from an improvement in their current account balances, trade balances, and terms of trade.

The reversion of South Asian migrant labor stocks in East Asia, GCC, and other Middle East and North African countries to their 2010 levels (Scenario 2) is estimated to significantly hurt returning migrants' and earlier migrants'

TABLE 3.4 Impact on income of new migrants and migrants who had arrived earlier (nonmovers)
US$ billions

	S1		S2		S3		S4	
	NEW MIGRANTS	EARLIER MIGRANTS	NEW MIGRANTS	EARLIER MIGRANTS	NEW MIGRANTS	EARLIER MIGRANTS	NEW MIGRANTS	EARLIER MIGRANTS
Bangladesh	0.7	−0.1	0.0	−6.1	0.7	−5.6	57.6	−11.6
India	0.6	−0.1	0.0	−13.5	0.6	−12.7	57.0	−19.9
Nepal	0.1	0.0	0.0	−2.7	0.1	−2.5	3.1	−3.0
Pakistan	1.0	−0.1	0.0	−7.3	1.0	−6.2	86.8	−15.4
Sri Lanka	0.2	0.0	0.0	−1.3	0.2	−1.3	11.1	−2.7
Rest of South Asia	0.0	0.0	0.0	−1.5	0.0	−1.5	0.2	−1.9
South Asia	**2.7**	**−0.3**	**0.0**	**−32.4**	**2.7**	**−29.8**	**215.6**	**−54.5**

Source: World Bank data.
Note: "Earlier migrants" refers only to migrants who were already in the destination, but did not move, making them distinct from natives and the new migrants who came due to the shock in countries abroad. Simulation results are relative to the baseline in 2027. S1 = Scenario 1; S2 = Scenario 2; S3 = Scenario 3; S4 = Scenario 4.

TABLE 3.5 Impact on remittances

	CHANGE (US$ BILLIONS)				PERCENT CHANGE			
	S1	S2	S3	S4	S1	S2	S3	S4
Bangladesh	0.4	−3.6	−2.8	29.5	2.8	−25.8	−20.4	213.2
India	0.9	−21.8	−19.5	86.7	0.9	−21.1	−18.9	83.9
Nepal	0.0	−0.9	−0.8	0.7	1.0	−28.4	−25.9	22.5
Pakistan	0.7	−5.0	−3.6	53.9	4.2	−32.4	−22.9	347.3
Sri Lanka	0.2	−0.9	−0.7	8.2	2.3	−12.9	−9.9	120.4
Rest of South Asia	0.0	0.0	0.0	0.1	0.0	−10.7	−10.6	30.2
South Asia	**2.1**	**−32.3**	**−27.5**	**179.1**	**1.5**	**−22.6**	**−19.2**	**125.1**

Source: World Bank data.
Note: Simulation results are relative to the 2027 baseline scenario. S1 = Scenario 1; S2 = Scenario 2; S3 = Scenario 3; S4 = Scenario 4.

TABLE 3.6 **Impact of alternative scenarios on GDP in origin and destination economies**

	BASELINE GDP, 2027 (US$ BILLIONS)	PERCENT CHANGE			
		S1	S2	S3	S4
Bangladesh	286.6	−0.02	0.95	0.90	−1.08
India	3,639.4	−0.01	0.63	0.60	−0.21
Nepal	39.3	−0.06	3.06	2.89	1.17
Pakistan	381.4	−0.01	0.40	0.39	0.43
Sri Lanka	97.0	−0.22	3.17	2.91	−5.29
Rest of South Asia	24.8	0.00	1.67	1.67	−0.34
South Asia total	**4,468.5**	**−0.01**	**0.71**	**0.68**	**−0.31**
Qatar	146.4	0.00	−2.74	−2.74	−2.73
Saudi Arabia	548.9	0.00	−8.23	−8.23	−8.22
United Arab Emirates	330.1	0.00	−7.87	−7.87	−7.87
Rest of GCC	195.7	0.00	−17.08	−17.08	−17.03
Rest of MENA	2,438.4	0.00	0.01	0.01	0.03
MENA total	**3,659.4**	**0.00**	**−2.96**	**−2.96**	**−2.94**
Malaysia	380.4	0.04	−0.20	0.03	0.00
Japan	4,718.5	0.01	0.00	0.01	0.55
Korea, Rep.	1,273.8	0.06	0.01	0.07	0.72
Hong Kong SAR, China	267.1	0.00	−0.02	0.00	0.96
Rest of East Asia	13,164.4	0.03	−0.04	0.03	3.29
East Asia and Pacific total	**19,804.2**	**0.03**	**−0.03**	**0.03**	**2.38**
Sub-Saharan Africa	1,620.9	0.00	0.00	0.00	0.01
Eastern Europe and Central Asia	2,752.9	0.00	−0.03	−0.03	0.61
Latin America and the Caribbean	5,573.9	0.00	0.00	0.00	0.01
Western OECD	38,028.0	0.00	0.00	0.00	0.26

Source: World Bank.
Note: Simulation results. Percent change relative to the baseline in 2027. S1 = Scenario 1; S2 = Scenario 2; S3 = Scenario 3; S4 = Scenario 4. GCC = Gulf Cooperation Council; GDP = gross domestic product; MENA = Middle East and North Africa; OECD = Organisation for Economic Co-operation and Development.

income and remittances as well as the host countries' economies. As total outward South Asian migration declines by 27 percent, remittances are estimated to fall by 22.6 percent or US$32.3 billion. The adverse effects of this decline in remittances, such as the deterioration of the current account balance and the worsening of terms of trade, are fully mitigated by the increase in the labor force in home countries, translating into an overall increase in South Asian GDP by 0.71 percent. The biggest benefits accrue to Sri Lanka and Nepal, where GDP is estimated to expand by more than 3 percent. In contrast, the shrinking labor force in GCC and other Middle East and North African host countries leads to a significant contraction in GDP. Overall, Middle East and North African GDP is estimated to decline by close to 3 percent, with a more pronounced adverse effect on Saudi Arabia and the rest of the GCC region. The decline in economic activity in host countries also hurts migrants who had arrived earlier, who experience a decline in their income of US$32.4 billion, or more than US$500 per capita, over the period 2017–27.

If the reversion of South Asian migrant labor stocks in Middle East and North African countries is accompanied by the acceleration of migration to East Asian countries (Scenario 3), the adverse effects on remittances and nonmovers are slightly alleviated. South Asian remittances decline by 19.2 percent, close to US$5 billion less than in Scenario 2. As in the first scenario, new migrants to East Asian countries benefit from an increase in their incomes of US$2.4 billion—close to US$13,700 per capita over the period 2017–27.

The growth benefits would be significant if migrant workers from South Asia could help keep the aggregate supply of unskilled workers in Hong Kong SAR, China; Japan; Korea; Europe and Central Asia; and OECD economies at 2017 levels, especially if South Asian migrants could also diversify away from GCC destinations. The almost 60 percent increase in South Asian outward migration would translate into a 125 percent, or US$179 billion, increase in remittances. The incomes of new migrants would be significantly boosted overall by US$215.6 billion, or more than US$7,300 per capita over the period 2017–27. In some South Asian countries, the beneficial effects of the increase in remittances and the improvements in terms of trade are outweighed by the decline in their labor forces, and translate into an overall decline in South Asian GDP of 0.31 percent (table 3.6). Among South Asian countries, Sri Lanka is hurt the most, with a 5.3 percent decline in GDP; Nepal and Pakistan benefit in aggregate terms.

GETTING TO MORE PRODUCTIVE, RESILIENT, AND SUSTAINABLE MIGRATION

Sending country interventions to improve information and invest in migrants' human capital

Several of the policy actions that could be taken in the premigration phase of the migration life cycle to reduce the vulnerability of migrants would directly reduce costs and improve access for poorer households.[9] One possible measure would be to enhance the information services offered by government entities in the predecision and predeparture phases of migration so that prospective and aspiring migrants have easier access to knowledge about opportunities and processes for legally migrating (such as requirements for government clearances, visa requirements and types, and passport applications). Some countries are already investing in this area, such as Nepal, through the Migrant Resource Centers and the Safer Migration Initiative supported by the Swiss Agency for Development and Cooperation and implemented by Helvetas. Another measure to enhance information would be to follow the Filipino example and require licensed recruitment agencies to advertise approved positions in a standardized fashion, while also requiring the relevant line agencies to replicate the standardized advertisement of approved positions across multiple platforms. Finally, measures to prepare migrants for overseas employment would also support their employability and would be particularly useful for aspiring migrants from poorer households who may not have invested as much in their human capital. Skills and human resource development are often within the core mandate of the ministries responsible for migration.[10] It would thus be relatively easy to broaden the programs offered by their line agencies to move beyond technical skills and language training to also focus on enhanced psychosocial characteristics—an area in which poorer migrants are often lagging.

Migrants' remittances could be better increased by reducing costs—following the measures just described—rather than necessarily addressing the direct costs of remitting. South Asia has some of the lowest-cost remittance transfer mechanisms in the world (aggregated across modes—banks, money transfer orders, post offices, and mobile operators).[11] The global average cost of remitting in 2019 was 6.9 percent, whereas in South Asia the average was 5 percent (World Bank 2019). These costs have been falling over time around the world, including in Bangladesh, Nepal, and Pakistan. As such, although efforts to reduce the barriers to remitting through legal means should continue, addressing fundamental issues such as the cost of migrating can have a number of benefits.

To reduce volatility and improve sustainability, sending countries will ultimately have to diversify their range of migration destinations. Despite the large economic capacity of countries in high-income Asia and their sophisticated labor migration policies, these countries have received relatively few South Asian migrants in recent decades. However, because of changing demographics, high-income Asian countries might substantially increase their intake of labor migrants from South Asia in the future. Labor migration programs, such as Korea's EPS program, show that further diversification toward high-income Asia could be beneficial for South Asian migrants and their home countries because of much lower migration expenditures and a lower risk of human rights violations by employers than in the GCC countries.

Entering these newer markets will require changes in the profile of the migrants being sent. Currently, most migrants from South Asia are in lower-skilled occupations, reflecting the demands of current destinations (primarily GCC countries and Malaysia). Destinations that offer higher wages and better protection for workers—such as Korea—require additional skills, even for jobs in labor-intensive sectors such as agriculture. These skills include language knowledge in addition to other noncognitive skills such as teamwork and collaboration. For other markets, such as Japan and Hong Kong SAR, China, where there is growing demand for caregivers (childcare and care of the elderly), the supply of such professionals will have to increase, as will the supply of skills development services to train aspiring migrants to become caregivers. Line agencies responsible for managed labor migration may also need to have the capacity to take proactive measures, such as identifying potential demand for different types of workers from new and existing markets. This information will be critical for reorienting the skills development architecture and for gaining a detailed understanding of the scope offered by those markets.

The managed migration systems all reflect an awareness of the need for investment in technical skills and have extensive skills development services in place. For example, in Bangladesh, the Bureau of Manpower Employment and Training is one of the largest providers of technical skills training programs in the country—even for the domestic market—in addition to its responsibilities for regulating recruitment agencies and providing clearances for outbound migrant workers. Under its skills development mandate, it administers 42 District Employment and Manpower Offices, 64 Technical Training Centers, 6 Institutes of Marine Technology, and 3 Apprenticeship Training Offices. The emphasis on technical skills for aspiring migrants has been credited with some preference on the part of Korean employers availing themselves of the Korea EPS.

Skills development programs need to be complemented by certification to signal technical ability, accompanied by due recognition in overseas markets. In the Philippines, under the rules and regulations of the Philippine Overseas Employment Administration, workers seeking overseas employment, including domestic workers, must undergo a skills test in a testing center accredited by the Technical Education and Skills Development Authority (TESDA) and acquire certification before being deployed. Upon completion of the course, there is an assessment, satisfactory completion of which is a precondition for issuance of the Overseas Employment Certificate (OEC) needed to leave the country. TESDA also supports Overseas Filipino Workers (OFWs) who are already in service by offering more than 50 categories of online courses, which are in demand internationally. After taking the course, an OFW can take an assessment in a recognized TESDA center and receive a certificate. In addition to managing the assessment and certification of competencies of OFWs, TESDA also maintains a database to link returning migrants to prospective employers and provides support services through the Permanent Returning Overseas Filipino Workers Network (Tayah 2016). Meanwhile, in Bangladesh, the Bureau of Manpower Employment and Training has been pursuing certification for its training programs that are recognized in overseas markets. In 2017, it revised its curricula in six Technical Training Centers to be eligible for certification from the UK City and Guilds vocational education firm.

Bilateral and multilateral frameworks can reduce costs and improve outcomes

Some institutional frameworks, such as high-quality BLAs, can serve to reduce costs while also providing avenues into new markets—both new destinations and new types of professions. One example is the Korea EPS, which is managed directly by the Human Resources Development Service of Korea and is open to Bangladesh and Nepal. Migrating to Korea for temporary work through this program costs the migrant approximately US$900. However, the migrants are paid Korean minimum wages, are able to change employers, have access to grievance redressal mechanisms, are covered by Korean labor laws against abuse and exploitation, and receive reintegration support (including a lump-sum payment) to Bangladesh upon completion of their contract period (Cho et al. 2018). The program is managed entirely by the Korean government, and it offers high-quality intermediation, whereby employers' needs for skills and workforce size are closely monitored to facilitate rigorous matching of migrant workers to employers.

Another managed migration program is the Bangladesh-Malaysia G2G program, which ran from 2012 to 2018, and which also improved migration-related outcomes while greatly reducing costs (Shrestha, Mobarak, and Sharif 2019). Under this program, the government of Bangladesh—under the auspices of an MOU with the government of Malaysia—sent 18,000 workers in two waves to Malaysia for temporary employment between 2013 and 2018. The program was directly managed by the Bangladesh Ministry of Expatriates' Welfare and Overseas Employment, with the government responsible for all intermediation. Temporary migrants to Malaysia who went through this program incurred substantially lower costs than other migrants, for example, US$520 versus US$4,500. Workers migrating through the G2G also borrowed less and were more likely to have contracts, official clearance from the ministry to migrate, and insurance than were workers migrating through the private sector. The G2G program also ensured better uptake of the predeparture orientation sessions necessary for a safer migration experience. Because of the reduced cost and debt burden, the study estimates that net earnings from a three-year migration, after deducting costs and interest payments, were 87 percent higher under the G2G program than via private channels.

Beyond BLAs, Global Skill Partnerships (GSPs) are a newer, innovative mechanism to structure the sending and receiving country relationship in the interests of both. GSPs have been included under the Global Compact for Safe, Orderly, and Regular Migration, a nonbinding agreement that was adopted in December 2018 by 164 countries under the auspices of the UN General Assembly. The idea of GSPs is that host countries provide technology and financial training for potential migrants before migration, giving them skill sets that companies will need. At the same time, sending countries are usually responsible for providing training to potential migrants. Their labor markets ultimately benefit from those course participants who do not end up migrating (Hooper 2019). Thus, GSPs may help mitigate the problems related to "brain drain" because costs are transferred to migrant-receiving countries and training is provided to migrants and nonmigrants alike (Hooper and Sumption 2016).

Although GSPs have been established in various countries, there is still no clear evidence of their impact. The Australia-Pacific Technical College financed vocational training in five Pacific Island developing countries to increase employment there and in Australia over the period 2007–15.[12] Although the program led to skill creation, it did not lead to skill mobility, given that fewer than 3 percent of the participants migrated to Australia and New Zealand (Clemens, Graham, and Howes 2015). The German development agency, GIZ, facilitates various programs to improve skills training in the health care sector in Kosovo and promotes labor migration from the country to Germany. The backbone of these bilateral labor programs are Kosovar training institutions specializing in nursing that offer a double-track education to locals. One track offers a three-year training program to meet domestic labor market needs in Kosovo; the other track offers skills and German language training aimed at sending students to Germany. The training institutions are usually financed by private sector employers in Kosovo and Germany as well as by German government development agencies (Clemens and Gough 2018). Such labor market programs could effectively interlink the labor market, education, and migration policies in the two countries (Sauer and Meyn 2019).[13]

The principles of the GSPs can be applied more generally to new investments, as illustrated by interventions in the Pacific islands. Tonga is receiving financing of US$20 million by the World Bank and the Australia-Pacific Partnership Trust Fund for a project that aims to provide access to secondary education and vocational training for economically disadvantaged Tongans ages 13 to 55.[14] The project contains a conditional cash transfer program for secondary school enrollment and attendance as well as a program to strengthen the provision of technical and vocational education and training and English language courses.[15] The goal is to prepare Tongans for the local labor market and for the skilled labor mobility programs of countries such as Australia and New Zealand. Scholarships are provided to encourage participation in and completion of skills courses (World Bank 2018b).[16]

Mutual recognition arrangements (MRAs) are another mechanism that some countries have used to recognize the qualifications of foreign workers, but they have limited use in many developing countries (Mendoza and Sugiyarto 2017). These arrangements can be horizontal (covering all occupations between signatories), such as the European Union Professional Qualifications Directive and the Trans-Tasman Mutual Recognition Arrangement between New Zealand and Australia. Vertical MRAs (covering only specific occupations) would include such arrangements as the MRA on Architecture between the United States and Canada, and the Caribbean Community Skills Certificate program. Some regional bodies such as the European Union (through its Professional Qualifications Directive) and the Association of Southeast Asian Nations (through the ASEAN Qualifications Reference Framework) can facilitate cross-country recognition of qualifications across multiple countries simultaneously (Fahmi, Balasingam, and Laguador 2019). A few MRAs have been signed by South Asian countries or institutions. For example, India signed an MRA with Singapore in 2017 for nursing, and Pakistan's Institute of Certified Internal Auditors has an MRA with the Institute of Certified Commercial Professional Accountants and Internal Auditors.

Strengthening institutions for both unilateral and bilateral interventions

Administrative capacity in sending countries will need to increase if G2G programs such as the EPS or the Bangladesh-Malaysia G2G program are to be used further in the future. The improved migration outcomes and lower costs of intermediation are attributed to the public provision of services such as job matching and screening. However, this public provision requires substantial investments in government capacity for sustained service delivery. The Bangladesh-Malaysia G2G program experienced excess demand from aspiring migrants, with about 1.4 million eligible migrants requesting to be placed in the 30,000 vacancies available under the program. The Ministry of Expatriates' Welfare and Overseas Employment's in-house recruitment agency, the Bangladesh Overseas Employment and Services Limited, administers programs similar to, albeit smaller than, the Korea EPS. However, the EPS is a channel for relatively modest migrant labor demand from Korea (relative to labor demand from GCC economies, for example) with a total of roughly 30,000 workers needed from all sending countries combined (Cho et al. 2018). Nepal's relative success, compared with its near neighbors, in maintaining and growing its EPS quotas is a reflection of its successful implementation of the MOU. The government of Nepal has also encouraged EPS workers to return home on time—countries with fewer overstays factor into the EPS formula for determining the migrant worker quota for a given country.

National policy frameworks and legislation can help focus action, but only if conscientiously implemented and enforced. Pakistan's Ministry of Overseas Pakistanis and Human Resource Development has developed a National Emigrants Policy (after several years of preparatory activity), but it has yet to be presented to the federal cabinet for formal approval. In Bangladesh, an Overseas Employment and Migrants Act was passed in 2013 to promote overseas employment and enhance safe migration while supporting the rights and welfare of migrant workers and members of their families. This act included a provision to enhance the regulatory oversight of recruitment agencies. However, the relevant implementing rules—the Recruitment License and Code of Conduct—were not officially circulated until January 2020.

ANNEX 3A: REGRESSION ANALYSIS

The model used to estimate the impact of costs on remittances by Pakistanis working in Saudi Arabia and the United Arab Emirates has the following standard linearized equation:

$$mthremitUSD2016_i = \alpha + \beta_1 rci_i + \beta_2 fornic\_to\_homeninc_i + \beta_3 level\_edu_i + \beta_4 work_i$$
$$+ \beta_5 months\_expect_i + \pi_i + \varepsilon_i.$$

The term $mthremitUSD2016_i$, the estimated monthly remittance during the year of work abroad in 2016 constant US\$ in corridor i, is regressed on rci_i, recruitment costs paid as a multiple of monthly income (recruitment cost indicator) in corridor i. A set of variables controls for recruitment costs in the respective migration corridor: $fornic\_to\_homeninc_i$ is the monthly foreign earnings as a multiple of home earnings earned before migrating; $level\_edu_i$ is the highest level of education completed; $work_i$ is the type of work the migrant does in the host country; $months\_expect_i$ is the number of months the migrant stayed in the host country for the most recent job; finally, π_i is host country fixed effects that capture specific country characteristics. The results are depicted in table 3A.1.

TABLE 3.A1 Results from ordinary least squares regression analysis

	(1)	(2)	(3)	(4)	(5)
rci_i	−14.51***	−12.32***	−11.66***	−11.63***	−10.65***
	(1.521)	(1.478)	(1.376)	(1.365)	(1.322)
$fornic\_to\_homeninc_i$		8.442***	7.851***	8.067***	7.517***
		(3.032)	(2.904)	(2.916)	(2.687)
$level\_edu_i$			17.09***	17.32***	15.74***
			(4.365)	(4.393)	(4.079)
$work_i$				0.132	0.229***
				(0.081)	(0.082)
$months\_expect_i$					3.729***
					(0.534)
Constant	358.7***	299.8***	235.8***	221.1***	121.4***
	(17.13)	(18.43)	(22.48)	(25.39)	(30.67)
Observations	630	512	512	512	512
R-squared	0.207	0.232	0.265	0.267	0.340

Source: KNOMAD-ILO Migration Costs Surveys 2015 and 2016.
Note: The dependent variable for all regressions is $mthremitUSD2016_i$ and includes receiving country fixed effects. Robust standard errors in parentheses. *** $p < 0.01$.

ANNEX 3B: EVENT STUDY

In the event study, migration from South Asia during the past two decades is analyzed on the basis of the following three indicator variables, defined as growth rates:

(1) Oil rent as a share of GDP of the host country, which indicates the economic situation of that country. The following host countries were selected: Bahrain, Japan, Korea, Kuwait, Malaysia, Oman, Qatar, Saudi Arabia, and the United Arab Emirates.

(2) Number of migrants deployed in the host country, which represents the demand for foreign labor migrants in the economy. For Bangladesh, India, Nepal, and Pakistan, the number of deployments for their respective top-five host countries was selected:

- Bangladesh: Malaysia, Oman, Singapore, Saudi Arabia, the United Arab Emirates,
- India: Kuwait, Oman, Qatar, Saudi Arabia, the United Arab Emirates
- Nepal: Kuwait, Malaysia, Qatar, Saudi Arabia, the United Arab Emirates
- Pakistan: Bahrain, Oman, Qatar, Saudi Arabia, the United Arab Emirates

(3) GDP per capita (constant 2010 US$) in the host country as a measure of the strength of the respective host economy. The following host countries were selected: Bahrain, Japan, Korea, Kuwait, Malaysia, Oman, Qatar, Saudi Arabia, and the United Arab Emirates.

(4) Remittances (current US$) are the average amount of remittances that households in Bangladesh, India, Nepal, and Pakistan receive from labor migrants abroad. No differentiation is made between geographical sources (host countries) of the remittances.

ANNEX 3C: SIMULATION MODEL

The model underlying the simulations is GMig—a comparative static, multiregion, multisector, and multifactor computable general equilibrium model that extends the standard Global Trade Analysis Project (GTAP) model (Hertel 1997) to incorporate bilateral migration flows. The GMig model (Walmsley 2002; Walmsley, Winters, and Ahmed 2007) relies on the GMig2 database, a modified version of the GTAP 9 database representing the global economy in 2011 that incorporates data on bilateral migrant labor and wages by skill and bilateral remittance flows (Walmsley, Ahmed, and Parsons 2005). For the purpose of the simulations, the GMig2 database has been aggregated into 20 countries or regions (table 3C.1) and 11 sectors (table 3C.2).

The core specification of the GMig model broadly replicates a standard global comparative static computable general equilibrium model. Production is specified as a series of nested constant elasticity of substitution functions using various inputs—unskilled and skilled labor, capital, land, and natural resources. Labor is assumed to be perfectly mobile across sectors, with an aggregate economywide wage clearing the labor markets. Demand by each domestic agent is specified at the so-called Armington level, that is, demand for a bundle of

TABLE 3C.1 **Regional aggregation**

	REGION CODE	DESCRIPTION
1	BGD	Bangladesh
2	IND	India
3	NPL	Nepal
4	PAK	Pakistan
5	LKA	Sri Lanka
6	XSA	Rest of South Asia
7	XGCC	Rest of GCC
8	QAT	Qatar
9	SAU	Saudi Arabia
10	UAE	United Arab Emirates
11	XMN	Rest of Middle East and North Africa
12	MYS	Malaysia
13	JPN	Japan
14	KOR	Republic of Korea
15	HKG	Hong Kong SAR, China
16	XEA	Rest of East Asia
17	SSA	Sub-Saharan Africa
18	ECA	Eastern Europe and Central Asia
19	LAC	Latin America and the Caribbean
20	WOECD	Western Organisation for Economic Co-operation and Development countries

TABLE 3C.2 **Sector aggregation**

	SECTOR CODE	DESCRIPTION
1	AGR	Agriculture
2	TWL	Textiles, wearing apparel, and leather
3	MNFC	Manufacturing
4	COG	Other extractives and minerals
5	EXTRACT	Coal, oil, and gas extraction
6	P_C	Petro-chemicals
7	CONS	Construction
8	SVCS	Services
9	TRDTRS	Trade and transport
10	ROS	Recreational services, including domestic
11	OSG	Other services

domestically produced and imported goods. Armington demand is aggregated across all agents and allocated at the national level between domestic production and imports by region of origin.

The GMig2 model extends the GTAP model to consider skilled and unskilled bilateral labor movement across countries. The model distinguishes between domestic and foreign workers by sector of employment. Foreign and domestic workers of the same skill type are treated as imperfect substitutes, but there is no distinction between foreign countries. Migration flows can be determined either exogenously or endogenously in response to changes in relative real wages. Endogenously, the supply of labor migration is assumed to respond to changes in the expected real wages between the sending and potential receiving region. Explicitly representing bilateral migration flows allows for the quantification of their impact on growth, remittances, and the real incomes of migrants and permanent residents.

GMig distinguishes between incomes of permanent residents, existing migrants, new migrants, and return migrants. The income of permanent residents depends on the change in income from nonlabor and labor endowments and remittances received from workers abroad. Permanent residents are assumed to receive all the income on capital and tax revenues. The income of an existing migrant is a function of the migrant's labor income less remittances sent to the home country. Similarly, the change in income of new migrants is also determined by their labor income less remittances, and less the labor income they received before they migrated.

Remittances sent from the host country back to the home country are assumed to be a constant proportion of income. An increase in the number of new migrants or their wages results in an increase in remittances. The outflow of remittances reduces the income of the migrants and increases the incomes of permanent residents in the home country. In turn, inflows of remittances have an impact on the balance of payments of the home country: an increase in remittances is associated with an improvement in the current account balance, which is offset by an appreciation of the real exchange rate and a decline in the trade balance, maintaining balance of payments equilibrium.

NOTES

1. These estimates are based on data from the Household Income and Expenditure Survey Bangladesh 2016/17 and the Nepal Household Risk and Vulnerability Survey 2016.
2. An important caveat to the statistical analysis is that although the results show associations, they do not necessarily support causality. Unobservable characteristics and omitted variables could also play a role, and could include nonpecuniary benefits or costs of moving abroad, which could make migrants willing to invest in higher costs in exchange for lower earnings and remittances.
3. Tobit regressions are run as a robustness check.
4. In the Nepal-Malaysia and Nepal–Saudi Arabia corridors, the results are not statistically significant and the standard errors are large, possibly because of the small sample size.
5. Chapter 1 discusses BLAs and MOUs in greater detail.
6. Based on key informant interviews and focus group discussions (Khadka 2018a, 2018b).
7. The magnitude of the results should be interpreted keeping in mind that they do not capture noneconomic benefits of the diversification of South Asian labor migration flows. Nonmonetary benefits such as better working and living conditions and less exposure to host country shocks are not captured. An awareness of the underlying assumptions and closure rules is very important in the interpretation of the results.
8. Note that these are estimates expressed in 2027 US dollars.
9. The measures are discussed in chapter 1.
10. For example, in Pakistan, migration-management responsibilities sit with the Ministry of Overseas Pakistanis and Human Resource Development, while in Bangladesh, one of the largest providers of technical skills training, the Bureau of Manpower Employment and Training, is also a core agency under the Ministry of Expatriates' Welfare and Overseas Employment.

11. Based on December 2019 data from Remittances Prices Worldwide, maintained by the World Bank.

12. Participating Pacific Island countries were Fiji, Papua New Guinea, Samoa, the Solomon Islands, and Vanuatu. The most common subjects taught at the Australia-Pacific Technical College were automotive, construction, electrical, manufacturing, hospitality and tourism, community, and health services (Clemens, Graham, and Howes 2015).

13. Various labor market programs between Germany and Kosovo in the health care sector are in place, but it is difficult to assess their effectiveness because of the lack of comprehensive data.

14. The project runs over the period 2018–23.

15. In the conditional cash transfer program for secondary school enrollment and attendance, the amount of cash transfers is 360 Tongan pa'anga (US$170) per school term or quarter, or 1,440 pa'anga (US$680) per year (World Bank 2018b).

16. The scholarship provided is up to 1,800 pa'anga (US$900) annually per beneficiary to cover tuition for the training course.

REFERENCES

Abella, Manolo, and Geoffrey Ducanes. 2009. "The Effect of the Global Economic Crisis on Asian Migrant Workers and Governments' Responses." *Asian and Pacific Migration Journal* 18 (1).

Abraham, Rhea. 2018. "Getting Qatar Ready for 2022: Reforms in Labor Immigration Policy and India's Options." Middle East Institute. https://www.mei.edu/publications /qatar-labor-immigration-policy-and-india.

Ahmed, Shamsun Naher. 1998. "The Impact of the Asian Crisis on Migrant Workers: Bangladesh Perspectives." *Asian and Pacific Migration Journal* 2 (3): 369–93.

Al-Lamki, Salma Mohammed. 2000. "Omanization: A Three Tier Strategic Framework for Human Resource Management and Training in the Sultanate of Oman." *Journal of Comparative International Management* 3 (1): 55–75.

Amnesty International. 2010. "Trapped: The Exploitation of Migrant Workers in Malaysia." Amnesty International, London.

Angelucci, Manuela. 2015. "Migration and Financial Constraints: Evidence from Mexico." *Review of Economics and Statistics* 97 (1): 224–28.

ADBI, OECD, and ILO (Asian Development Bank Institute, Organisation for Economic Co-operation and Development, and International Labour Organization). 2019. *Building Partnerships for Effectively Managing Labor Migration: Lessons from Asian Countries.* Tokyo: ADB Institute.

Bossavie, Laurent, Joseph-Simon Görlach, Çağlar Özden, and He Wang. 2021. "Temporary Migration for Long-term Investment." Background paper for *Toward Safer and More Productive Migration for South Asia*, World Bank, Washington, DC.

Bhuyan, Owassim Udin. 2018. "Malaysia Freezes Hiring Workers from Bangladesh thru Govt Channel." New Age. http://www.newagebd.net/article/44294/malaysia-freezes -hiring-workers-from-bangladesh-thru-govt-channel.

Bryan, Gharad, Shyamal Chowdhury, and Ahmed Mushfiq Mobarak. 2014. "Underinvestment in a Profitable Technology: The Case of Seasonal Migration in Bangladesh." *Econometrica* 82 (5): 1671–748.

Buckley, Michelle, Adam Zendel, Jeff Biggar, Lia Frederiksen, and Jill Wells. 2016. *Migrant Work & Employment in the Construction Sector.* Geneva: International Labour Office.

Callen, Tim, Reda Cherif, Fuad Hasanov, Amgad Hegazy, and Padamja Khandelwal. 2014. "Economic Diversification in the GCC: Past, Present, and Future." Staff Discussion Note 14/12, International Monetary Fund, Washington, DC.

Carey, Glen. 2013. "Saudi Arabia Tackles Illegal Labor in Job-Creation Push." Bloomberg. https://www.bloomberg.com/news/articles/2013-04-04/saudi-arabia-tackles -illegal-labor-in-job-creation-push.

Cho, Yoonyoung, Anastasiya Denisova, Soonhwa Yi, and Upasana Khadka. 2018. "Lessons from Korea's Employment Permit System: Bilateral Arrangement of Temporary Labor Migration." World Bank, Washington, DC.

Clemens, Michael A., and Kate Gough. 2018. "A Tool to Implement the Global Compact for Migration: Ten Key Steps for Building Global Skills Partnerships." CGD Brief, Center for Global Development, Washington, DC.

Clemens, Michael A., Colum Graham, and Stephen Howes. 2015. "Skill Development and Regional Mobility: Lessons from the Australia-Pacific Technical College." *Journal of Development Studies* 51 (11): 1502–17.

Coogle, Adam. 2015. "Detained, Beaten, Deported: Saudi Abuses against Migrants during Mass Expulsions." Human Rights Watch.

Dajani, Haneen. 2011. "Pay Rises of Up to 45% for All Federal Government Employees." The National. https://www.thenational.ae/uae/pay-rises-of-up-to-45-for-all-federal -government-employees-1.380953.

De Bel-Air, Françoise. 2018. "Demography, Migration and Labor Market in Saudi Arabia." Explanation Note. Gulf Labour Markets, Migration and Population (GLMM) Programme Publications, European University Institute (EUI) and Gulf Research Center (GRC).

Deloitte. 2018. "Has the Industry Turned the Corner? Deloitte GCC Powers of Construction 2018." https://www2.deloitte.com/xe/en/pages/real-estate/articles/gcc-powers-construction-2018 .html.

Dustmann, Christian, and Joseph-Simon Görlach. 2016. "The Economics of Temporary Migrations." *Journal of Economic Literature* 54 (1): 98–136.

Dustmann, Christian, and Oliver Kirchkamp. 2002. "Migration Duration and Activity Choice after Re-Migration." *Journal of Development Economics* 67 (2): 351–72.

Economic Times. 2007. "India, Qatar Ink Pact to Protect Rights of Expatriate Workers." November 20. https://economictimes.indiatimes.com/jobs/india-qatar-ink-pact-to-protect -rights-of-expatriate-workers/articleshow/2556740.cms?from=mdr.

Fahmi, Zita M., Usharani Balasingam, and Jake M. Laguador. 2019. "ASEAN Qualification Reference Framework: Harmonization of ASEAN Higher Education Area." In *ASEAN Post-50: Emerging Issues and Challenges*, edited by Aida Idris and Nurliana Kamaruddin, 101–34. Singapore: Palgrave Macmillan.

Forstenlechner, Ingo, and Emilie Jan Rutledge. 2011. "The GCC's 'Demographic Imbalance': Perceptions, Realities and Policy Opinions." *Middle East Policy Council* XVIII (4): 25–43.

Habibi, Nader. 2009. "The Impact of the Global Economic Crisis on Arab Countries: A Year-End Assessment." Crown Center for Middle East Studies, Brandeis University.

Hertel, Thomas. 1997. *Global Trade Analysis: Modeling and Applications*. Cambridge: Cambridge University Press.

Hertog, Steffen. 2012. "A Comparative Assessment of Labor Market Nationalization Policies in the GCC." In *National Employment, Migration and Education in the GCC*, edited by Steffen Hertog, 65–106. Berlin: Gerlach Press.

Hooper, Kate. 2019. "Towards a Global Compact for Migration: A Development Perspective." Policy Brief, Migration Policy Institute.

Hooper, Kate, and Madeleine Sumption. 2015. "Reaching a Fair Deal on Talent: Emigration, Circulation and Human Capital in Countries of Origin." In *A Fair Deal on Talent: Fostering Just Migration Governance: Lessons from around the Globe*, 105–31. Gütersloh, Germany: Verlag Bertelsmann Stiftung.

IOM (International Organization for Migration). 2011. *Labour Migration from Colombo Process Countries: Good Practices, Challenges and Ways Forward*. Geneva: International Organization for Migration.

Khadka, Upasana. 2018a. "The Migrant's Journey—Bangladesh." Unpublished.

Khadka, Upasana. 2018b. "The Migrant's Journey—Nepal." Unpublished.

Khaleej Times. 2015. "New Human Resources Authority Set Up in Abu Dhabi." November 22. https://www.khaleejtimes.com/nation/government/new-human-resources-authority -set-up-in-capital.

Khamis, May, and Abdelhak Senhadji. 2010. *Impact of the Global Financial Crisis on the Gulf Cooperation Council Countries and Challenges Ahead.* Washington, DC: International Monetary Fund.

Kibira, Nazil. 2011. "Working Hard for the Money: Bangladesh Faces Challenges of Large-Scale Labor Migration." Migration Policy Institute. https://www.migrationpolicy.org/article /working-hard-money-bangladesh-faces-challenges-large-scale-labor-migration.

KNOMAD-ILO Migration Costs Survey 2015 & 2016. World Bank, Washington, DC.

Lokshin, Michael, Mikhail Bontch-Osmolovski, and Elena Glinskaya. 2011. "Work-Related Migration and Poverty Reduction in Nepal." In *Migration and Poverty: Toward Better Opportunities for the Poor,* edited by Edmundo Murrugarra, Jennica Larisson, and Marcin Sasin, 35–62. Washington, DC: World Bank.

Malit, Froilan T., Jr., and Ali Al Youha. 2013. "Labor Migration in the United Arab Emirates: Challenges and Responses." Migration Policy Institute. https://www.migrationpolicy.org /article/labor-migration-united-arab-emirates-challenges-and-responses.

Mendoza, D. R., and G. Sugiyarto. 2017. *The Long Road Ahead: Status Report on the Implementation of the ASEAN Mutual Recognition Arrangements on Professional Services.* Manila: Asian Development Bank.

Netto, Anil. 2001. "Malaysia: Ban on Bangladesh Workers Pushes Search for Cheap Labour." Interpress Service News Agency. http://www.ipsnews.net/2001/02/malaysia-ban-on -bangladesh-workers-pushes-search-for-cheap-labour/.

Peck, Jennifer R. 2017. "Can Hiring Quotas Work? The Effect of the Nitaqat Program on the Saudi Private Sector." *American Economic Journal: Economic Policy* 8 (1): 316–47.

Pillai, Patrick. 1999. "The Malaysian State's Response to Migration." *Sojourn: Journal of Social Issues in Southeast Asia* 14 (1): 178–97.

Randeree, Kasim. 2012. "Workforce Nationalization in the Gulf Cooperation Council States." Center for International and Regional Studies. School of Foreign Service in Qatar, Georgetown University.

Ruppert Bulmer, Elizabeth, Ami Shresta, and Michelle Marshalian. 2020. *Nepal Jobs Diagnostic.* Jobs Series 22, World Bank, Washington, DC.

Saif, Ibrahim. 2009. "The Oil Boom in the GCC Countries, 2002–2008: Old Challenges, Changing Dynamics." Carnegie Papers, Carnegie Middle East Center, Beirut.

Sarker, Rayhena. 2016. "Migration and Employment: A Study of Bangladeshi Male Migrant Workers in Malaysia." In *International Migration in Southeast Asia: Continuities and Discontinuities,* edited by Kwen Fee Lian, Md Mizanur Rahman, and Yabit bin Alas, Vol. 2, 125–48. Singapore: Springer.

Sauer, Michael, and Andreas Meyn. 2019. "Mobility and Skills Partnership: Linking Labour Migration and VET Policies in Kosovo." In *Politics & Governance.*

Shrestha, Maheshwor, Ahmed Mushfiq Mobarak, and Iffath Anwar Sharif. 2019. *Migration and Remittances: The Impacts of a Government Intermediated International Migration Program.* Washington, DC: World Bank.

Tayah, Marie-Jose. 2016. "Skills Development and Recognition for Domestic Workers across Borders." International Labour Organization, Geneva. www.ilo.org/wcmsp5/groups/public /---ed_protect/---protrav/---migrant/documents/briefingnote/wcms_533536.pdf.

UAE Ministry of Labour. 2007. "The Protection of the Rights of Workers in the United Arab Emirates, Annual Report." UAE Ministry of Labour, Dubai.

Wahba, Jackline. 2015. "Selection, Selection, Selection: The Impact of Return Migration." *Journal of Population Economics* 28 (3): 535–63.

Walmsley, Terrie L. 2002. "Incorporating International Ownership of Endowments into a Global Applied General Equilibrium Model." *Economic Modelling* 19 (5): 679–707.

Walmsley, Terrie, Angel Aguiar, and S. Amer Ahmed. 2017. "Labour Migration and Economic Growth in East and South-East Asia." *World Economy* 40 (1): 116–39.

Walmsley, Terrie L., S. Amer Ahmed, and Chris Parsons. 2005. "The Impact of Liberalizing Labor Mobility in the Pacific Region." Working Paper 283449, Purdue University, Center for Global Trade Analysis, Global Trade Analysis Project.

Walmsley, Terrie L., Alan L. Winters, and S. Amer Ahmed. 2007. "Measuring the Impact of the Movement of Labor Using a Model of Bilateral Migration Flows." GTAP Technical Paper 28, Global Trade Analysis Project, Purdue University.

Wickramasekara, Piyasiri. 2016. *Review of the Government-to-Government Mechanism for the Employment of Bangladeshi Workers in the Malaysian Plantation Sector*. Geneva: International Labour Organization.

World Bank. 2018a. "Institutional Assessment of Migration Systems in Bangladesh: Initial Findings Meant to Inform Future Areas for Bank Support on Policy Reforms and Capacity Building." World Bank, Washington, DC.

World Bank. 2018b. "Skills and Employment for Tongans Project." International Development Association Project Appraisal Document. Report PAD2432, World Bank, Washington, DC.

World Bank. 2019. "Indonesia: Information Dissemination to Achieve Safe Labor Migration." World Bank, Washington, DC.

4 Harnessing the Development Potential of Return Migration

INTRODUCTION

The temporary nature of labor mobility is a prominent feature of migration from South Asia and many other countries of origin. Low-skilled labor migrants from South Asia typically work for a few years in destination countries before returning to home labor markets. The existing literature, however, typically treats migration as a permanent, one-time event. One reason behind the lack of focus on temporary and return migration is the large data requirements for this type of analysis, combined with the scarcity of relevant microdata (Ahmed et al. 2021; Dustmann and Görlach 2016; Wahba 2014). As a result, studies of labor migration as a temporary phenomenon are few, particularly for South Asia, where temporary migration prevails but suitable microdata are particularly scarce.

Temporary migration from South Asia not only affects migrants' welfare during their migration episode, but also has longer-term dynamic effects after migrants have returned home. Making migration safer and more productive should not only involve interventions before and during migration, but also at the postmigration stage. By bringing financial and human capital back home, temporary migration can increase workers' productivity, help return migrants start up entrepreneurial activities, and help migrants gain access to higher-paying employment back home (Bossavie et al. 2021; Dustmann and Kirchkamp 2002; Piracha and Vadean 2009; Reinhold and Thom 2013; Wahba 2015a). As such, temporary migration can benefit the migrants themselves, their households, and the home economy even after the migration episode has ended.

Interventions to maximize the benefits of return migration cannot, therefore, be developed in isolation: they must be linked to the other stages of the migration cycle. Policies targeted at return migrants need to consider the dynamic nature of temporary migration and its role in workers' active life cycles. They must also take into account the heterogeneity of migration experiences and temporary migrants' wide variety of circumstances of return. These differences mean a wide range of policy interventions need to be implemented; for example, a migrant who was forced to return may need a very different set of interventions from those needed by somebody who returns voluntarily after accumulating enough savings to start up a business.

This chapter relies heavily on a survey specifically designed for this book, the World Bank Bangladesh Return Migrant Survey 2018/19 (BRMS 2018/19) (box 4.1). The survey is unique in South Asia: it retrospectively collected very detailed information on the entire employment and migration history of temporary migrants after they had returned home.[1] This approach permits analysis of return migration as an integral part of migrants' entire life cycles. The chapter also uses data from standard national household surveys—from Bangladesh, Nepal, and Pakistan—that include migration modules, and from the KNOMAD-ILO Migration and Recruitment Costs Surveys conducted for specific corridors between South Asian countries and high-income destinations. Although these surveys only capture a portion of the migration and employment history of return migrants, they provide valuable information on the postreturn outcomes of temporary migrants, which can be linked to basic parameters of the migration experience such as duration of stay and migration costs.

This chapter describes the regulatory and institutional features of low-skilled migration from South Asia that make return mandatory; highlights the interconnections between choice of destination, duration of stay, activity after return,

---

BOX 4.1

The Bangladesh Return Migrant Survey 2018/19

The Bangladesh Return Migrant Survey 2018/19 (BRMS 2018/19) is a unique household survey data set in South Asia designed to support this book and conducted from November 2018 to June 2019. It covered 5,000 households with at least one member who had returned from work overseas after 2009. It used the 2011 Bangladesh Census as a sampling frame to be representative of returning migrants in rural and semi-urban areas of Bangladesh. The survey reflects an understanding that temporary migration decisions are part of workers' life-cycle optimization processes, and it incorporates several attractive features for the study of temporary labor migration.

The survey collected information on the entire employment history (both in Bangladesh and abroad) of return migrants from the time they left school. This approach permits reconstruction of the full employment trajectories of migrant workers. The survey includes detailed information on all migration episodes, including destination country, duration of stay, labor market outcomes at destination, and reasons for returning, among others. To the best of the authors' knowledge, it and the Mexican Migration Project are the only data sets that capture retrospective information on the entire work history of temporary migrants. Unlike most surveys of temporary migrants, it also collects detailed information on the costs of each

migration episode, including cost breakdowns by item and sources of finance.

The BRMS 2018/19 also collects information on migrants' expectations regarding wages and savings, enabling a comparison to be made between these expectations and actual migration outcomes to identify whether expectations have been met. Again, to the best of the authors' knowledge, this is the only survey on temporary migrants to date that captures this type of information. This cost information provides a measure of the incidence and extent of disappointment among temporary migrants so as to investigate its association with behavior and choices, such as duration of stay abroad.

The survey captures information on the experience abroad during the most recent migration episode, such as remittances sent, monthly expenses and savings, difficulties encountered abroad, and overall impressions of the migration experience. Information about future intentions to migrate abroad is collected. Finally, the survey also includes a detailed module on household enterprises and assets. The survey sample size is larger than analogous surveys in countries of origin, allowing a more thorough and illuminating investigation to be made of the heterogeneity of migrant experiences. The BRMS 2018/19 is described in more detail in Ahmed et al. (2021).

and intention to remigrate; analyzes the home labor market outcomes of return migrants; and discusses potential policies to increase the benefits of return migration for the migrants themselves, their households, and the home economy.

PREVALENCE OF RETURN MIGRATION IN SOUTH ASIA

Permanent migration of low-skilled migrants from South Asia is prohibited in the main destination countries. In general, conditions of entry and legal status in the destination country affect migrants' return decisions (Wahba 2014). In various destination countries, migrants with permanent residence rights have been shown to return considerably less often than migrants with temporary residence rights (OECD 2008). Meanwhile, the main countries that host migrants from South Asia—primarily in the Gulf Cooperation Council (GCC) and Southeast Asia—only grant temporary residence rights to low-skilled labor migrants. In the GCC countries, the acquisition of citizenship by a migrant worker is effectively prohibited, irrespective of duration of residence (Fargues 2011; Fargues and De Bel-Air 2015; Wahba 2015b).[2]

Stays in the main destinations are strictly tied to labor contracts. Low-skilled workers from South Asia cannot migrate to the GCC or Southeast Asia without holding a labor contract, usually fixed term, and an accompanying work permit. In addition, their stay at destination is strictly conditional on holding a valid employment contract and work permit. Temporary migrants can have their labor contracts and work permits renewed at destination if the employer still wants their services. However, expiration of the employment contract without renewal, or a layoff by the employer at destination, automatically entails return to the home country.[3]

As a result, the main reason for returning home among migrants from South Asia is the end of their employment contract abroad. In this institutional setting, losing a job, or expiration of an employment contract, will be the principal reasons for return. The termination of employment abroad is reported as the main reason for returning home by labor migrants from Bangladesh and Nepal, according to the BRMS 2018/19 and the 2017/18 Labor Force Survey for Nepal. Because of the regulations governing migration to the main destinations, labor migrants from South Asia are therefore particularly vulnerable to labor demand shocks in destination countries. The risk of job loss for labor migrants is exacerbated by the heavy dependence of labor demand on international oil prices in the main GCC destinations.

Restrictions on family migration to the main destinations increase the incentives to return. In the GCC countries, work permits do not allow the spouse and family to accompany the migrant unless the migrant's income is above a given threshold set significantly higher than the mean wage of low-skilled migrants.[4] In any case, even these state-mandated minimums often prove insufficient to cover the actual costs of living of an entire family in a GCC country (Gardner 2011). Similarly, in Malaysia and Singapore, holders of temporary low-skilled work permits are not allowed to bring dependents or to marry while at destination. As a result, the vast majority of labor migrants from South Asia leave their families behind.[5] These restrictions are a significant nonpecuniary cost for migrants. By increasing the relative value of consumption and leisure at home (Dustmann and Kirchkamp 2002), a close family and social milieu there provides another incentive to stay at destination for a shorter period. Evidence from Bangladesh shows that family structure at origin has a bearing on duration of stay abroad: migrants who were married before departure return on average two years earlier than their unmarried colleagues.

Forced returns have risen in recent years and are expected to rise further because of the tightening of regulations in several destination countries. A sizable share of temporary migrants from South Asia are forced to return, mainly from deportation for overstay. In Bangladesh, for example, about 12 percent of return migrants report that the reason for returning was being expelled from the host country because of work permit or visa issues, according to the responses to the BRMS 2018/19. Recent years have been marked by a tightening of policies regarding repatriation of illegal migrants in the European Union and the GCC countries (World Bank 2018a). In the European Union, the number of potential returnees—rejected asylum seekers and migrants lacking valid documents—rose from 1.4 million in 2011 to about 5.5 million in 2017. In Saudi Arabia, deportations increased from 594,000 in 2012 to 665,000 in 2013, falling only slightly to 461,000 in 2017. Cumulatively, about 3.9 million migrants were deported from Saudi Arabia between March 2011 and August 2018, an annual average rate of more than 500,000 (World Bank 2018a).

Forced returns have also increased sharply in the context of the COVID-19 (coronavirus) pandemic, which has highlighted the specific support needs among the population of forced returnees. Migrants from South Asia are concentrated in destination countries that were strongly hit by the dual shock of the COVID-19 pandemic and a collapse in oil prices. The reduction in materials, capital, and intermediate inputs due to disrupted business and transport activities has substantially affected supply (Arezki and Nguyen 2020). Because the labor-intensive, low-skilled sectors have been hit disproportionately—and migrants can only stay with a valid employment contract—hundreds of thousands of labor migrants have been returning to South Asia. An estimated 250,000 Bangladeshis returned to the country between January and April of 2020, and estimates suggest that up to 2 million may have returned in subsequent months. Similarly, the government of Nepal has been preparing to repatriate 400,000 displaced workers (IOM 2020). By May of 2020, about 60,000 Pakistanis were registered to return from the United Arab Emirates alone (Al Jazeera 2020). Once back home, return migrants can face multiple challenges, including lack of employment opportunities, limited access to social safety nets, and even discrimination by community members fearful that migrants may transmit COVID-19. In addition, when they return unexpectedly and prematurely, as during the pandemic, returnees often face the additional challenge of large debt burdens with high interest rates as a consequence of high migration costs. Although the COVID-19 pandemic underscored these needs, they did exist earlier, and they still apply to migrants who unexpectedly return to their home countries for other reasons.

At present, the return patterns of South Asian migrants cannot be tracked. No administrative records show how long migrants from South Asia stay overseas and when they return home (Ahmed at al. 2021),[6] which has been a major impediment to gain a better understanding of temporary migrants' decisions to return and to identify policies that could help the development potential of return migration to be realized. Administrative data in the home countries (Bangladesh, Nepal, and Pakistan) record exits but not returns. Receiving countries in the GCC and Southeast Asia have similarly not made any administrative data recording the entry and exit of temporary migrants accessible. The only micro-data sources available in South Asia—offering some evidence on the duration of stay of temporary migrants—are national household surveys and dedicated surveys capturing temporary migrants upon their return, such as the recent BRMS 2018/19. Comprehensive return migrant surveys, however, remain very scarce globally, including for South Asia.

Duration of stay at destination for South Asian migrants estimated from survey data is typically a couple of years (figure 4.1). A few nationally representative household surveys allow estimation of duration of stay at destination, albeit only for a selected subset of temporary migrants who went overseas.[7] The Nepal Living Standards Survey 2010/11 asks any household member present at the time of the survey who ever went abroad to provide their date of departure and return. The median duration of stay abroad of return migrants captured by the survey is two years. The more recent 2017/18 Labor Force Survey in Nepal collects information on how long absentees from the household have been overseas, but not on the duration of completed stays (episodes of residence) for return migrants. The median duration of stay abroad of a family member currently absent from the household for work overseas is also two years. For Bangladesh, the average duration of stay at destination of migrants who were still overseas at the time of the survey (current migrants) and those who had already returned (return migrants) is five years (for both categories), according to the BRMS 2018/19 and the Household Income and Expenditure Survey 2016/17. For Pakistan, the only source available for estimating duration of stay is the 2015 KNOMAD-ILO Migration and Recruitment Costs Survey, which collects information on the number of months spent at destination for specific migration corridors. For return migrants from Pakistan who had worked in Saudi Arabia and the United Arab Emirates, the average duration of stay at destination is two years and one and a half years, respectively.[8]

INTERCONNECTIONS BETWEEN MIGRANTS' DEPARTURE, DESTINATION, DURATION OF STAY, AND ACTIVITIES AFTER RETURN

Although return is mandatory for low-skilled migrants from South Asia, duration of stay overseas varies substantially. Initial labor contracts and work permits in the main host countries of South Asian migrants are typically granted for one or two years. However, temporary migrants may extend their stay by renewing their labor contract with their employer. According to the BRMS 2018/19, only 1 percent of temporary migrants had more than one employer while at destination, suggesting that an extension or renewal of the existing labor contract is the main way to extend duration of stay at destination.[9] As a result, duration of stay varies substantially among temporary migrants returning to Bangladesh, for example (figure 4.2). Roughly a quarter of migrants stayed abroad less than two years, while 23 percent stayed in their last destination abroad for work for more than 10 years. The median and average durations of stay among migrants to all destinations are 4.7 and 6.5 years, respectively. However, stays of longer than 10 years are not uncommon (except in Qatar). Less variation in duration of stay is observed among temporary migrants from Nepal and Pakistan. The median duration of stay is 2 years for return migrants in both countries and stays of more than 10 years are rare.[10]

FIGURE 4.1

Number of years spent overseas by temporary migrants from South Asia

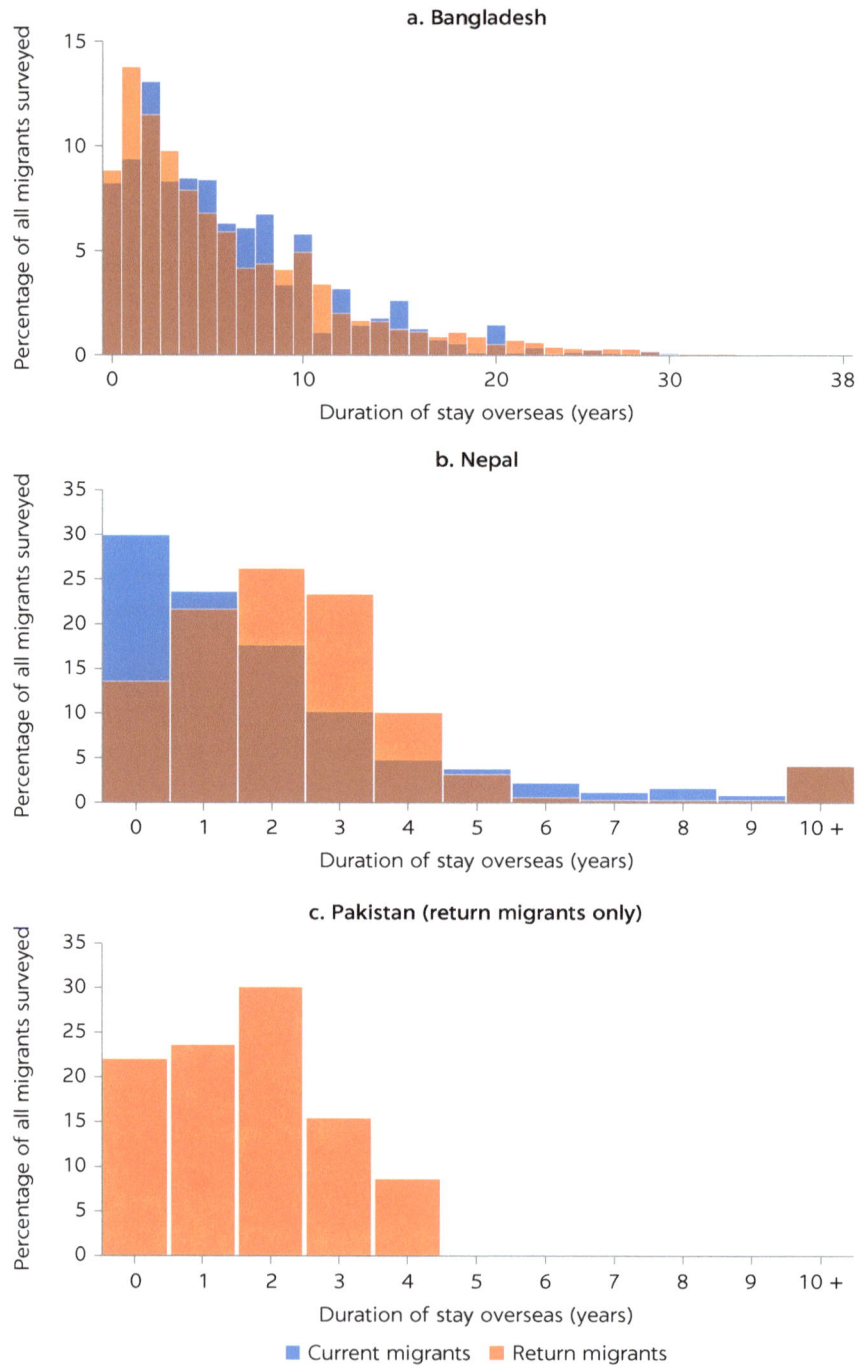

a. Bangladesh

b. Nepal

c. Pakistan (return migrants only)

■ Current migrants ■ Return migrants

Sources: World Bank calculations from the Bangladesh Household Income and Expenditure Survey 2016/17 and Bangladesh Return Migrant Survey 2018/19 for current migrants and return migrants in Bangladesh, respectively; from the Labor Force Survey 2018 and National Living Standards Survey 2010/11 for current migrants and return migrants from Nepal, respectively; and from the KNOMAD-ILO Migration and Recruitment Costs Survey for Pakistan.

Note: Statistics are for males ages 18–59 and account for sampling weights. Current migrants are defined as workers who were overseas for work at the time of the survey. Return migrants are defined as workers who went overseas for work in the past but had returned to the home country at the time of the survey. The duration of stay of current migrants refers to migration spells that have not been completed yet. Statistics for Pakistan only include return migrants from Saudi Arabia and the United Arab Emirates.

FIGURE 4.2

Number of years spent abroad by return migrants from Bangladesh, by country of destination

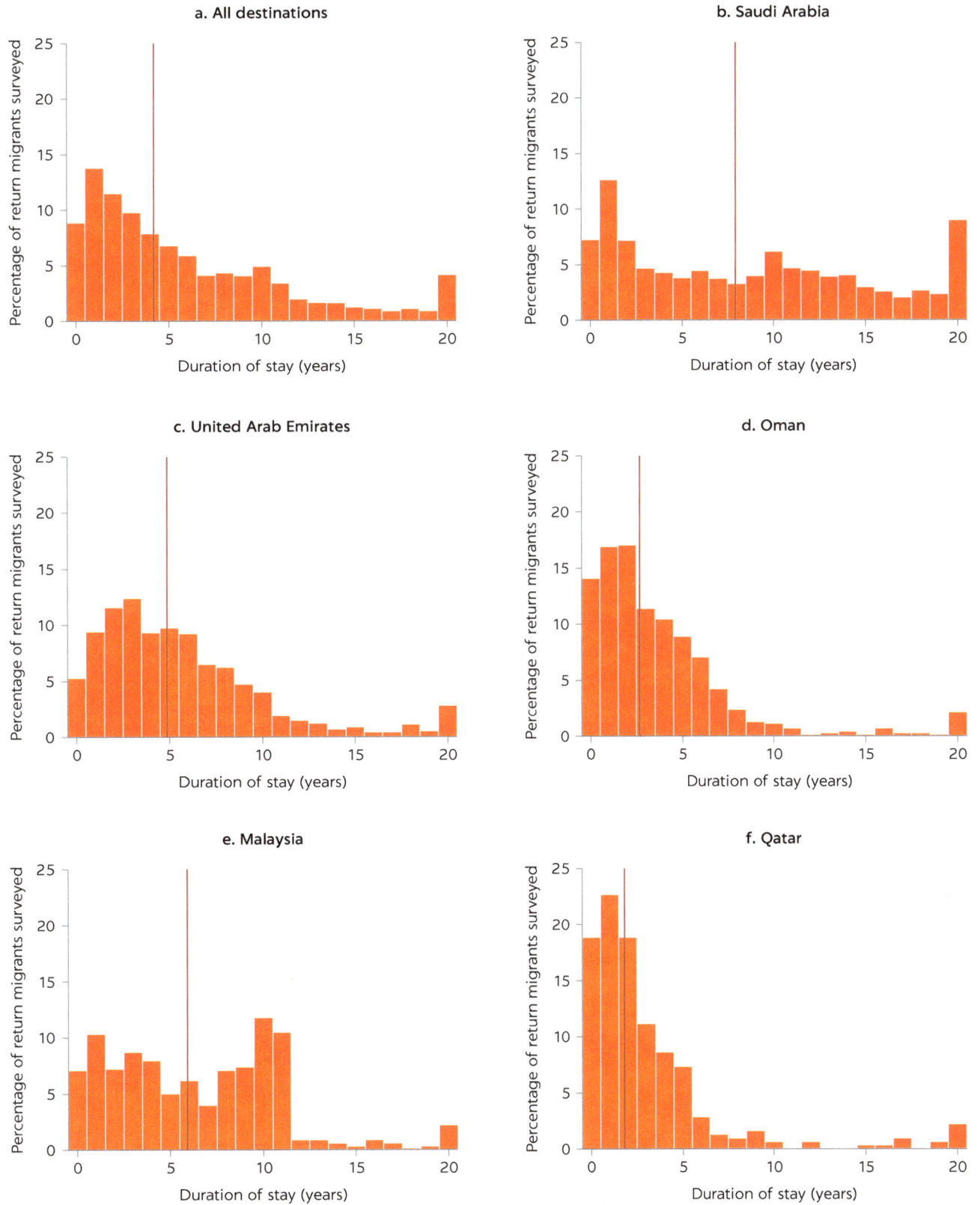

Sources: Ahmed et al. (2021) based on data from the Bangladesh Return Migrant Survey 2018/19.
Note: Statistics are for males ages 18–59. The y-axis shows the percentage of migrants who have stayed overseas for a given number of years. Vertical red lines show median duration of stay by destination.

Duration of stay varies by destination, but also among migrants returning from the same destination. Among temporary migrants from Bangladesh, the median duration of stay in Saudi Arabia is 8.4 years, but only 2.1 years in Qatar—two of the top five destinations for temporary migrants (figure 4.2). Clearly, the length of stay is influenced by factors specific to a country, especially regulations. Duration of stay, however, also varies among temporary migrants who have returned from the same destination (having been exposed to the same legal constraints). Shorter stays of one or two years are the most common in all top destination countries, but longer stays of more than five years are also very common in all destinations (except Qatar). In Malaysia, a high concentration of stays between 8 and 10 years is observed, followed by a sharp drop in stays beyond 10 years because of the regulation capping the cumulative duration of stay of temporary migrants. Therefore, labor migrants are able to adjust their duration of stay to maximize intertemporal utility, even when legal restrictions on duration of stay are tight.

Duration of stay at destination is influenced by a number of factors. When returns are planned as part of the migrant's life-cycle optimization strategy, duration of stay at destination can be affected by the relative purchasing power of savings at home and in the host country (Dustmann 1995, 1997, 2003), location-specific preferences for consumption (Djajic and Milbourne 1988; Hill 1987), and longer-term benefits that accrue from the human and financial capital accumulated in the host country (Stark 1991). Returns, however, may be unplanned and may occur because of unexpected changes in economic or noneconomic conditions at home (Dustmann 2003; Dustmann and Kirchkamp 2002), imperfect information resulting in lower earnings and savings than originally expected (Borjas and Bratsberg 1996), or early termination of employment by the employer.

Migrants' labor market outcomes at destination influence return decisions. In a life-cycle framework in which migrants choose duration of stay to maximize lifetime gains from migration, employment outcomes and wages at destination affect return decisions (Akee and Jones 2019; Bijwaard and Wahba 2014, 2019; Bossavie et al. 2021; Dustmann 2003; Dustmann and Kirchkamp 2002; Yang 2006). If migrants simply balanced the marginal benefits of working abroad with its marginal cost, they would extend their stay overseas in response to higher wages (the life-cycle hypothesis; Dustmann 2003).[11] However, if they were target savers and planned to return home upon attainment of their target, an increase in earnings overseas would make them return earlier (the savings targeting hypothesis; Mesnard 2004).[12]

Labor migrants from South Asia with higher wages at destination return later. Figure 4.3 plots the relationship between average monthly earnings at destination and duration for specific migration corridors for temporary migrants from Bangladesh, Nepal, and Pakistan. Except for Nepal, where the sample is restricted to the Nepal-Qatar corridor, the association between earnings and duration of stay at destination is positive overall. This finding holds when looking at all destinations together as well as when individual corridors are considered. Although this evidence is only descriptive, it suggests that the life-cycle hypothesis prevails for temporary migration from South Asia.

Workers who paid more to migrate also tend to return home later. In addition to being associated with the wage benefits of migration, labor migrants' duration of stay at destination is linked to migration costs. In a setting in which migrants optimize their duration of stay at destination and target net earnings, large fixed

FIGURE 4.3

Correlations between monthly earnings at destination and duration of stay of temporary migrants

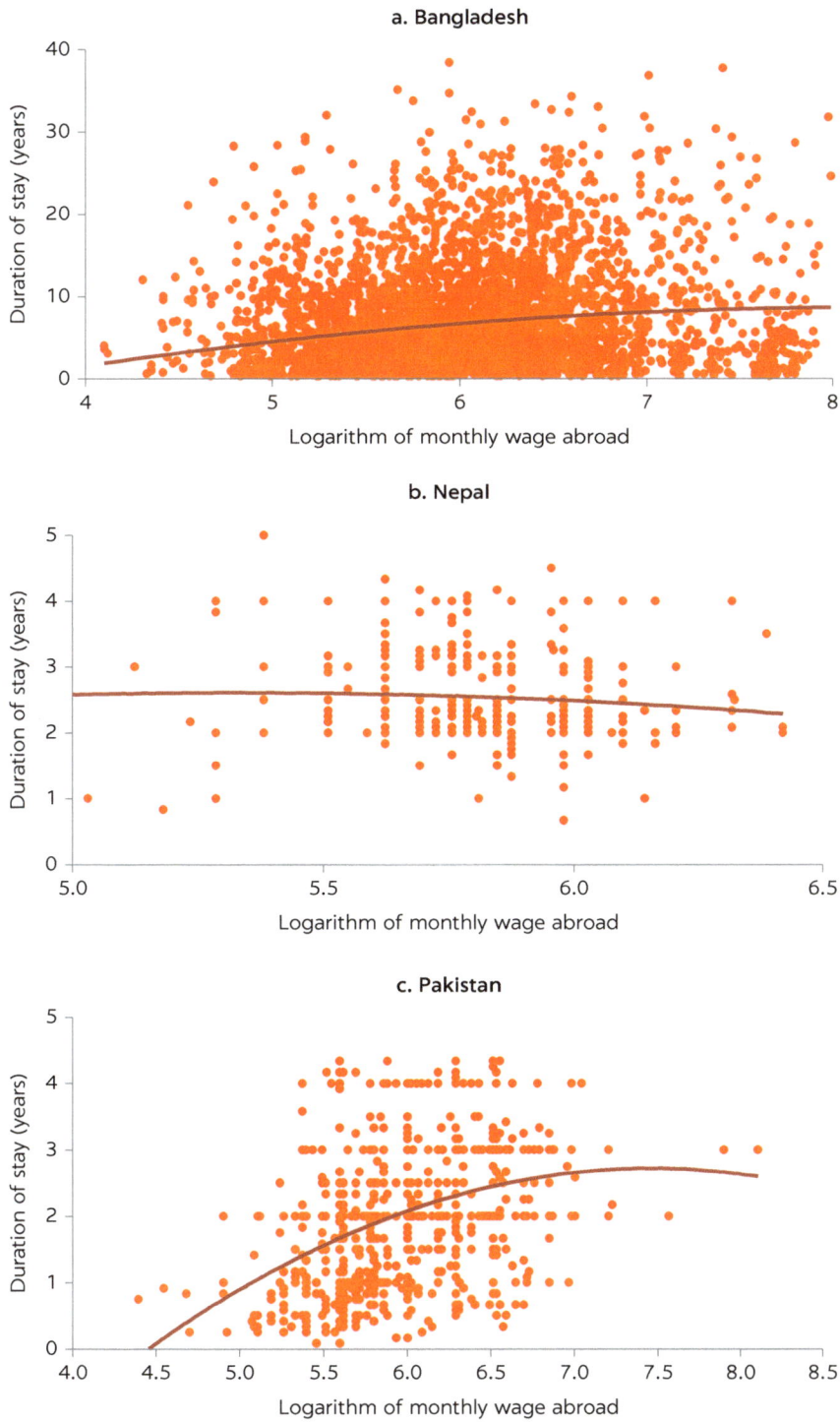

a. Bangladesh

b. Nepal

c. Pakistan

Sources: World Bank calculations from the KNOMAD-ILO Migration and Recruitment Costs Surveys 2015 and 2016 for Nepal and Pakistan, and from the World Bank Bangladesh Return Migrant Survey 2018/19 for Bangladesh.
Note: Wages overseas are in 2016 constant US dollars and reported on a logarithmic scale. The red curves show the relationship between wages abroad and duration of stay overseas estimated from the available data points.

costs of migration increase the incentive to stay longer at destination to make the labor migration episode profitable. Initial costs of migration of labor migrants from South Asia are positively associated with duration of stay at destination (figure 4.4),[13] indicating that migrants target total earnings from their migration episode by adjusting their duration of stay on the basis of monetary costs incurred. In a context in which regular stay in the main destinations is strictly tied to having an employment contract, higher migration costs can thus provide incentives for migrants to overstay irregularly if their contracts are not renewed.

Many temporary migrants return earlier than originally planned, and some of these unanticipated returns are involuntary. According to the BRMS 2018/19, more than 40 percent of return migrants to Bangladesh returned earlier than originally planned or before the term of their employment contract. The principal reason for returning early is being expelled from the destination country, closely followed by low wages and being laid off by the employer (figure 4.5). Thus, many unanticipated returns are involuntary, being linked to irregular overstay or to being laid off, both events a consequence of tight regulation of guest labor in the main destinations. The fact that a large share of temporary migrants cannot stay at destination as long as expected has important implications for their expected versus actual gains from migration. Given the very high migration costs paid before migrating, some migrants do not stay sufficiently long at destination to even cover these upfront costs.

Disappointment due to inaccurate expectations of wages overseas contributes to unanticipated returns. Despite the large wage differentials between wages at home and at destination, low wages overseas are also a common reason for early return among temporary migrants from Bangladesh (figure 4.5). About a quarter of temporary migrants who returned earlier than anticipated report low wages as the main reason, suggesting imperfect (and therefore misleading) information received by migrants before departure about wages to be earned overseas. Estimates from the BRMS 2018/19 suggest that there is a general sense of disappointment due to mismatches between expected and actual wages. Migrants from Bangladesh systematically overestimate the wages they will earn abroad: before departure, more than three-quarters of migrants overestimate the wage they expect by a margin of more than 30 percent (figure 4.6). Similarly, the vast majority of return migrants report being able to save less at destination than expected before departure. Temporary migrants from Nepal fall prey to a similar miscalculation (Shrestha 2020).

Returns can also be temporary, although migrants from South Asia typically migrate overseas only once. In migration corridors outside South Asia, some temporary migrants engage in repeated or circular migration (Constant and Zimmerman 2011; Piracha and Vadean 2009). Because of data constraints, however, rigorous analyses of repeat migration are very scarce.[14] In the main sending countries from South Asia, surveys typically only ask about the most recent migration episode, and administrative data fail to reveal multiple trips by a single migrant (which would involve using a unique individual identifier). One exception is the BRMS 2018/19, which reports that only 3 percent of return migrants have completed more than one migration episode overseas. The KNOMAD-ILO Migration and Recruitment Costs Surveys for Pakistan and Nepal also ask whether individuals had undertaken any other trips abroad for work before the more recent migration episode. About 14 percent and 21 percent of return migrants from Pakistan and Nepal, respectively, report that they have completed more than one migration episode. Thus, only a minority of low-skilled workers

FIGURE 4.4

Correlations between total migration costs and duration of stay overseas of temporary migrants

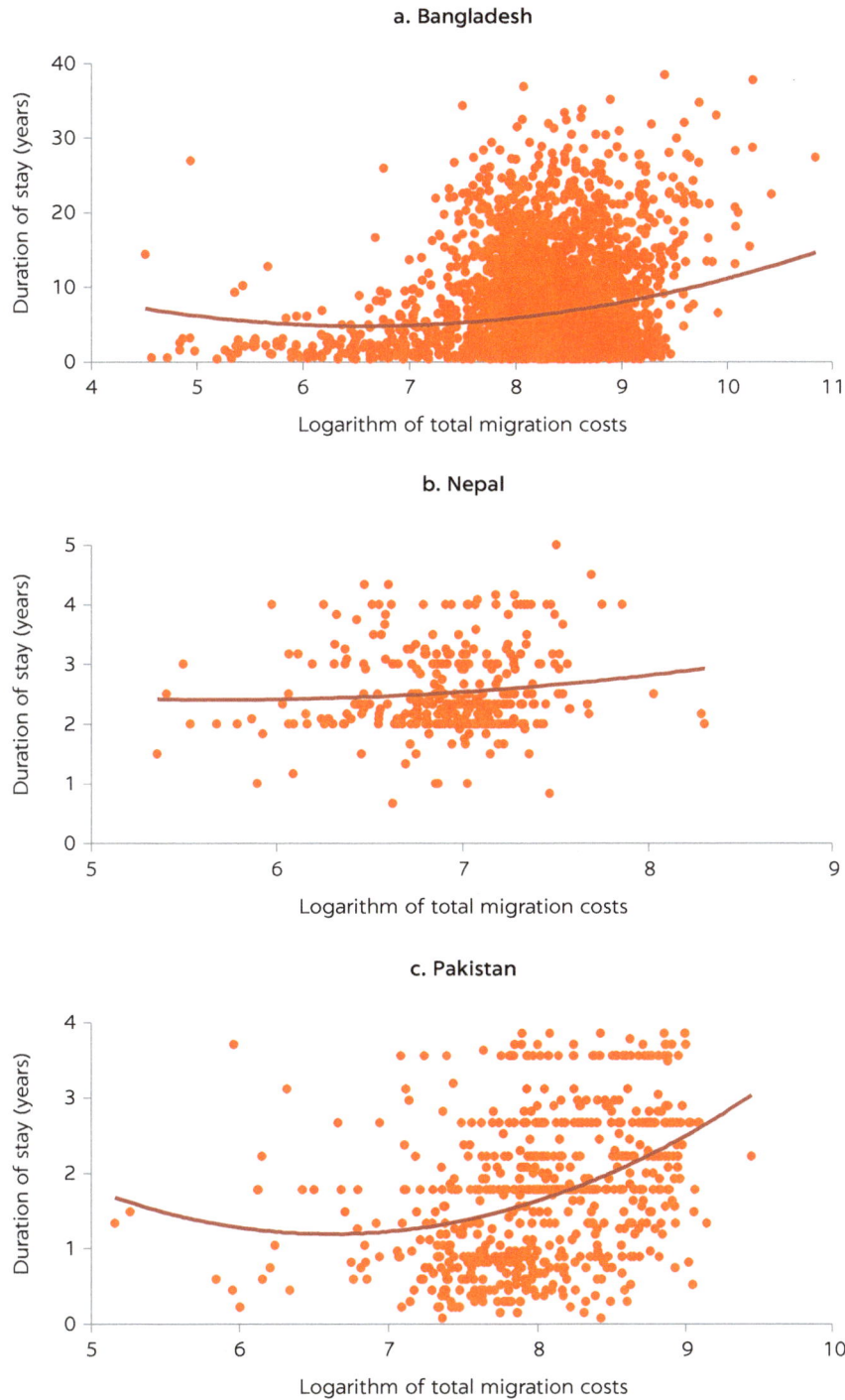

a. Bangladesh

b. Nepal

c. Pakistan

Sources: World Bank calculations from the KNOMAD-ILO Migration and Recruitment Costs Surveys 2015 for Nepal and Pakistan, and from Bangladesh Return Migrant Survey 2018/19 for Bangladesh.

Note: Total migration costs are in 2016 constant US dollars and reported on a logarithmic scale. The red curves represent the relationship between migration costs and duration of stay overseas estimated from the available data points.

FIGURE 4.5

Primary reason for returning earlier than originally planned among return migrants from Bangladesh

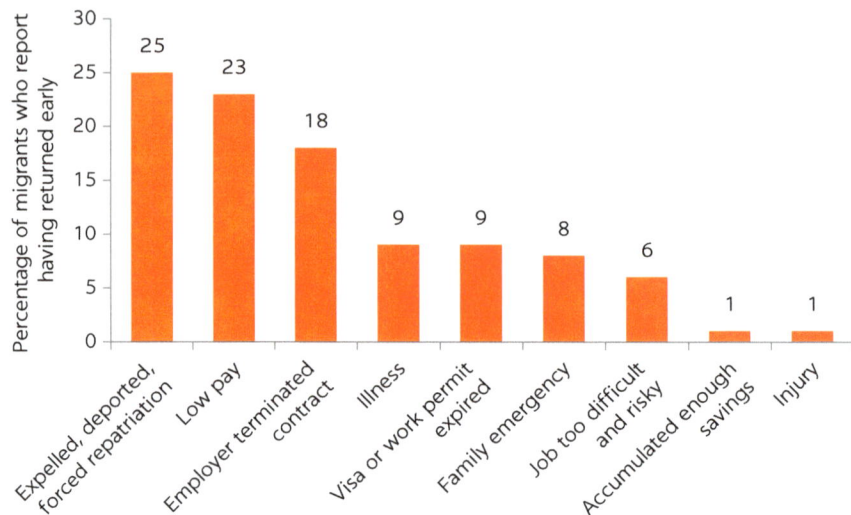

Sources: Ahmed et al. (2021) based on Bangladesh Return Migrant Survey 2018/19.
Note: Statistics are for males ages 18–59 who reported returning earlier than originally planned, or before the term of their employment contract.

FIGURE 4.6

Wage levels expected before departure compared with wages actually earned overseas by temporary migrants from Bangladesh

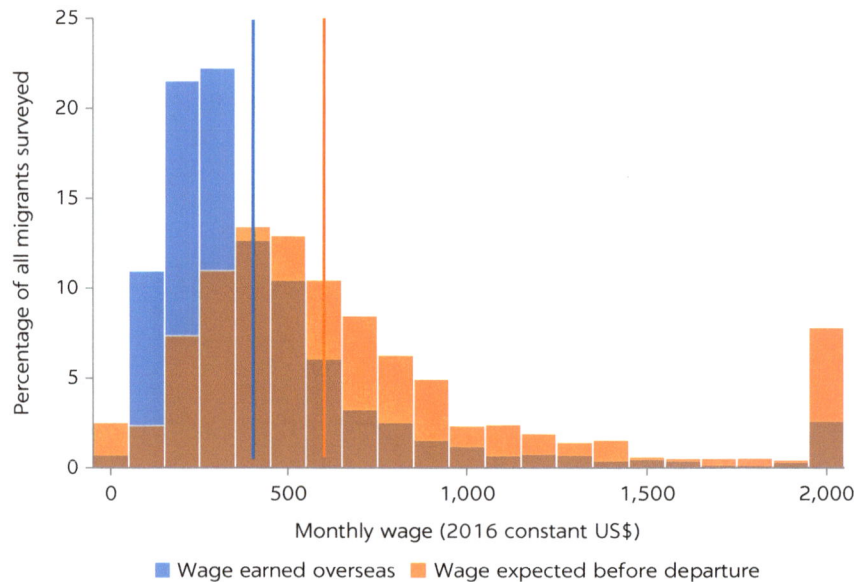

■ Wage earned overseas ■ Wage expected before departure

Sources: Bossavie et al. (2021) based on the Bangladesh Return Migrant Survey 2018/19.
Note: Statistics are for males ages 18–59. The y-axis shows the percentage of migrants who earned or expected the corresponding wage values overseas (on the x-axis). Vertical lines represent median values.

from South Asia migrate more than once; this finding may be partly driven by the very high upfront costs of migration in the region.

Temporary migrants who are forced to return and do more poorly in domestic labor markets are more likely to intend to remigrate. Intentions to remigrate among return migrants seem to strongly depend on whether returns are voluntary or not. For Bangladesh, the BRMS 2018/19 reports significant variation in intention to remigrate depending on the main reason for return.[15] Migrants who returned because of unexpected or involuntary circumstances, such as a family emergency, being expelled, or being laid off by the employer, are more likely to intend to migrate again. In contrast, a minority of migrants who returned because they had accumulated enough savings report that they intend to migrate again. Remigration is also linked to labor market outcomes after return: the intention to remigrate overseas is likely to affect investments in home labor markets, and this intention is, in turn, affected by underlying home labor market conditions. In Bangladesh, return migrants who are not employed back home, or who take precarious jobs such as day labor or unpaid family work, are more likely to intend to remigrate (figure 4.7, panel a). In contrast, returnees who become self-employed, particularly those who set up a business with paid employees after return, are less likely to intend to remigrate. Return migrants who earn more after returning home are also less likely to intend to remigrate (figure 4.7, panel b). This evidence is consistent with temporary migration being a way to overcome credit constraints so as to launch entrepreneurial activities after return (Bossavie et al. 2022).

FINANCIAL AND HUMAN CAPITAL GAINS FROM RETURN MIGRATION

The benefits of return migration for home economies in South Asia partly depend on who returns home. Workers who choose to migrate overseas for work are a select group within the working-age population (World Bank 2018b). Furthermore, in contexts in which return migration is not mandatory, migrants who return home are, in turn, a select group within that already select subset of workers (Wahba 2015a). Differences in characteristics between return migrants and nonmigrants are thus the result of a double selection, first at the emigration stage and then at the return stage. Whereas most studies report that migrants are more skilled than workers who do not migrate overseas (positive selection), returning migrants have been found to be negatively selected among labor migrants, meaning that they tend to be less skilled or educated than migrants who did not return and stayed abroad (Ambrosini at al. 2015; Bijwaard and Wahba 2014; Borjas and Bratsberg 1996; de Coulon and Piracha 2005; Fernández-Huertas Moraga 2011; Kaestner and Malamud 2014; Reinhold and Thom 2013; Wahba 2015a). In South Asia, however, the negative selection of return migrants among the pool of migrants overseas is expected to be largely overridden by the regulatory imperative that all low-skilled migrants must ultimately return from the main destinations.

Return migrants from South Asia are higher skilled than nonmigrants. They attained higher levels of schooling than workers in Bangladesh, Nepal, and Pakistan who have not migrated (figure 4.8). The share of return migrants who have not attended school is much lower than for nonmigrants in all three countries. In Pakistan, return migrants have completed, on average, 7.9 years of schooling compared with 6.3 years for nonmigrants. In Nepal, return migrants completed 7.9 years of schooling compared with 7.1 years for nonmigrants. In Bangladesh, the average number of years of schooling is 6.6 for return migrants and 5.3 for nonmigrants. The positive selection of return migrants is largely driven by a positive selection in emigration, as discussed in chapter 1, meaning that South Asian workers who migrate overseas are more educated than those

FIGURE 4.7

Share of return migrants in Bangladesh who intend to migrate again in the next five years

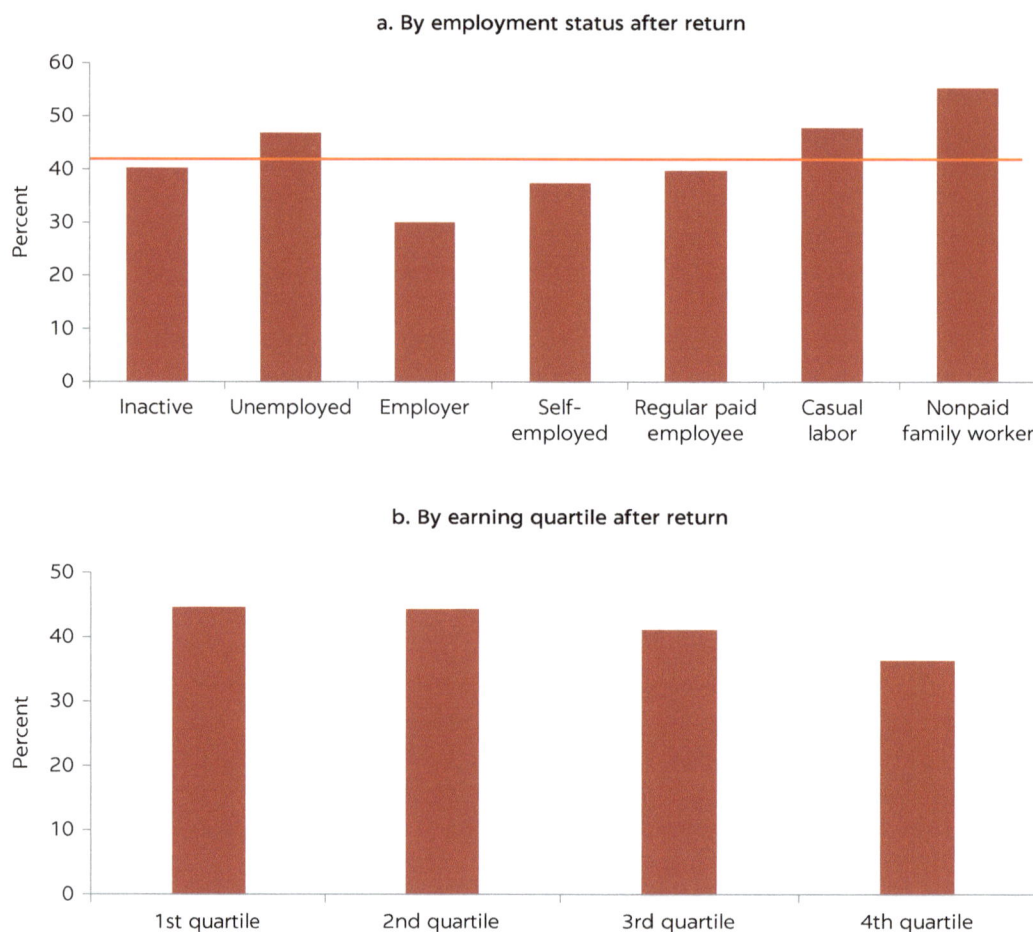

a. By employment status after return

b. By earning quartile after return

Sources: Ahmed et al. (2021) based on the Bangladesh Return Migrant Survey 2018/19.
Note: Statistics are restricted to males ages 18–59. Individuals are classified as having the intention to remigrate if they report being either "rather likely" or "very likely" to remigrate overseas in the next five years (as opposed to "not likely at all," "rather unlikely," or "neither likely nor unlikely"). Higher earnings quartiles refer to higher levels of earnings in home labor markets. The horizontal line represents mean value.

who do not migrate. Figure 4.8, however, shows that return migrants attained lower levels of schooling than migrants who are currently overseas. In Bangladesh, for example, the share of return migrants with no education is significantly higher than that of temporary migrants who are still abroad. This cross-sectional evidence, however, does not necessarily imply a negative selection of return migrants among workers who migrate overseas, given that it may be confounded by cohort effects: return migrants are, on average, older and migrated earlier than current migrants, and belong to cohorts of migrants whose educational attainment is lower in the first place.

In addition to being more skilled before migrating, return migrants can acquire new skills abroad, resulting in greater labor productivity in home labor markets. The return of labor migrants is a potential source of growth for origin countries through the accumulation of human capital overseas (Docquier and Rapoport 2012). The greater productivity of return migrants in home labor markets is supported by the existence of a positive wage premium relative to

FIGURE 4.8

Educational attainment of male workers from South Asia, by migration status

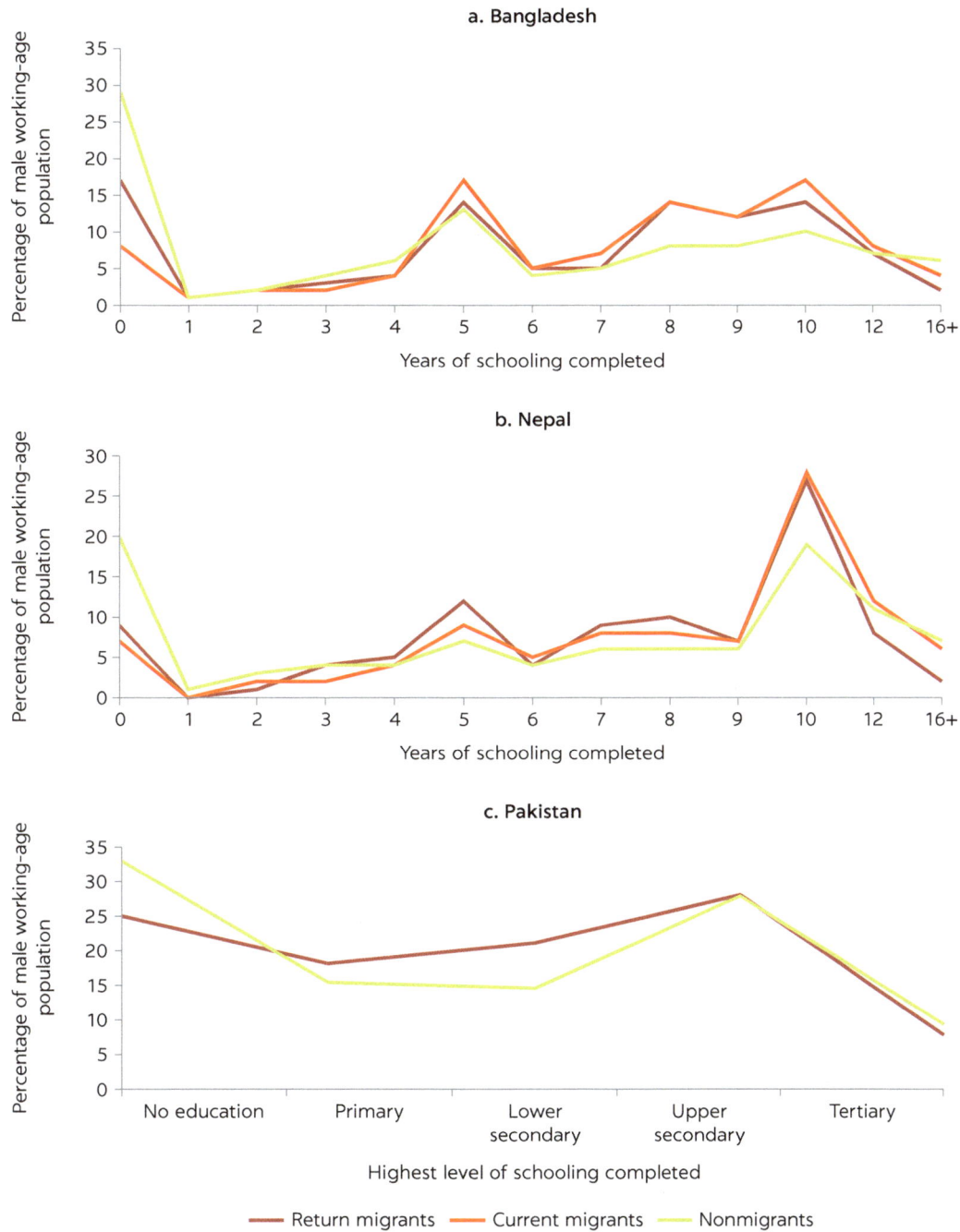

a. Bangladesh

b. Nepal

c. Pakistan

Legend: Return migrants — Current migrants — Nonmigrants

Sources: World Bank calculations based on the Bangladesh Household Income and Expenditure Survey 2016/17 and the Bangladesh Return Migrant Survey 2018/19, and the Labor Force Survey 2017/18 for Nepal and Pakistan.
Note: Statistics are for males ages 18–59 and weighted by household weights. Statistics for Bangladesh are for rural and semi-urban areas only. Current migrants are defined as individuals who were overseas at the time of the survey. Return migrants are defined as individuals who went overseas in the past but were back in the home country at the time of the survey. Nonmigrants are defined as individuals who have not migrated internationally (so includes internal migrants). Statistics for Pakistan do not include current migrants because they are not captured by the Labor Force Survey. Individuals who came back from overseas more than 10 years before the survey are excluded for Pakistan.

nonmigrants, which was reported in contexts outside South Asia. Although part of the premium can be attributed to differences in characteristics between return migrants and nonmigrants, it has been shown that return migrants benefit from their experience abroad in ways that translate into higher wages back home (Bossavie and Ozden 2022; De Vreyer, Gubert, and Robilliard 2010; Dumont and Spielvogel 2008; Lacuesta 2010; Reinhold and Thom 2013; Wahba 2015b). The human capital accumulated abroad can be occupation specific or sector specific. It can also be more general, such as language skills or soft skills, or confidence and motivation, which can increase productivity in a variety of jobs (Wahba 2014). The extent to which migrants and home countries benefit from return migration depends on whether returning migrants can use the experience gained abroad in the home labor market (Dustmann, Fadlon, and Weiss 2011; Mayr and Peri 2009). It has also been shown that highly educated returnees benefit more from the skills they acquired abroad (McCormick and Wahba 2001), and that the destination country has some bearing on the benefits of return migration (Debnath 2016).

Given the occupations in which migrants from South Asia are customarily employed at destination, however, it is unclear whether migration does increase human capital in ways that significantly raise productivity at home. Although most of the literature focuses on human capital gained by migrants abroad, it does not establish whether temporary migration work in low-skill occupations in the GCC or Southeast Asia usually generates human capital gains among temporary migrants. As shown in chapter 1, the occupations of South Asian migrants in destination countries are largely blue-collar jobs in the construction sector. Although most temporary migrants from South Asia are employed in the construction sector overseas, very few of them remain in the construction sector after returning home (Ahmed et al. 2021; Bossavie and Wang 2021), suggesting that return migrants do not take advantage of the occupation- or sector-specific skills that may have been acquired abroad. The physicality and tedium of the occupations they are employed in overseas may limit opportunities for human capital accumulation and reduce the likelihood that migrants will continue working in these same occupations at an older age once they return home. With regard to language skills, however, data from Bangladesh suggest that migrants are able to improve their proficiency in the language of the destination country. Very few temporary migrants report being able to speak or understand the language used in their workplace—Arabic in most cases—before departure, but more than two-thirds of return migrants report being able to speak and understand at least some simple sentences in the language used in their workplace overseas.

Return migrants from South Asia earn somewhat higher wages than nonmigrants, but the return wage premium is smaller than that in other origin countries.[16] Return migrants from South Asia who are engaged in wage work earn higher wages than wage workers who never migrated. The wage premium of return migrants is positive in all three countries and larger in Pakistan than in Bangladesh or Nepal (figure 4.9). In all three countries, the estimated wage premium is not much affected by controlling for other workers' observable characteristics. The returnee wage premium is 16 percent in Pakistan, 6 percent in Nepal, and 5 percent in Bangladesh. In comparison, the wage premium estimated by Wahba (2015) for Egyptian returnees who mostly migrated to the GCC countries is 46 percent before accounting for selection in return migration, and 16 percent

FIGURE 4.9

Estimated hourly wage premium earned by return migrants relative to nonmigrants

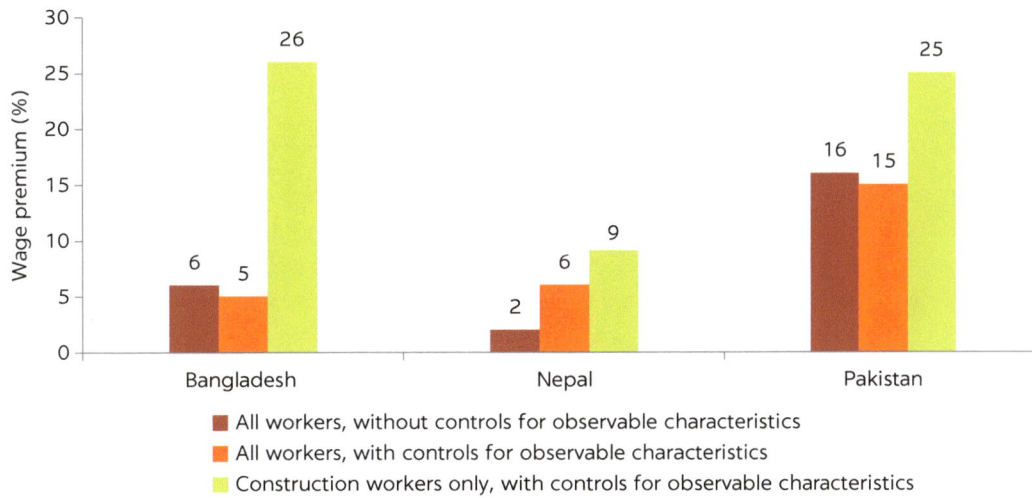

Sources: World Bank calculations based on the Labor Force Survey 2017/18 for Nepal; the Labor Force Survey 2017/18 for Pakistan; and the Bangladesh Return Migrant Survey 2018/19 and the Household Income and Expenditure Survey 2016/17 for Bangladesh.
Note: Statistics are for males ages 18–59 who are paid employees (as opposed to self-employed) and account for sampling weights. Statistics for Bangladesh are for rural and semi-urban areas only. The estimated wage premium is the additional earnings return migrants receive in home labor markets relative to workers who have never migrated, expressed as a percentage of nonmigrants' earnings. The wage premium for return migrants was estimated by regressing the logarithm of monthly earnings of employed workers on a dummy variable for being a return migrant. The specification with control variables also includes years of schooling attained, current age and its square, an urban dummy, and regional dummies as additional regressors.

after accounting for selection. In a different context, Lacuesta (2010) estimates an 11 percent wage premium for return migrants to Mexico compared with nonmigrants with similar observable characteristics. Therefore, although the wage premium for return migrants in Pakistan is in line with estimates in other contexts, the returnee wage premium in Bangladesh and Nepal is on the low end of estimates in the literature. When the analysis is restricted to workers employed in the construction sector–the main sector of employment of temporary migrants overseas–the returnee wage premium increases significantly in Bangladesh and Pakistan. The minority of return migrants who find employment in construction after return to these two countries thus enjoy significantly higher wages compared to workers in the same sector who never migrated. In Nepal, the wage premium earned by return migrants remain small, even in the construction sector. However, it is wise to keep in mind the methodological constraints on interpretation of the estimated wage premium for return migrants (box 4.2).

Return migrants in South Asia are more likely to start self-employment activities than nonmigrants, except in Nepal. The lack of access to credit is an important constraint to entrepreneurship in South Asia (Kuntchev et al. 2012). When options for formal wage employment at home are limited, temporary migration can be a way for aspiring entrepreneurs to mitigate credit constraints at home by accumulating financial capital abroad to start a business after return (Bossavie et al. 2021; Dustmann and Kirchkamp 2002). Several studies for developing economies find that return migrants are more likely to set up businesses than nonmigrants (Dustmann and Kirchkamp 2002; Mesnard 2004; Piracha and Vadean 2010; Wahba and Zenou 2012). In addition, duration of stay at destination has been shown to increase the likelihood of a small business being

Estimating the returns to temporary migration in home labor markets: Data requirements and methodological challenges

Estimating the gains that temporary international migration brings to the home country labor market involves several methodological challenges. As discussed in Wahba (2015a), the first issue to tackle is selection in outmigration, given that temporary migrants are not randomly selected within the home country populations. In particular, labor outmigrants may be selected according to characteristics that cannot be observed in the data, such as motivation or unobserved ability. In the context of migration to the Gulf Cooperation Council countries, prior studies such as Wahba (2015a) have used global oil prices as an instrument for outmigration.

In addition to selectivity in outmigration, return migrants may also be a select group among the pool of international labor migrants. Migrants who return to the home country may systematically differ from those who decide to stay longer at destination because, for example, they have been less successful abroad as a result of factors that may also affect their labor market outcomes back home. This second type of selection is likely to be less prominent for migrants from South Asia, who ultimately must return home given labor regulations at destinations. However, as highlighted by Bossavie et al. (2021), duration of stay at destination of temporary migrants from South Asia varies substantially, in ways that are related to migrants'

characteristics. Therefore, a cross-sectional sample of return migrants may capture selected groups of return migrants. To address the endogeneity in return decisions, Yang (2006) uses fluctuations in exchange rates as an instrument, whereas Wahba (2015a) uses conflict and war-related shocks in destination countries.

Additionally, labor force participation after return is selective, which further complicates the estimation of the returns (benefits) to past migration episodes. When estimating the returns to past migration abroad using earnings back home, selection issues are further exacerbated by the fact that national household surveys only capture earnings for wage employees. Earnings of the self-employed are thus not observed, which further complicates the interpretation of the returnee wage premium. This issue presents a particular problem in the context of return migration in developing economies because temporary migration has been shown to facilitate the start-up of self-employed activities among return migrants as a way to circumvent credit constraints (Bossavie et al. 2021; Dustmann and Kirchkamp 2002; Wahba 2015a). Thus, to obtain reliable estimates of the labor earnings premium for the population of return migrants, self-employed earnings, which are not available in standard household survey data sets, also need to be observed.

established back home (Bossavie et al. 2021; Ilahi 1999; Kilic et al. 2009). Figure 4.10 depicts the distribution of the occupational status of return migrants in Bangladesh, Nepal, and Pakistan compared with nonmigrants. In Bangladesh and Pakistan, the incidence of self-employment, particularly nonagricultural self-employment, is significantly larger among return migrants than nonmigrants. In rural Pakistan, 30 percent of return migrants are self-employed in sectors other than agriculture as opposed to 18 percent of nonmigrants. In urban areas, 46 percent of return migrants are self-employed in nonagriculture as opposed to 33 percent of nonmigrants. In Nepal, however, the incidence of self-employment among return migrants is about the same as for nonmigrants, perhaps indicating that migrants from Nepal do not benefit as much from their migration experience as do workers from Bangladesh or Pakistan, or that starting up self-employment after return is not the main driver of temporary migration from Nepal.

FIGURE 4.10

Self-employment of return migrants and nonmigrants

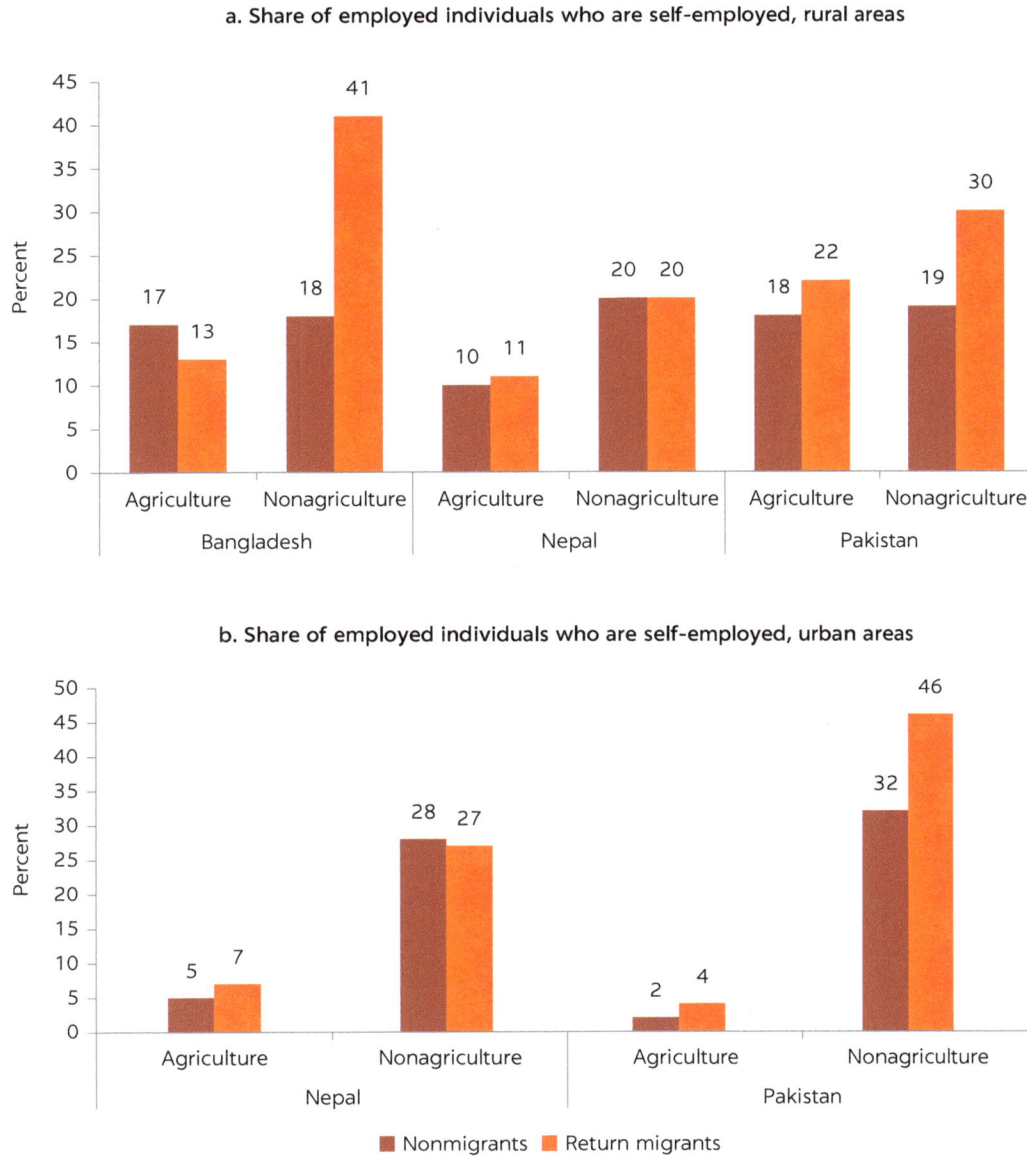

a. Share of employed individuals who are self-employed, rural areas

b. Share of employed individuals who are self-employed, urban areas

◼ Nonmigrants ◼ Return migrants

Sources: World Bank calculations based on the Labor Force Survey 2017/18 for Pakistan and Nepal and the Household Income and Expenditure Survey 2016/17 and the Bangladesh Return Migrant Survey 2018/19 for Bangladesh.
Note: Statistics are for males ages 18–59 and account for sampling weights. Return migrants are defined as individuals who went overseas in the past but were back to the home country at the time of survey. Nonmigrants are defined as individuals who have not migrated internationally (thus including internal migrants). The Bangladesh Return Migrant Survey only covers rural and semi-urban areas; therefore, statistics for Bangladesh are not reported for urban areas.

Scarce data on South Asian migrants' employment history shows that many temporary migrants move from nonemployment before migration to self-employment after return. Surveys that collect information on the entire employment history of temporary migrants, including before and after migration, are very scarce globally, including for South Asia. The BRMS 2018/19 is a recent exception, and it shows massive transitions of workers from not being employed before migration into nonagricultural self-employment after return (figure 4.11).

FIGURE 4.11

Employment status of temporary migrants from Bangladesh before migration and after return

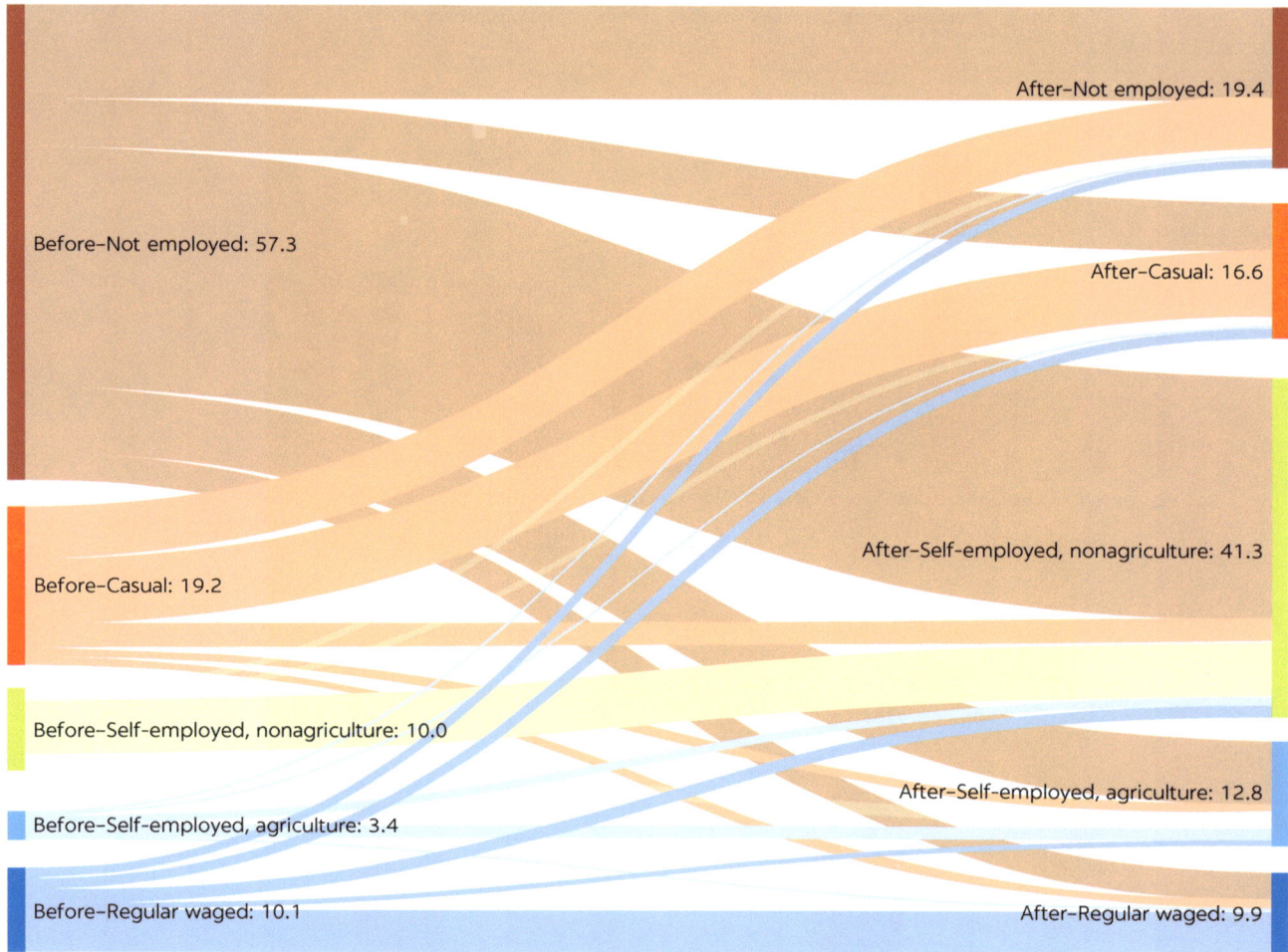

Sources: Ahmed et al. (2021) based on the Bangladesh Return Migrant Survey 2018/19.
Note: Statistics are for males ages 18–59.

According to the BRMS 2018/19, only 43 percent of temporary migrants from Bangladesh were employed before going abroad, while 82 percent are employed two years after returning home. The sharp increase in employment rates after return largely results from return migrants starting up small businesses. Among individuals who were not employed in Bangladesh before migrating overseas, 82 percent were employed in Bangladesh after returning, and among the employed, 81 percent were self-employed (figure 4.11). Transitions into nonagricultural self-employment are particularly striking, increasing from 10 percent before migration to 41 percent after return.[17] Similar transitions into nonagricultural self-employment after return have been shown for Pakistan (Ilahi 1999).

Savings from employment overseas play a critical role in starting up self-employment activities, offering a means for overcoming credit constraints at home. Figure 4.12 shows a strong positive association between cumulative earnings abroad and the likelihood of self-employment after return to Bangladesh. The likelihood of starting up nonagricultural self-employment after return is also positively associated with savings accumulated abroad in Pakistan (Ilahi 1999), suggesting that some of the savings accumulated during migration are channeled into

FIGURE 4.12

Share of return migrants who are self-employed in Bangladesh as a function of total earnings overseas

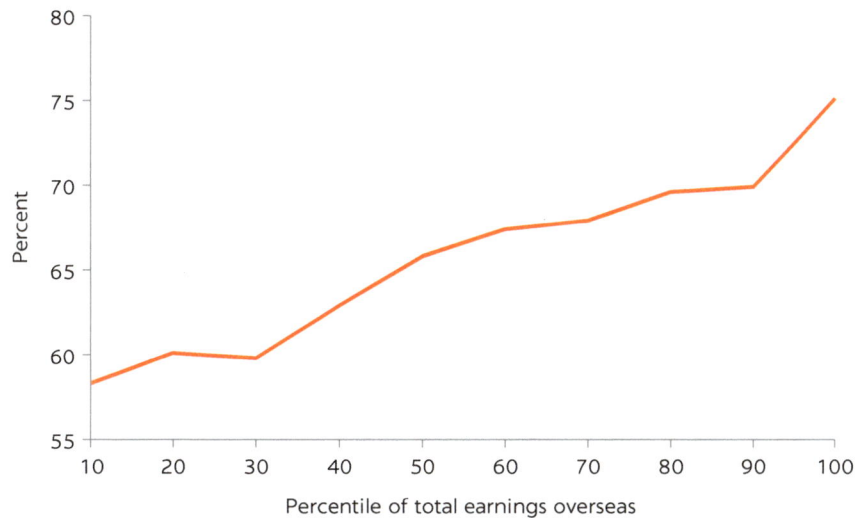

Sources: Bossavie et al. (2021) based on the Bangladesh Return Migrant Survey 2018/19.
Note: Statistics are for males ages 18–59. Higher percentiles shown on the x-axis correspond to higher levels of earnings overseas. The percentage of return migrants who are self-employed is calculated as a proportion of returnees who are employed after return.

starting up self-employment activities. The BRMS 2018/19 indicates that many migrants used the capital accumulated abroad to start their self-employment activity (figure 4.13). Almost half of the return migrants who at the time of the survey were self-employed reported that their earnings overseas were the main source of funding to start up their self-employed activity (Bossavie et al. 2022).

The benefits of return migration for the home economy and migrants themselves, however, may be reduced by several factors. The home economy may not take full advantage of the growth potential of return migration for a number of reasons. First, there may be adjustment costs and job search frictions associated with return migration. For example, return migrants may bring back skills that do not match the demands of the home economy, which can adversely affect the reintegration of temporary migrants in home labor markets and limit productivity gains (Lucas 2008). Second, returnees may have high reservation wages, and may therefore not be willing to work for home labor market wages. Third, if return migrants intend to migrate overseas again, and if the skills demanded overseas are different from those in demand by home labor markets, there may be little incentive to acquire experience and skills in home labor markets.

The employment rates of return migrants are lower than nonmigrants shortly after return. Figure 4.14 shows that the employment rates of return migrants are lower than for nonmigrants in Bangladesh, Nepal, and Pakistan. The difference in employment rates between the two groups is statistically significant and is larger in Nepal and Pakistan than in Bangladesh. Two main reasons could explain the lower employment rates observed among return migrants. First, return migrants may deliberately choose leisure time upon returning as part of their life-cycle plan, after spending years away from their families and friends (Dustmann and Kirchkamp 2002). According to this hypothesis, return migrants stay inactive for some time after returning before seeking employment. Second,

FIGURE 4.13

Main source of finance of self-employment activities among temporary migrants from Bangladesh

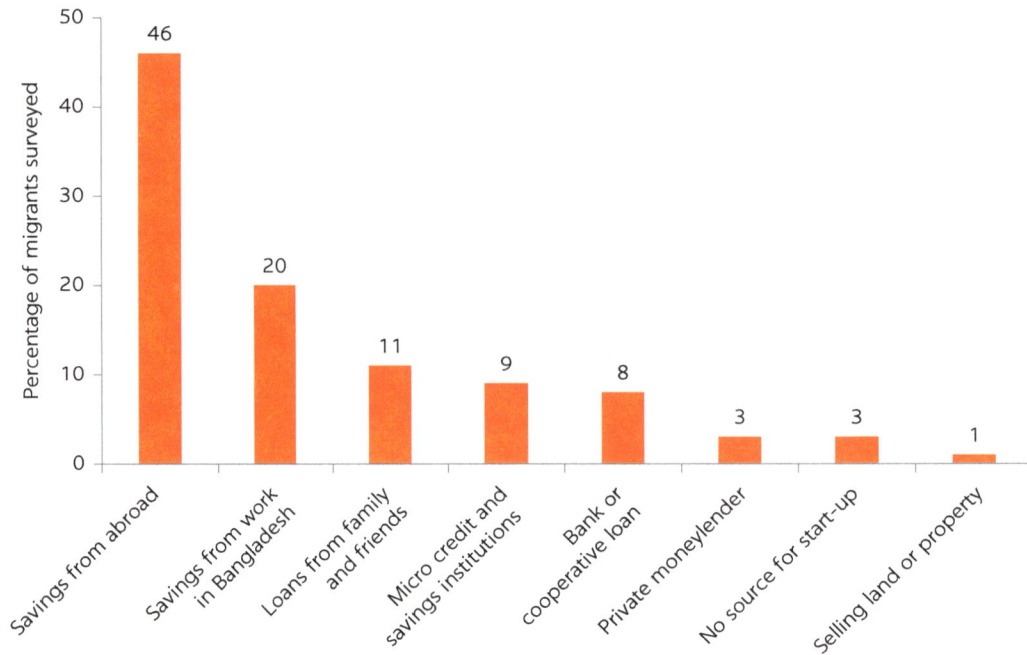

Sources: Ahmed et al. (2021) from Bangladesh Return Migrant Survey 2018/19.
Note: Statistics are for males ages 18–59.

return migrants may want to start working immediately after return, but job search frictions may prevent them from finding wage employment back home. For those who become self-employed after return, setting up a self-employed activity may not be immediate.

One way to determine whether lower employment rates among return migrants are driven by a lower willingness to work or by job search frictions is to break down the employment rate into its labor force participation component and its unemployment component.[18] As shown in panels b and c of figure 4.14, lower employment rates appear to be mostly driven by higher unemployment rates among return migrants in Nepal and Pakistan, rather than by lower labor force participation. The unemployment rate of return migrants is higher than that of nonmigrants in both countries, although the unemployment gap is significantly larger in Nepal and Pakistan than it is in Bangladesh. In Pakistan, the labor force participation rate of return migrants and of nonmigrants is the same, indicating that lower employment rates among return migrants are mostly driven by job search frictions. In Nepal, lower levels of labor force participation coupled with job search frictions appear to be driving the lower employment rates among returnees. Therefore, job search frictions and a lower willingness to engage in economic activities shortly after return both seem to explain the lower employment rates of returnees.

However, the lower rates of employment among return migrants are mostly transitory. The gap in employment between nonmigrants and return migrants is wide during the first year after return, but in all three countries employment rates among return migrants progressively converge a few years after return to

FIGURE 4.14

Labor market status of return migrants compared with nonmigrants

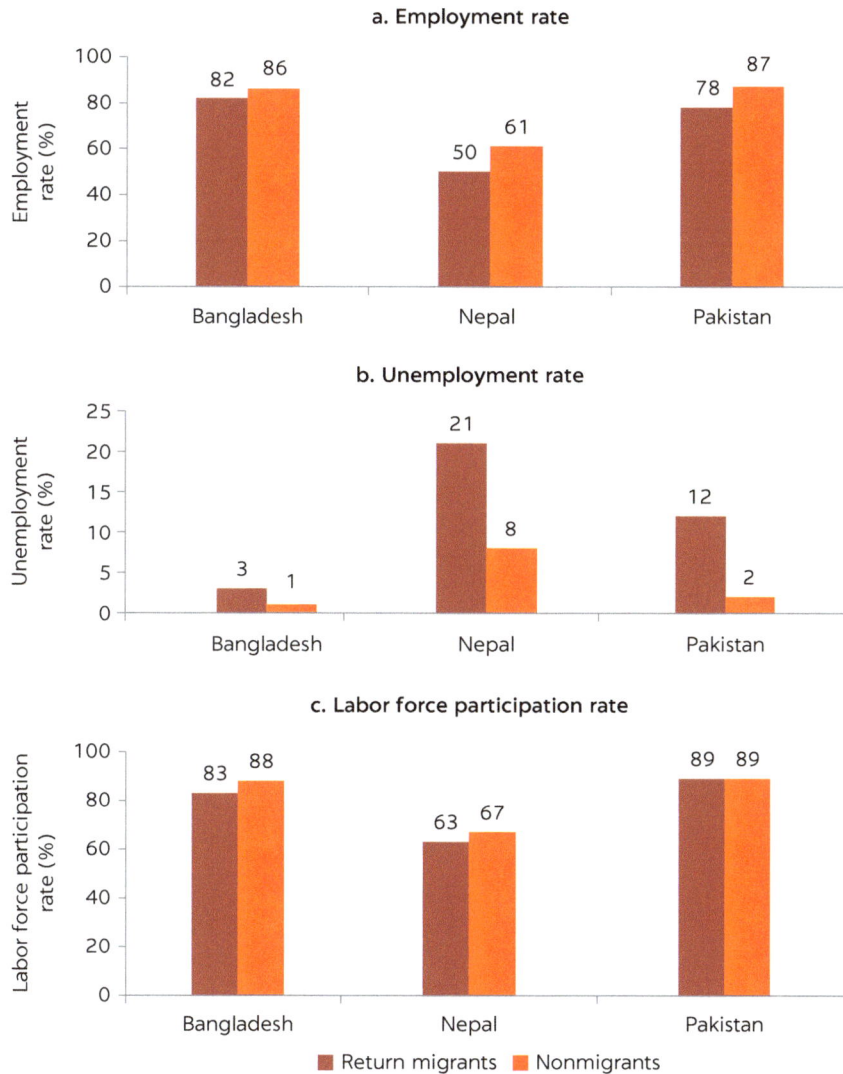

a. Employment rate

b. Unemployment rate

c. Labor force participation rate

■ Return migrants ■ Nonmigrants

Sources: World Bank calculations based on the Labor Force Survey 2017/18 for Pakistan; Household Income and Expenditure Survey 2016/17 for Bangladesh; and Labor Force Survey 2017/18 for Nepal.
Note: Statistics are for males ages 18–59 and account for sampling weights. Statistics exclude individuals who returned from India. The employment rate is calculated as the ratio of the number of individuals employed in the past week to the working-age population. The unemployment rate is calculated as the ratio of the number of individuals who were seeking employment in the past week to the population in the labor force (employed and unemployed individuals). The labor force participation rate is calculated as the ratio of the number of individuals who were either employed or seeking work in the past to the total working-age population. Return migrants are defined as individuals who went overseas in the past but were back in the home country at the time of the survey. Nonmigrants are defined as individuals who have not migrated internationally (thus including internal migrants).

those of nonmigrants (figure 4.15). That convergence happens the fastest in Bangladesh, taking roughly one year. In other words, although the employment rate of return migrants who have recently returned to Bangladesh is significantly lower than that of nonmigrants, the employment rate of those who have been back in Bangladesh for more than a year is virtually identical to that of

FIGURE 4.15

Labor market status of return migrants, by number of years since returning

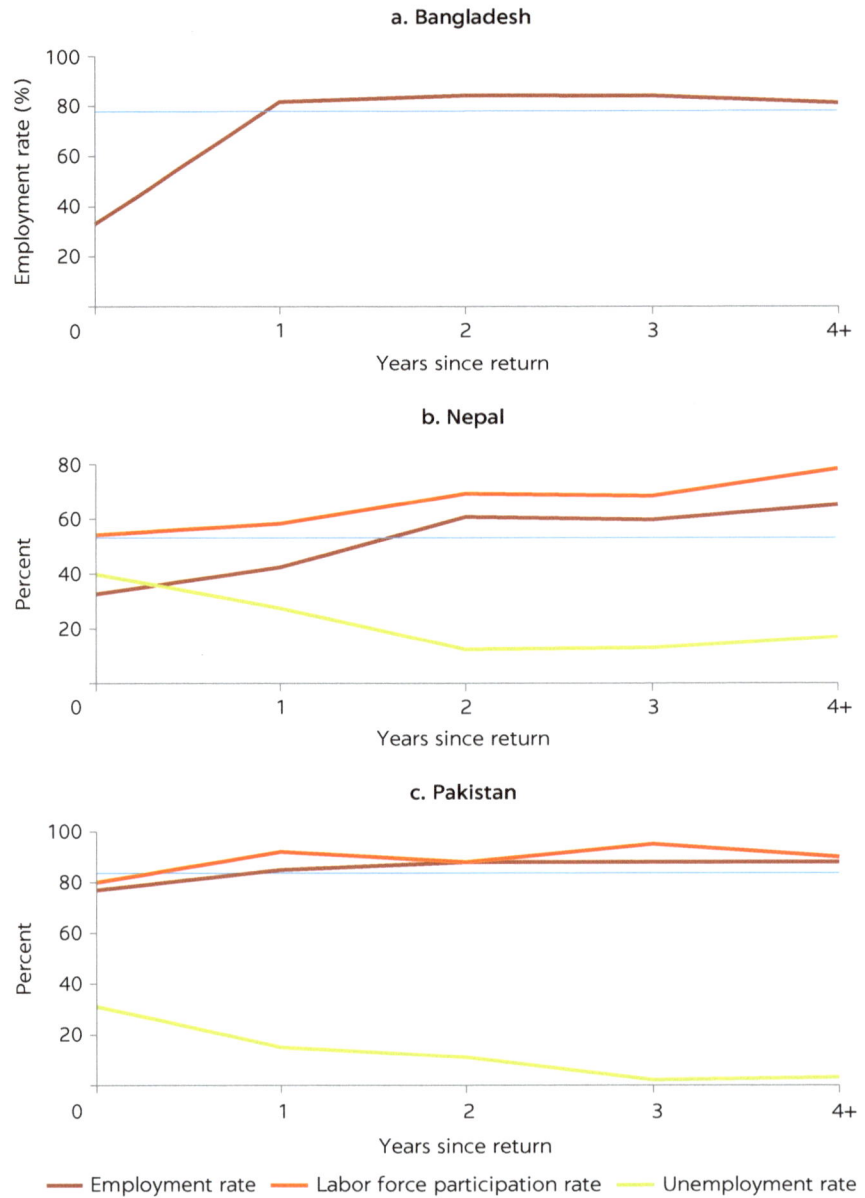

a. Bangladesh

b. Nepal

c. Pakistan

— Employment rate   — Labor force participation rate   — Unemployment rate

Sources: World Bank calculations based on the Bangladesh Return Migrant Survey 2018/19 and the Household Income and Expenditure Survey 2016/17 for Bangladesh; and the 2017/18 Labor Force Surveys for Nepal and Pakistan.

Note: Statistics are for males ages 18–59 and account for sampling weights. Statistics for Bangladesh are for rural and semi-urban areas. The horizontal straight blue line shows the employment rate of the nonmigrant population. The employment rate is calculated as the ratio of the number of individuals employed to the working-age population. The labor force participation rate is calculated as the ratio of the number of individuals who are either employed or looking for a job to the working-age population. The unemployment rate is calculated as the ratio of the number of individuals who are looking for employment to the number of those who are economically active, that is, who are either employed or looking for employment.

nonmigrants. In Nepal and Pakistan, the convergence in employment rates also occurs, but about two years after return, driven by both an increase in labor force participation and a decline in unemployment rates over the years following return. In Pakistan unemployment rates only converge to those of nonmigrants three years after return, while in Nepal it is only after four years. The faster transition of return migrants into employment in Bangladesh may be explained by the higher share of return migrants who start up in self-employment as opposed to looking for wage employment.

The benefits of return migration for migrants and the home economy are also reduced by high migration costs, which negatively affect the ability to start self-employment activities after return. With credit constraints on entrepreneurship at home, temporary migration can allow migrants to accumulate savings faster to start up in business after return (Dustmann and Kirchkamp 2002; Kilic et al. 2009; Mesnard 2004). In this context, higher migration costs require migrants to stay longer at destination to accumulate the assets needed, as shown for Bangladeshi migrants (Bossavie et al. 2021). Given the tight regulations on duration of stay in the main destinations and their vulnerability to exogenous shocks affecting labor demand at destination, migrants from South Asia are not always able to extend their duration of stay to accumulate sufficient savings. As a result, higher migration costs reduce the net returns to episodes of migration, and thus the ability of migrants to start up in business subsequently. Conversely, a drop in migration costs has been shown to lower the age at which workers migrate, to decrease duration of stay overseas, and to increase self-employment after return in Bangladesh (Bossavie et al. 2021).

POLICIES TO ENHANCE THE BENEFITS OF RETURN MIGRATION

Interventions targeted at return migrants are increasingly in demand by policy makers in sending countries. McKenzie and Yang (2015) classify programs targeted at return migrants into three categories: (1) policies to remove the regulatory, bureaucratic, and informational barriers that inhibit return migration; (2) policies intended to change the financial and other incentives to return; and (3) policies intended to make return migrants more productive and reintegration easier. Given the regulations requiring temporary stay in the destinations under discussion, the first two categories do not readily apply to the South Asian context. However, the reintegration and employment of return migrants in productive activities upon return has been a growing concern among policy makers in South Asia, exacerbated by the COVID-19 pandemic, the tightening of regulations in the European Union and by measures in some GCC countries to reduce economic reliance on low-skilled labor. In addition, an increase in forced returns from some GCC and European Union countries was observed in recent years (World Bank 2018a).

Dedicated agencies that facilitate returnee initiatives are, however, very rare globally and nonexistent in South Asia. One of the very few comprehensive nationwide programs for developing economies is the Overseas Filipino Worker reintegration program provided by the Philippines (box 4.3). In 2007, the government established the National Reintegration Center for Overseas Filipino Workers as a "one-stop center" for helping returnees reintegrate. Initiatives include providing expedited access to credit for creating a business, capacity development training, and family counseling. The program attempts to address

Comprehensive programs targeted at return migrants: The Overseas Filipino Worker in the Philippines

The Philippines currently provides the world's most comprehensive range of programs targeted at return migrants. The programs include a number of reintegration services for migrants provided by the Overseas Workers Welfare Administration and the National Reintegration Center for Overseas Filipino Workers (OFWs). The reintegration center offers two livelihood and self-employment programs for return migrants who seek to create income-generating opportunities. The government also offers services to returning migrants who were displaced from work abroad by conflict, policy change, illegal recruitment, or human trafficking as part of Balik Pinay! Balik Hanapbuhay! (BPBH), a noncash livelihood support program that provides skills or entrepreneurial training and starter kits. The Enterprise Development and Loan Program (EDLP), run in partnership with the Land Bank of the Philippines and the Development Bank of the Philippines, also helps support enterprise development through entrepreneurial training and fixed interest loans.

Other reintegration programs include the OFW-M3 program for financial literacy and entrepreneurship training, the Assist WELL (Welfare, Employment, Legal, Livelihood) program to train domestic workers to become teachers and other professionals, and the Financial Awareness Seminar–Small Business Management Training program. The success of these reintegration programs, however, is not well documented, and existing evidence is restricted to a very small sample of beneficiary interviews. Based on those interviews, the Philippines Commission on Audit found that neither the BPBH nor the EDLP met their objective for 2015. Out of 36 BPBH interviewees, 15 said that the businesses started were no longer in existence. Interviews showed that most borrowers from the EDLP (known as the Reintegration Program when it was audited) were not able to sustain their income-generating activities.

both the economic and social needs of return migrants. Training programs are offered for those who would like to start up small businesses, and a psychosocial component includes services such as family counseling, stress debriefing, and community organizing programs intended to help the migrant fit back into life in the Philippines (Tornea 2003).

Existing programs targeted at return migrants in South Asia are small and have been focused on forced returnees. In Bangladesh, the Prottasha program was put in place by both the International Organization for Migration and the European Union to reintegrate migrants who were forced to return from Europe after holding irregular immigration status. The support for return migrants was provided in the returnees' home districts and consisted of four main interventions: (1) social support, including psychosocial support; (2) awareness-raising programs; (3) economic empowerment; and (4) institutional development. The third component included entrepreneurship and motivational skills training, vocational skills training, access to finance, and referrals to economic reintegration services. As of March 2019, 774 returnees had been identified for reintegration assistance. A similar program was implemented in Ethiopia following the forced return of 163,000 migrants. The effectiveness of the intervention is unclear, however, given that no impact evaluation has been undertaken to assess its impact on return migrants and their households. In Nepal, the government, together with the International Organization for Migration, put in place a return assistance program for stranded migrants. The program lasted from 2015 to 2018 and consisted of a package of support interventions to facilitate returnees' integration. Those services included financial support to fulfill basic consumption needs after return as well as support to access livelihood opportunities. However, the impact of this program has not been evaluated either.

Programs focused on forced returnees have been developed in response to the COVID-19 pandemic. The COVID-19 context has further highlighted the need for support among the population of forced returnees in South Asia. In Bangladesh, 87 percent of migrant workers who returned in the first quarter of 2020 were found to either lack any source of earnings since returning or to be dependent on family members or minor agricultural activities (BRAC 2020). Owing to the high levels of debt taken on to migrate and the unexpectedly short duration of stay at destination (because of the pandemic), most return migrants are reportedly liquidating savings or taking loans from various formal or informal sources. There were also reports of difficulties faced by returnees in Nepal attempting to reintegrate into local labor markets during the pandemic (Barker et al. 2020). To address these pressing needs, origin countries in South Asia have developed programs to support the reintegration of migrants forced to return because of the pandemic. In Bangladesh, a program implemented by the Wage Earners Welfare Board under the Ministry of Expatriates' Welfare and Overseas Employment (MoEWOE) delivers services to eligible return migrants who are interested in either sustainable reintegration into the domestic labor market or access to services to prepare for remigration. The program also supports an upgrade to and integration of the migration management systems (databases, services, and systems) within the MoEWOE, which streamlines the delivery of social protection services for aspiring migrants, currently deployed migrants, and return migrants and enhance the safety and productivity of future migrants. In Nepal, the flagship employment support program—the Prime Minister Employment Program—was extended to provide support to migrants who unexpectedly returned because of the pandemic.

Effective policies for return migrants require systematic data collection on their migration history, including outcomes before, during, and after migration. For lack of data, important knowledge gaps remain regarding temporary migrants in South Asia. Administrative data sources in the region do not record temporary migrants once they return to the home country, but only when they leave the country. In addition, the individual labor market activities of temporary migrants in destination countries are typically unknown because administrative data from host countries cannot be linked to home-country administrative data on migrants. As a result, administrative data are currently of very limited use to anyone keen to understand temporary migration from South Asia and to design adequate supporting policies. Some nationally representative surveys in countries of origin have covered temporary migrants after their return, but sample sizes are typically small and detailed information on labor market outcomes at destination is typically lacking (Ahmed et al. 2021). National household surveys must therefore be expanded or modified so that detailed labor migration modules capture the necessary granularity of data on return migrants. In addition, surveys targeting return migrants, such as the BRMS 2018/19 in Bangladesh, could be replicated and generalized to other migrant-sending countries. Those surveys allow in-depth information to be collected on the migration and employment history of temporary migrants at a level of detail that cannot be achieved by standard national household surveys.

Policies targeted at return migrants must distinguish between planned and unplanned returns and similarly between forced and voluntary returns. These distinctions are vital because the circumstances behind migrants' returns have very different implications for the type of policies needed to maximize the benefits of return migration for both the migrant and the home country. From a policy perspective, the type of interventions needed to support temporary migrants who voluntarily return after accumulating sufficient savings overseas may greatly differ from what is needed for migrants who were expelled from the host country, returned earlier than intended (because the experience abroad failed to meet expectations), or were laid off by their employer at destination. Migrants who unexpectedly return early face specific issues because they have often accumulated a large amount of debt (resulting from high migration costs that most probably will not have been recouped) after earning at destination for a short period. Whereas voluntary returns can be accompanied by more standard labor interventions, such as labor intermediation or support for entrepreneurship, forced returns may require social assistance interventions that include support for repatriation and cash grants to meet basic needs and commence the process of livelihood restoration. Meanwhile, interventions aimed at improving savings management and financial literacy throughout the migration life cycle can improve the welfare of all migrants, irrespective of the reason for returning home (Doi, McKenzie, and Zia 2014).

For temporary migrants who return voluntarily, labor market intermediation and support for entrepreneurship activities may facilitate reintegration into home labor markets. Although the employment rates of return migrants ultimately get close to those of nonmigrants a few years after return, the employment levels of return migrants are lower in the earlier years, suggesting that labor market intermediation targeted at return migrants could be considered to smooth the transition of return migrants who are seeking wage employment back home. Labor market intermediation interventions should take into account the specifics of the situation of return migrants who have been away from the home labor market for some time. They may have skills and experience that diverge from the needs of home markets, or, to the contrary, could make them more productive at home. Given that starting up self-employment is quite frequent among return migrants (Bossavie et al. 2021, 2022), small business advice and savings management training could be useful to help migrants invest or channel their financial capital more effectively. A similar outcome could also be achieved by referring return migrants to existing services aimed at supporting small-scale self-employment.

Strengthening the management and investment of savings by temporary migrants can increase the benefits of return migration. Evidence from the BRMS 2018/19 shows that return migrants typically lack basic financial literacy, which can impede the accumulation of savings abroad and productive investment after returning home. Interventions to address this issue could include basic financial literacy training to support savings and the management of labor earnings abroad. These interventions should ideally take place at each stage of the migration life cycle, including at the predeparture stage, periodically throughout the stay abroad, and after return. Financial literacy interventions taking place in destination countries have been shown to increase financial knowledge among migrants (Gibson, McKenzie, and Zia 2014) and in some cases to increase migrants' actual savings (Seshan and Yang 2014). In addition, these financial literacy interventions can have a greater impact on savings when they are delivered to both the migrant and their close household member (Doi, McKenzie, and Zia 2014).

The effectiveness of current return and reintegration policies for migrants who return voluntarily has been a subject of debate for years, and rigorous evidence of their impact is lacking. The few programs targeted at those who return voluntarily are on a small scale and their impact has not been evaluated. In addition, the few large-scale programs, such as the ones that have been implemented in China and India, are primarily targeted at high-skilled migrants (Debnath 2016; Jonkers 2008). Although China, India, the Republic of Korea, and Taiwan, China, may have benefited from implementing various return policies, not all developing economies might benefit to the same extent, because, for example, of imperfect labor market conditions or less accessible credit markets for returnee entrepreneurs. Moreover, the policies that have worked for some developing economies might not work for the entire developing world given that each economy has a unique set of migration and return patterns and domestic labor market conditions that warrants a customized policy solution. Others have argued that successful return occurs when the factors at home as well as in the host economy are conducive to return (Wickramasekara 2002).

The effectiveness of programs facilitating entrepreneurship among returnees is also poorly documented. Given the large proportion of returnees that take up entrepreneurship activities after return in South Asia (Bossavie et al. 2021, 2022), there is a case for putting in place interventions that support such activities. Some reintegration programs involve training or credit, or both, to start small enterprises. The rationale behind these programs is to help overcome financial or skill constraints that limit the ability of migrants to work productively. McKenzie and Yang (2015), however, outline some drawbacks. First, there is no rigorous evidence available on the effectiveness of these programs. It must be understood that not everybody wants to be an entrepreneur, and many return migrants will have been working in wage jobs previously, with no experience of running a business. Second, existing evaluations of training programs have had at best mixed results, even among those individuals interested in setting up businesses (McKenzie and Woodruff 2017), and there is limited reason to expect return migrants to be particularly good at running businesses. Third, that being the case, it is unclear why such programs should be targeted explicitly at return migrants rather than being part of a portfolio of training and work assistance options offered to all in a given region.

For returnees who seek wage employment, it is yet to be determined whether programs aimed at reducing job search frictions are effective. One potential barrier to maximizing the benefits of return migration (for the migrants themselves or indeed for the home economy) is the existence of these job search frictions. In that respect, one option would be to adapt standard labor market interventions and employment services to support the reinsertion of return migrants who seek wage employment. To reduce frictions and facilitate the transition from overseas to home labor markets, some governments have attempted to make it easier for domestic firms to locate emigrant workers who may be interested in returning, and vice versa. For example, Jamaica's returning residents program has a data bank of migrants abroad that prospective employers can use for recruitment purposes; Bulgaria runs an annual job fair to try to initiate direct contacts between Bulgarian emigrants and leading companies in Bulgaria; and Moldova has held job fairs in Italy to provide information about job opportunities back in Moldova. It is again unclear how successful any of these efforts have been for increasing return migration or improving the jobs that return migrants get because their impact has not been evaluated.

Policies facilitating the recognition of skills gained abroad could both strengthen the reintegration of return migrants and increase the gains that accrue from future migration. Through their work experience abroad, migrants acquire skills and experience that can be valuable in another migration experience. Those skills can be destination specific but may also be transferable to other destination countries and may potentially generate higher earnings the next time around. This possibility applies not only to technical skills, such as those acquired in the construction sector overseas, but also language skills. Among temporary migrants returning to Bangladesh, about two-thirds of those who moved to GCC countries report after returning that they were able to formulate and understand at least simple sentences in Arabic, and about one-third were able to formulate and understand complex sentences. A better command of the work language used at destination is likely to increase labor productivity in any future migration episode, even where manual labor at destination predominates, through, for example, a better understanding of instructions given in the workplace. A few countries have attempted to make return migrants more productive by facilitating the recognition of qualifications and skills gained abroad. For example, Argentina's RAICES program offers the translation and accreditation of qualifications formally earned abroad. One promising policy area in the context of temporary and repeated migration involves international recognition of the skills and experience gained abroad so that migrants can benefit from that certification in subsequent migration episodes.

NOTES

1. For more details about the return migrant survey, see Ahmed et al. (2021).
2. According to the sponsorship system that regulates migration to the GCC, labor migrants can only enter and stay in the country through a sponsor, that is, a local employer who takes on both legal and economic responsibility for the migrant worker.
3. Return to the home country is mandatory, but temporary migrants sometimes choose to stay irregularly in the destination country. In recent years, however, the GCC countries have been tightening monitoring and sanctions, which has resulted in an increase in deportations.
4. Kuwait's and the United Arab Emirates' monthly minimum salaries for the family visa, for example, are set at 250 Kuwaiti dinars (US$888) and 10,000 dirhams (US$2,723), respectively.
5. According to the BRMS 2018/19, 96 percent of temporary labor migrants from rural Bangladesh migrated abroad alone.
6. This data availability constraint, however, is not specific to South Asia. Administrative and survey data for countries around the world do not typically allow researchers to track migrants once they leave the destination country, which makes estimation of return rates difficult (Wahba 2014; Dustmann and Görlach 2016).
7. See Ahmed et al. (2021) for a comprehensive cross-country overview of survey data sets that allow the capture of temporary migrants globally.
8. However, such patterns may be partly driven by sampling and the way the question on past migration is asked in the KNOMAD-ILO Recruitment Costs Surveys in Nepal and Pakistan.
9. Although there is no explicit restriction on the number of work permit renewals in the GCC countries, cumulative duration of stay is capped at 10 years in Malaysia and Singapore, the two main countries that host low-skilled migrants in Southeast Asia.
10. Such patterns may be partly driven by sampling and the way the question on past migration is asked in surveys for Nepal and Pakistan.

11. It is assumed that substitution effects dominate income effects associated with higher wages.

12. Studies looking at the relationship between earnings at destination and return decisions report mixed findings. Borjas (1989) and Yang (2006) find that higher earnings are associated with less return migration, whereas Dustmann (2003) finds that migrants' optimal duration of stay decreases with wages. Constant and Massey (2003) and Gibson and McKenzie (2011) find no significant association between return decisions and labor earnings at destination. Mixed findings are partly driven by the difficulty of isolating the causal relationship between labor earnings at destination and return decision, given that earnings and return are likely to be strongly correlated with migrants' observable and unobservable characteristics. The few studies that attempt to isolate a causal relationship find that the life-cycle hypothesis prevails empirically (Bijwaard and Wahba 2019; Wahba 2015b; Yang 2006). In addition, both low- and high-income migrants have been found to return earlier than the average migrant, but low-income migrants tend to return even sooner (Bijwad and Wahba 2014).

13. The positive association between costs of migration and duration is statistically significant at the 1 percent level for all corridors.

14. The work by Piracha and Vadean (2009) is, to the best of the authors' knowledge, the only paper that looks at these questions, using data from Albania.

15. Piracha and Vadean (2010) find evidence of a strong association between reasons for return and intentions to remigrate in Albania.

16. This association, however, cannot be interpreted as causal, given that the authors are unable to control for unobservable factors that could affect the decision to migrate and labor earnings after returning home, such as unobserved ability not captured by level of schooling, motivation, social networks, or other factors.

17. The relationship between temporary migration and entrepreneurship back in Bangladesh is explored in detail in Bossavie et al. (2021).

18. Unemployment is defined as not being employed but looking for employment. Labor force participation is defined as being either employed or looking for employment, as opposed to being economically inactive.

REFERENCES

Ahmed, S. Amer, Faiz Ahmed, Laurent Bossavie, Çağlar Özden, and He Wang. 2021. "Low-Skilled Temporary Migration and Development: A New Dataset from Bangladesh." Background paper for *Toward Safer and More Productive Migration for South Asia*, World Bank, Washington, DC.

Akee, Randall, and Maggie R. Jones. 2019. "Immigrants' Earnings Growth and Return Migration from the US: Examining Their Determinants Using Linked Survey and Administrative Data." Working Paper 25639, National Bureau of Economic Research, Cambridge, MA.

Al Jazeera. 2020. "Pakistan Concerned at Workers Returning from UAE with Coronavirus." May 6, https://www.aljazeera.com/news/2020/05/pakistan-concerned-workers-returning-uae-coronavirus-200506081618984.html.

Ambrosini, William J., Karin Mayr, Giovanni Peri, and Dracos Radu. 2015. "The Selection of Migrants and Returnees: Evidence and Long-Term Implications." *Economics of Transition and Institutional Change* 23 (4): 753–93.

Arezki, Rabah, and Ha Nguyen. 2020. "Coping with a Dual Shock: COVID-19 and Oil Prices." VoxEU, CEPR, London.

Barker, Nathan, C. Austin Davis, Paula López-Peña, Harrison Mitchell, Ahmed Mobarak, Karim Naguib, Maira Reimão, Ashish Shenoy, and Corey Vernot. 2020. "Migration and the Labour Market Impacts of COVID-19." Yale Research Initiative on Innovation and Scale, Yale University, New Haven, CT.

Bijwaard, Govert, and Jackline Wahba. 2014. "Do High-Income or Low-Income Immigrants Leave Faster?" *Journal of Development Economics* 108 (C): 54–68.

Bijwaard, Govert, and Jackline Wahba. 2019. "Immigrants' Wage Growth and Selective Out-Migration." *Oxford Bulletin of Economics and Statistics* 81 (5): 1065–94.

Borjas, George J. 1989. "Immigrant and Emigrant Earnings: A Longitudinal Study." *Economic Inquiry* 27 (1): 21–37.

Borjas, George J., and Bernt Bratsberg. 1996. "Who Leaves? The Outmigration of the Foreign-Born." *Review of Economics and Statistics* 78 (1): 165–76.

Bossavie, Laurent, Joseph-Simon Görlach, Çağlar Özden, and He Wang. 2021. "Temporary Migration for Long-Term Investment." Background paper for *Toward Safer and More Productive Migration for South Asia*, World Bank, Washington, DC.

Bossavie, Laurent, and He Wang. 2021. "Return Migration and Labor Market Outcomes Evidence from South Asia." Background paper for *Toward Safer and More Productive Migration for South Asia*, World Bank, Washington, DC.

Bossavie, Laurent, and Çağlar Özden. 2022. "Impacts of Temporary Migration on Development in Origin Countries." World Bank, Washington DC.

Bossavie, Laurent, Joseph-Simon Goerlach, Çağlar Özden, and He Wang. 2022. "Institutional Voids, Credit Markets and Temporary Migration: Evidence from Bangladesh." Policy Research Working Paper 9930, World Bank, Washington DC.

BRAC. 2020. "A Survey on the Impact of COVID 19 Pandemic on the Life and Livelihoods of Returnee Migrants." Unpublished, BRAC, Dhaka.

Constant, Amelie, and Douglas S. Massey. 2003. "Self-Selection, Earnings and Out-Migration: A Longitudinal Study of Immigrants to Germany." *Journal of Population Economics* 16 (4): 631–53.

Constant, Amelie F., and Klaus F. Zimmermann. 2011. "Circular and Repeat Migration: Counts of Exits and Years Away from the Host Country." *Population Research and Policy Review* 30 (4): 495–515.

Debnath, Priyanka. 2016. "Leveraging Return Migration for Development: The Role of Countries of Origin—A Literature Review." KNOMAD Working Paper Series 17, World Bank, Washington, DC.

de Coulon, Augustin, and Matloob Piracha. 2005. "Self-Selection and the Performance of Return Migrants: The Source Country Perspective." *Journal of Population Economics* 18 (4): 779–807.

De Vreyer, Philippe, Flore Gubert, and Anne-Sophie Robilliard. 2010. "Are There Returns to Migration Experience? An Empirical Analysis Using Data on Return Migrants and Non-Migrants in West Africa." *Annals of Economics and Statistics* 97/98: 307–28.

Djajic, Slobodan, and Ross Milbourn. 1988. "A General Equilibrium Model of Guest-Worker Migration: The Source Country Perspective." *Journal of International Economics* 25 (3–4): 335–51.

Docquier, Frederic, and Hillel Rapoport. 2012. "Globalization, Brain Drain, and Development." *American Economic Review* 50 (3): 681–730.

Doi, Yoko, David McKenzie, and Bilal Zia. 2014. "Who You Train Matters: Identifying Combined Effects of Financial Education on Migrant Households." *Journal of Development Economics* 109 (2): 33–55.

Dumont, Jean-Christophe, and Gilles Spielvogel. 2008. "Return Migration: A New Perspective." In *OECD International Migration Outlook 2008*, 161–222. Paris: OECD Publishing.

Dustmann, Christian. 1995. "Savings Behavior of Return Migrants." *Zeitschrift für Wirtschafts- und Sozialwissenschaften* 115: 511–33.

Dustmann, Christian. 1997. "Return Migration, Uncertainty and Precautionary Savings." *Journal of Development Economics* 52 (2): 295–316.

Dustmann, Christian. 2003. "Return Migration, Wage Differentials, and the Optimal Migration Duration." *European Economic Review* 47 (2): 353–69.

Dustmann, Christian, Itzhak Fadlon, and Yoram Weiss. 2011. "Return Migration, Human Capital Accumulation and the Brain Drain." *Journal of Development Economics* 95 (1): 58–67.

Dustmann, Christian, and Joseph-Simon Görlach. 2016. "The Economics of Temporary Migrations." *Journal of Economic Literature* 54 (1): 98–136.

Dustmann, Christian, and Oliver Kirchkamp. 2002. "Migration Duration and Activity Choice after Re-Migration." *Journal of Development Economics* 67 (2): 351–72.

Fargues, Philippe. 2011. "Immigration without Inclusion: Non-Nationals in Nation-Building in the Gulf States." *Asian and Pacific Migration Journal* 20 (3–4): 273–92.

Fargues, Philippe, and Françoise De Bel-Air. 2015. "Migration to the Gulf States: The Political Economy of Exceptionalism." In *Global Migration: Old Assumptions, New Dynamics,* edited by Diego Acosta Arcarazo and Anja Wiesbrock, 139–66. Santa Barbara, CA: ABC-CLIO.

Fernandez-Huertas Moraga, Jesus. 2011. "New Evidence on Emigrant Selection." *Review of Economics and Statistics* 93 (1): 72–96.

Gardner, Andrew M. 2011. "Gulf Migration and the Family." *Journal of Arabian Studies* 1 (1): 3–25.

Gibson, John, and David McKenzie. 2011. "The Microeconomic Determinants of Emigration and Return Migration of the Best and Brightest: Evidence from the Pacific." *Journal of Development Economics* 95 (1): 18–29.

Gibson, John, David McKenzie, and Bilal Zia. 2014. "The Impact of Financial Literacy Training for Migrants." *World Bank Economic Review* 28 (1): 130–61.

Hill, John K. 1987. "Immigrant Decisions Concerning Duration of Stay and Migratory Frequency." *Journal of Development Economics* 25 (1): 221–34.

Ilahi, Nadeem. 1999. "Return Migration and Occupational Change." *Review of Development Economics* 3 (2): 170–86.

IOM (International Organization for Migration). 2020. "IOM Assists Vulnerable Returning Migrants Impacted by the COVID-19 Pandemic." Press Release, July 21.

Jonkers, Koen. 2008. "A Comparative Study of Return Migration Policies Targeting the Highly Skilled in Four Major Sending Countries." Technical Report, MIREM-AR, 2008/05. European University Institute, Robert Schuman Centre for Advanced Studies.

Kaestner, Robert, and Ofer Malamud. 2014. "Self-Selection and International Migration: New Evidence from Mexico." *Review of Economics and Statistics* 96 (1): 78–91.

Kilic, Talip, Calogero Carletto, Benjamin Davis, and Alberto Zezza. 2009. "Investing Back Home: Return Migration and Business Ownership in Albania." *Economics of Transition and Institutional Change* 17 (3): 587–623.

Kuntchev, Veselin, Rita Ramalho, Jorge Rodríguez-Meza, and Judy S. Yang. 2012. "What Have We Learned from the Enterprise Surveys Regarding Access to Finance by SMEs?" World Bank, Washington, DC.

Lacuesta, Aitor. 2010. "A Revision of the Self-Selection of Migrants Using Returning Migrant's Earnings." *Annals of Economics and Statistics/Annales d'Économie et de Statistique* 97/98: 235–59.

Lucas, Robert E. B. 2008. *International Migration and Economic Development: Lessons from Low-Income Countries.* Cheltenham: Edward Elgar.

Mayr, Karin, and Giovanni Peri. 2009. "Brain Drain and Brain Return: Theory and Application to Eastern-Western Europe." *B.E. Journal of Economic Analysis and Policy* 9 (1): 1–52.

McCormick, Barry, and Jackline Wahba. 2001. "Overseas Work Experience, Savings and Entrepreneurship amongst Returnees to LDCs." *Scottish Journal of Political Economy* 48 (2): 164–78.

McKenzie, David, and Christopher Woodruff. 2017. "Business Practices in Small Firms in Developing Countries." *Management Science* 63 (9): 2967–81.

McKenzie, David, and Dean Yang. 2015. "Evidence on Policies to Increase the Development Impacts of International Migration." *World Bank Research Observer* 30 (2): 155–92.

Mesnard, Alice. 2004. "Temporary Migration and Self-Employment: Evidence from Tunisia." *Brussels Economic Review* 47 (1): 119–38.

OECD (Organisation for Economic Co-operation and Development). 2008. *International Migration Outlook 2008.* Paris: OECD Publishing.

Piracha, Matloob, and Florin Vadean. 2009. "Circular Migration or Permanent Return: What Determines Different Forms of Migration?" IZA Discussion Paper 4287, Institute of Labor Economics (IZA), Bonn.

Piracha, Matloob, and Florin Vadean. 2010. "Return Migration and Occupational Choice: Evidence from Albania." *World Development* 38 (8): 1141–55.

Reinhold, Steffen, and Kevin Thom. 2013. "Migration Experience and Earnings in the Mexican Labor Market." *Journal of Human Resources* 48 (3): 768–820.

Seshan, Ganesh, and Dean Yang. 2014. "Motivating Migrants: A Field Experiment on Financial Decision-Making in Transnational Households." *Journal of Development Economics* 108 (2): 119–27.

Shrestha, Maheshwor. 2020. "'Get Rich or Die Tryin': Perceived Earnings, Perceived Mortality Rates, and Migration Decisions of Potential Work Migrants from Nepal." *World Bank Economic Review* 34 (1): 1–27.

Stark, Oded. 1991. *The Migration of Labor.* Cambridge, MA: Blackwell.

Tornea, Vivian F. 2003. "Reintegration Program for Migrant Workers." *Review of Women's Studies* 13 (2): 203–20.

Wahba, Jackline. 2014. "Return Migration and Economic Development." In *International Handbook on Migration and Economic Development,* edited by Robert Lucas, 327–49. Cheltenham: Edward Elgar.

Wahba, Jackline. 2015a. "Selection, Selection, Selection: The Impact of Return Migration." *Journal of Population Economics* 28 (3): 535–63.

Wahba, Jackline. 2015b. "Who Benefits from Return Migration to Developing Countries?" *IZA World of Labor* 123.

Wahba, Jackline, and Yves Zenou. 2012. "Out of Sight, Out of Mind: Migration, Entrepreneurship and Social Capital." *Regional Science and Urban Economics* 42 (5): 890–903.

Wickramasekara, Piyasiri. 2002. "Asian Labour Migration: Issues and Challenges in an Era of Globalization." International Migration Paper 57, International Migration Programme, International Labour Organization, Geneva.

World Bank. 2018a. "Migration and Development Brief 30." World Bank, Washington, DC.

World Bank. 2018b. *Moving for Prosperity: Global Migration and Labor Markets.* Washington, DC: World Bank.

Yang, Dean. 2006. "Why Do Migrants Return to Poor Countries? Evidence from Philippine Migrants' Responses to Exchange Rate Shocks." *Review of Economics and Statistics* 88 (4): 715–35.